THE
EMERGENCE
OF
CHARISMATIC
BUSINESS
LEADERSHIP

RICHARD S. TEDLOW

RosettaBooks®

NEW YORK, 2021

First edition published 2021 by RosettaBooks

Cover design by Mimi Bark
Interior design by Alexia Garaventa

ISBN-13 (print): 978-1-9481-2284-9
ISBN-13 (ebook): 978-0-7953-5310-9

Library of Congress Cataloging-in-Publication Data:
Names: Tedlow, Richard S., author.
Title: The emergence of charismatic business leadership / Richard S. Tedlow.
Description: New York : RosettaBooks, 2021.
Includes bibliographical references and index.
Identifiers: LCCN 2021021443 (print) | LCCN 2021021444 (ebook)
ISBN 9781948122849 (hardcover) | ISBN 9780795353109 (ebook)
Subjects: LCSH: Leadership--United States--Case studies.
Management--Technological innovations
Strategic planning--United States--Case studies.
Success in business--United States--Case studies.

Classification: LCC HD57.7 .T435 2021 (print)
LCC HD57.7 (ebook) | DDC658.4/092--dc23

www.RosettaBooks.com
Printed in Canada

RosettaBooks®

This book is dedicated to my wonderful wife, Donna M. Staton, MD, MPH. Donna is a sweet and loving soul with a passion for global child health and the environment. She is an inspiration in her devotion to those less fortunate than we in America's middle class.

CONTENTS

PART I

THE GREAT TRANSFORMATION

In the years following World War II, the biggest American businesses were faceless bureaucracies. This characteristic is captured by their names: General Motors, Standard Oil, United States Steel, and so forth. If I told you the names of the chief executive officers of these firms in, say, 1955, you would not recognize them. Indeed, few people in 1955 knew who they were. I choose 1955 because *Time* magazine selected the CEO of General Motors as its "Man of the Year" then. He was chosen because of the position he held, not because of the person he was. The job had a man rather than the man having a job.

In 1956, William H. Whyte published a brilliant book entitled *The Organization Man*. According to Whyte, the key to success in the large American company was "fitting in." He cites, for example, a documentary about the research laboratory of a major chemical corporation in which the narrator proudly observes, "No geniuses here; just a bunch of average Americans working together."[1]

The contrast to our world today could not be more striking. The names of large companies now often have personality: Amazon, Apple, Facebook, etc. The names of the people who are leading or who have recently led these corporations are known all over the country and indeed the world: Bezos, Jobs, Zuckerberg. The shunning of genius and the celebration of the average are inconceivable at these companies.

This great transformation has been essential in order to sustain the vibrancy of the American business world. Why has it taken place? What made it possible? An important part of the answer to these questions is the rise of charismatic business leadership.

There were charismatic business leaders in the 1950s and 1960s, just as there are CEOs today who are not charismatic. We are describing a general tendency away from the CEO as the chief mechanic of the business who kept the wheels of the company turning while working out of the public gaze to the CEO as a man or woman with a mixture of charm, guile, brilliance, and cruelty who remakes the industry and in some cases society as a whole and in the process becomes a celebrity.

What is charisma? It is a mercurial word for a mercurial concept. By looking at leaders who have it and those who do not, we will try to encapsulate its meaning. We will begin with Steve Jobs, who is invariably described as charismatic without that adjective ever being defined.

CHAPTER 1

STEVE JOBS, A LIFE IN THREE ACTS
ACT ONE: END AND BEGINNING

When Steve Jobs died on October 5, 2011, Apple was inundated with condolence messages from all over the United States and from around the world. Some of them were touching. Others probably were also, but one could not be certain because they arrived in such a variety of languages that it was difficult to find people who could translate them. Yet more problematic were the notes we (I worked at Apple from 2010 to 2018) received in alphabets no one could recognize.

These notes were sent not only to Apple headquarters in Cupertino, California, but to Apple retail stores around the world. The stores posted them on their windows. In addition, some people left bouquets of flowers in front of the stores. Pause to consider this. People left flowers at stores because of the death of a CEO.

No one knows how many notes were received. According to the "Remembering Steve" page on apple.com, "Over a million people from all over the world have shared their memories, thoughts, and feelings about Steve."[1] As he was dying, people made a pilgrimage to his home in Palo Alto. One of his daughters has written that "A few people he didn't know came to the doors wanting to see him... wandering into the garden or empty-handed. A stranger in a sari begged to talk with him. A man came in through the gate and said he had flown in from Bulgaria just to see my father."[2]

After his death, California governor Jerry Brown declared October 16 to be Steve Jobs Day. The president of the United States and the first lady, Barack and Michelle Obama, posted a condolence note.[3]

Jobs's death had been long anticipated. He was diagnosed with pancreatic cancer in October of 2003. He postponed surgery until July 31, 2004. The following day he sent a blast email to Apple employees informing them of the surgery and declaring that he would have a full recovery. In the meantime, Tim Cook would manage the company, "so we shouldn't miss a beat."[4]

On June 12, 2005, Jobs delivered the commencement address at Stanford. Saying anything worth hearing on such occasions is next to impossible. Jobs succeeded. "I want to tell you three stories from my life," he began. One of these was the story of his cancer and his brush with death. The heart of his advice was "Stay hungry. Stay foolish." As of this writing, the address has been viewed almost thirty-eight million times on YouTube.[5]

Much has been said and written about Jobs. No one has questioned whether he could tell a story. He was a great storyteller that day at Stanford. Not everything he said was quite true, but charismatic people often get away with walking the border between reality and fantasy.

By early 2008, it was clear that his cancer had metastasized. This was a truth that could not be finessed. Jobs lost weight and was in pain much of the time. On August 24, 2011, he informed Apple's board of directors that the day had come when he "could no longer meet my duties and expectations as CEO."[6] It was all over except the waiting. And that came to an end on October 5.

Dying from cancer is dreadful beyond words. In more than one instance, there is a denial of death until the last breath is drawn. Was this really the end? This disease had afflicted Jobs in 2003. He kept coming back.

As recently as January of 2010, he had delivered the keynote introducing yet another transformative product, the iPad. Would there be any more such products? What would happen to Apple? The company had fired Jobs on September 17, 1985. Twelve years less one day thereafter—September 16, 1997—he came back to save Apple when it was a month or two away from bankruptcy. Only he could have done it. How would the world go on without him?

Why was the death of Jobs an event of global import? Only a tiny handful of the millions of people who sent those notes had ever met him. And although there is a legion of legends about Jobs dating back to Apple's birth, he was not thought of by those who knew him or only knew of him as either nice or particularly kind. Why did all those people feel close enough to him to project their own feelings onto him? Why did they feel that he belonged to them... that he was theirs?

Is it because Jobs touched so many people through his products? Is it because the products were designed with pride and beauty, thereby in a sense honoring the purchaser, in a way that the products of competitors were not? Is it because he left behind a beautiful family? Is it because he reached the height of success when his life was taken from him? Is it because he succeeded despite starting with no advantages?

Jobs was born on February 24, 1955. His parents were Abdulfattah Jandali, a Syrian immigrant, and Joanne Schieble, who grew up on a farm in Wisconsin. He was Muslim; she was Roman Catholic. They met at the University of Wisconsin, where he was a teaching assistant for a course she was taking in graduate school in political science. They were both twenty-three, and they were unmarried.[7]

Jandali has said that he wanted to marry Schieble, but her parents disapproved. Her father was dying, and she did not want to upset him. Schieble was living for a time with Jandali (the son of a wealthy man) in Homs, Syria. She left Syria for San Francisco, took up residence in a home for unwed mothers, and put her son up for adoption immediately after his birth without consulting Jandali.

The couple who adopted Schieble's son was "Catholic, well-educated, and wealthy," ideal from Schieble's point of view. Unfortunately, the adopting couple changed their minds. They decided they wanted a girl.[8]

The next couple who wanted to adopt the infant were Clara and Paul Jobs, and they were not the future Joanne Schieble had in mind for her son at all. The problem was not only that they were Protestant rather than Catholic. The problem was that they were working-class people who had not graduated from high school, much less college.

Schieble refused to sign the adoption papers and went to court to prevent the adoption. She only relented after weeks when the Jobs couple presented her with a signed pledge that they would establish a fund for her child's college education. Steve never did earn a college degree.

Thus, Jobs was born to an unwed mother. He was "illegitimate." That word means nothing today. Numerous couples in the United States and abroad choose to have children and raise them without getting married these days. But Jobs was born in 1955, and such liberality was not typical then. Historically, illegitimate children were at times denied rights of inheritance and even some civil rights. The Jobs couple lived in a lower-middle-class world. Most of the children Steve encountered were quite legitimate. He was different in a way that mattered back then.

Later in 1955, Schieble's father died. He was the reason she had not married Jandali. The two were wed that year. Their next child—and this child they kept—was a girl named Mona, who grew up to become the successful novelist Mona Simpson.

Jobs was half Syrian. He matured into a good-looking man, but there was something a bit different about his looks from the standard issue White middle-class kid. He did not look quite like his peers.

From the circumstances of his birth and upbringing, Steve Jobs started out in life different from most other kids.

Fast forward to 1983. Apple was founded on April 1, 1976. By the time Jobs was twenty-three, he was rich. Two years later he was worth a quarter of a billion dollars and was already world famous. Not bad for a college dropout. Jobs said that he was not money motivated.[9] This is not the whole truth, but it certainly was the image he cultivated, and it was one of the building blocks of his charisma. He was young, rich, and good-looking, and he made his money not by climbing some boring corporate ladder but through creating a thrilling new product.

From the start, Apple looked like a winner. Its sales increased by orders of magnitude each year from 1977 to 1980 inclusive. Profits kept pace. In 1980, with sales of over $117 million and profits of $11.7 million, Apple had its initial public offering. It was a spectacular success, creating about three hundred millionaires, more than any other IPO in history to that time.[10]

But Apple wasn't only about the money. Apple was a cause, a crusade to change the world by putting technology in the hands of the average person. Steve Jobs had dropped acid and lived in an ashram in India. He was marching to the beat of his own drummer. He had no intention of playing by the rules. He had every intention of changing them.

As he himself put it, "When you grow up, you get told the world is the way it is and your life is to live inside the world... Try not to bash into the walls too much... Try to have a nice family life, have fun, save some money. But that's a very limited life. Life can be much broader once you discover one simple fact. And that is that everything around you that you call life was made up by people no smarter than you. And you can change it. The minute you understand that, you can poke life and something will pop out the other side. You can change it. You can mold it. That may be the most important thing. To shake off this erroneous notion that life is there, and you're just going to live in it."[11]

This was true for Jobs. He wasn't afraid to "poke life." What he doesn't say in this passage is that living as he describes takes courage, and pain often accompanies the freedom he cherishes. The choices he made are not for everybody. They are for the chosen few charismatic leaders.

All that said, an organization growing as quickly as Apple was in those years had to be managed. It is not easy to imagine the young Steve Jobs as a general manager. He had neither the inclination nor the skill. The company was managed from 1981 to 1983 by a hardware engineer named Mike Markkula, thirteen years older than Jobs, who was the first investor in Apple and had opened the doors to other funders in the earliest days of the company. Neither Markkula nor his wife wanted him to continue as an operating manager. So the search began for an executive who could manage a bunch of young people driven by a visionary with a fanatic desire to invent the future.

The first choice was Don Estridge, the creator of the IBM PC. This was an intriguing idea. Estridge had set up a skunk works in Boca Raton, Florida, far removed from IBM headquarters in Armonk, north of New York City. He and his team built a computer, which, introduced on August 12, 1981, was outselling Apple by late 1982.

Jobs offered Estridge the position personally. He had succeeded in building IBM's PC by working around the company's stifling bureaucracy. His team was as devoted to him as Jobs's was to him at Apple. Both were mission driven, and both were rule breakers. But Estridge was not interested. He was proud of working for IBM, even though his affection was unrequited.[12]

Jobs and Markkula next turned to Gerry Roche, a well-known corporate headhunter, to find someone to run Apple. "Steve Jobs told me very specifically that he wanted someone who understood consumer marketing because that's where computers were going," remembered Roche. "One of the lessons my recruiting experience has taught me," he observed, "is that the people I like most are the people I cannot get! The better the person, the harder they are to get." When dealing with Roche, playing hard to get was the way to go. Which is precisely what the man he wanted as Apple's CEO did.[13]

John Sculley was sixteen years older than Jobs, and his background was altogether different. Educated at St. Mark's, an exclusive New England prep school, Brown, and Wharton, Sculley came from a family that was well-off. They lived on the Upper East Side of Manhattan, the "silk stocking" district. His father was a Wall Street lawyer. He described his mother as a "renowned horticulturist and a prize-winning flower arranger."[14]

Sculley worked his way up the corporate ladder of Pepsi-Co, and in early 1983 he was the president of the Pepsi-Cola division. That was when Roche contacted him. Sculley was a high-profile executive because Pepsi-Cola was a high-profile, advertising-intensive product. He reported that he was receiving a lot of calls from headhunters and did not bother to return most of them. But Gerry was different. "You would not fail to return a call from Gerry Roche."[15] So he did, and the mating game began.

The opening gambit was from Gerry. "John... I know you don't want to leave Pepsi, and I hate to ask a favor of you. But please trust me. Would you make a trip to California and at least meet these guys?"[16] Unsurprisingly, Sculley flew to California.

Sculley's first stop was in Los Angeles to visit his two children from his first marriage. His daughter was nineteen and his son seventeen. They lived with their mother, who it is safe to assume was wealthy. She was the stepdaughter of Don Kendall, the CEO of PepsiCo and the man to whom Sculley reported.

He took his children to a computer store, and in response to their asking why he was interested in computers, he off-handedly remarked that he was going to see Steve Jobs. "Steve Jobs?" exclaimed his daughter excitedly. "You're going to meet Steve Jobs?"

"I was astonished that Jobs could prompt such a reaction, particularly from my children. They had grown up in a Hollywood environment; they went to school with the sons and daughters of movie and television stars. Celebrities couldn't turn their heads. But the mere mention of Steve Jobs seemed something else."[17] That is because charisma is more than celebrity.

It did not take long for Sculley to be "smitten." He did play hard to get, "but I was captivated and intrigued at the possibility of going to Silicon Valley to make a new life for myself, to share in Steve's dreams."[18] What were those dreams? Steve wanted to build a company that was a highway to the future rather than a brick wall that stifled imagination.

Sculley had spent his professional life at a company located on a fantastic 144-acre campus littered with priceless works of art in the Westchester suburb of Purchase, New York.[19] PepsiCo was a $7.5 billion company in 1982, ranked forty-ninth on the Fortune 500. It was an eastern establishment outfit whose executives took good care of themselves. Corporate jets were the order of the day. Everyone wore suits. When Sculley visited Apple on his trip to California, he was the only person in a suit. To this day, one rarely sees men dressed in suits on Apple's campus.

PepsiCo's products were not items one could love. Production was not a problem. PepsiCo was all marketing. The beverage division sold the sizzle, the "Pepsi Generation." When Sculley himself took the "Pepsi Challenge," he preferred Coke.[20] PepsiCo had seen a lot of success under its imperious CEO, Kendall.

The key question was how success was measured. "At Pepsi," according to Sculley, "the locker-room war stories were about competition. How a manager seized a quarter of a share point in a state or region. How a company hero worked day and night over a weekend to get the syrup dispensers to work in vending machines in time for some special event."[21]

At Pepsi, in other words, process and financial results were everything. It was a traditional company managed with traditional metrics. That "special event" meant showmanship. That "quarter of a share point" meant cash falling to the bottom line. You could love the company. You could enjoy your colleagues. You could spend your high salary, and you could bask in the joy of winning while always at risk of losing. It was "the thrill of victory and the agony of defeat" in a game that was important only to the players.

There was nothing special about the product. As Sculley himself said, the difference in taste between a Pepsi and a Coke was "subtle."[22] The means to the end were everything, and the end was profit. Sculley, a graduate of the Wharton Business School, had a copy of Michael Porter's classic *Competitive Strategy* in the posh library of his posh home in Greenwich, Connecticut.[23] Sculley was a man of business books. Jobs was a dreamer.

Jobs, the world he was building at Apple, and the culture of Silicon Valley could not have been more different from the business world in which Sculley became successful. At one point in the recruitment process, Jobs asked him, "Do you want to spend the rest of your life selling sugared water or do you want to change the world?" This became "one of the most famous lines in business."[24]

Sculley left Pepsi for Apple in the spring of 1983. When he arrived in Cupertino in May, "At the age of forty-four, I was one of the oldest Apple employees... The average age of an Apple worker was all of twenty-seven. In many companies, that would be years of service."[25]

The computer industry had been in a constant state of turmoil for almost a decade. New faces on the scene. New technologies being developed. Companies being founded. Companies failing. Most important, from Apple's point of view, was IBM's introduction of its PC. On the one hand, IBM's market entry legitimized the industry as nothing else could. Here was the giant—the creator of the IBM 360 in the mid-1960s, which transformed computing—making a statement that the mass-market desktop personal computer was not just a hobbyist's toy. It was here to stay.

Apple took out a full-page advertisement in the *Wall Street Journal* headlined, "Welcome, IBM. Seriously."[26] Apple's engineers had no respect for the technology of the IBM PC. This led the whole company to underestimate IBM. Bill Gates, who in addition to being a brilliant autodidact in software was as shrewd a businessperson as America has produced, was at Apple's headquarters when IBM announced its product. "They didn't seem to care," he said of the Apple people. "It took them a year to realize what had happened."[27]

Why was John Sculley really hired at Apple? There are a number of reasons publicly advanced. One was that Apple was producing computers for consumers, and he had a track record as a successful consumer product marketer. The second was that Steve was too young to run a $2 billion public company. The phrase often heard was the need for "adult supervision." These things are true. But the real reason Sculley was hired was to manage Steve. In that assignment, his failure was complete.

Partnerships have worked in business. There is no better example than Bill Hewlett and Dave Packard. But they were both engineers. They were both founders of the company they ran. They were age mates. And they were both able to keep their egos in check. Sculley and Jobs were none of the above.

Sculley was the wrong man for his responsibilities. The marketing he knew was for a non-ego-intensive, trivial impulse purchase. By contrast, a desktop computer for a consumer in 1983 cost between $2,000 and $3,000. It was an expensive bet the customer made, a bet on a complex consumer durable.

"What I hadn't realized," Sculley later wrote, "was that Apple never would be a consumer products company. It was a computer company in a technology industry." The industry sustained $2 billion in losses in 1983 and 1984 caused by inventory mismanagement. "Companies either built too much inventory and the industry slowed down, or they had badly forecasted sales. In consumer products, you don't worry about the value of inventories because their value usually remains constant. At Pepsi, you produce a soda the night before and ship it the next day."[28]

As far as managing Jobs was concerned, Sculley couldn't do it. Nobody could. When Sculley joined Apple, he was president and chief executive officer, reporting directly to the board. Steve was the chairman of the board and vice president of the corporation in charge of the Macintosh division. He was also Apple's largest stockholder and appeared as Number 286 on the first *Forbes* 400 list in 1982. In formal terms, Sculley reported to Steve as chairman of the board, and Steve reported to Sculley as chief executive officer. Steve needed a disciplinarian, and Sculley was not the man to play that role. "None of Steve's behavior alarmed me," he observed, "maybe because I so clearly saw my younger self in him."[29] Hopeless. An executive coach can't afford to be smitten by his student.

At first things went well. Too well. At a private dinner for Apple insiders, Sculley remarked, "Apple has one leader—Steve and me."[30] As late as November 26, 1984, *Business Week* featured Jobs and Sculley on its cover with the title "Apple's Dynamic Duo."

But the situation was already shaky. Business had suddenly softened. Sales increased, but profits declined for the first time in fiscal 1984. The alliance between Jobs and Sculley—if it was ever real in the first place—collapsed. Gut-clutching rancor overwhelmed their saccharine relationship. After endless twists, turns, and tears, Steve was forced out. The process of expelling him from Apple, according to one source, "was complete and designed to humiliate."[31] He submitted his letter of resignation on September 17, 1985. He never spoke to Sculley again.

Sculley succeeded in engineering the firing of a man who became one of the greatest CEOs in the history of American business. What went wrong? According to Jobs, "it was very painful. What can I say? I hired the wrong guy."[32] According to Sculley, the rift was the result of a difference of opinion between the two concerning the Mac, which Steve wanted to market more aggressively but which Sculley was convinced was a product that was technically outdated and could not succeed.[33]

The truth is that Steve was not a man to share the spotlight. And Sculley did not appreciate how different Steve was from the people with whom he was used to doing business. "I had come from a world," he wrote in 1987, "in which top executives were relatively anonymous, dull creatures..."[34] One wonders how the folks back at Pepsi felt when they read that sentence. At any rate, that was not the world of high technology, of Apple, or of Jobs.

For his part, Jobs was famously a man of extremes. If he loved you, he knew how to make you feel that you were the most wonderful person on Earth. But the love could turn to hate in a flash. One friend, Andy Hertzfeld, who worked with Steve on the Macintosh, said that this is the way it had to be. "Steve is the opposite of loyal. He's anti-loyal. He has to abandon the people he is close to."[35] As with other charismatic executives, Jobs created a persona that was different from his true self. That persona could make you feel specially anointed. But when he no longer needed you, you discovered that you were never genuinely close to him.

Sculley said of Jobs that "he could tell you things that only you knew about yourself."[36] Jobs's chronic cruelty was all the more effective because of his unique insight into the fears and insecurities that we all have. These he would exploit brutally and without guilt.

Debi Coleman came to Apple in 1981 and began working on the Mac team as the controller when the division was created in 1982. Jobs, she said, "would shout at a meeting, 'You asshole, you never do anything right.' It was like an hourly occurrence. Yet I consider myself the absolute luckiest person in the world to have worked with him."[37]

Why?

One of the puzzles about Jobs is how he was able to attract people of unquestioned talent, drive them to work harder than any sane person should, torment them with sadistic glee, and yet wind up with them devoted to him. Why did people put up with this behavior even after they had accumulated what in Silicon Valley is inelegantly called "fuck-you money"? Why did they stay even though their ability rendered them employable in many other companies?

Two stories from this phase of his career illustrate that Jobs not only rubbed people's faces in the mud, he was also uniquely able to endow their efforts with a sanctity no one else could.

When the design of the original Macintosh—Jobs's special project—was complete, he assembled the team for a meeting. "Real artists sign their work," he said. He called each of the forty-five members of the design team forward, one at a time, to sign their names on a sheet of paper. Jobs himself was the last to sign. The signatures were engraved inside each Mac. "No one," biographer Walter Isaacson has written, "would ever see them, but the members of the team knew their signatures were inside..."[38]

After the ceremony, Jobs toasted the team with champagne. According to Bill Atkinson, whom Jobs hired as Apple employee Number 51 and who created MacPaint among numerous other accomplishments, "With moments like this, he got us seeing our work as art."[39]

The second story deals with the 1984 television advertisement announcing the debut of the Mac. Steve didn't conceive the ad, nor did he write it. All he wanted was something "insanely great." Steve's instructions? "I want something that will stop people in their tracks. I want a thunderclap." He got one. He championed the advertisement against some very skeptical people, and it turned out to be the greatest television advertisement in history.[40]

The advertising agency that created it was Chiat/Day. Lee Clow of the agency deserves special mention. The ad was directed by Ridley Scott (now Sir Ridley). Sources provide a wide range of the cost of production. The best guess is probably $750,000.[41] The advertisement was sixty seconds long, but there is so much going on during that period that it is difficult to describe. The viewer feels as if he or she has seen a full-length movie.

The ad shows rows of colorless, lifeless men looking like zombies and watching a giant screen in an auditorium from which a Big Brother–like figure babbles nonsense in a stern, commanding voice. The men sit passive, transfixed, like patients etherized.

As the Big Brother figure—loveless, sexless, without feeling, evil—drones on, an attractive, athletic young woman with short, light-blond hair is seen running from goon oppressors, dashing into the auditorium, approaching the screen, spinning around perhaps three or four times to build up momentum with the huge sledgehammer she is carrying, and then letting it go with a barely audible gasp. The hammer smashes into the giant screen, which explodes in a blinding flash of light.

Emanating from the shattered screen comes a powerful gust of wind blowing into the faces of the prison-like assemblage, each one of whom sits mute, stupid, impotent. This altogether gripping mini-drama is followed by a voiceover: "On January 24th, Apple Computer will introduce Macintosh. And you'll understand why 1984 won't be like *1984*."[42]

The person wielding the sledgehammer is a woman. She is strong, independent, alone, sinewy, unafraid. A powerful woman representing the positive potential of technology through Apple saves humankind from the oppressive potential of technology represented by Big Brother, who could easily be thought to stand for IBM. The ad was slated for the Super Bowl, watched by more people than any other event in the American television year.

Jobs showed the ad to the board shortly before the Super Bowl aired. They didn't merely dislike it. They hated it. It didn't do anything an advertisement is supposed to do. It didn't communicate anything about the product. It looked like it was filmed in a concentration camp.

Sculley himself, according to one source, "got cold feet."[43] Apple had apparently (accounts differ on this point) purchased one sixty-second and one thirty-second spot. Chiat/Day was told to sell them back to the network. The thirty-second spot was unloaded. But the agency said it could not resell the other. Actually, the agency didn't try. Clow and his colleagues believed in it. So did Steve. Which is lucky.

The ad was shown during the third quarter of a boring game. Viewers were watching it almost out of a sense of duty. After all, this was the Super Bowl. Suddenly, the ad appeared. The ad began by not beginning. Viewers were expecting an instant replay of an Oakland Raider touchdown (the Raiders led the whole game and won easily). Instead, "television screens went black for an ominous two full seconds." Then came the advertisement.[44]

"Even the sports announcers lost their composure," according to Sculley. "One said, 'Wow, what was that?'" Sculley said that when the cost of the advertisement leaked, some angry shareholders wrote to the company complaining of what they thought was a waste of money. The complaints didn't last long.[45]

The advertisement made news. All the networks covered it and replayed it. It is probably not an exaggeration to say that it became the talk of the nation. Both *TV Guide* and *Advertising Age* selected it as the greatest commercial of all time.[46]

And it is great. This was an era in which technology was coming into your home. But you could control it because you identified not with the automatons marching to the orders of Big Brother but with the athletic, fit, colorful, powerful woman (played by English athlete and actress Anya Major) who put a sledgehammer through his face. The advertisement captured Apple's central message from its founding to today—you are in control of your technology. Only Steve would have permitted the creation of such an advertisement, and only he would have effectively defended it against its critics.

The "reality distortion field" is a phrase often used to describe life around Steve Jobs.[47] The phrase was coined by Guy L. Tribble (known as Bud), a key member of the original Mac team. Here is Tribble's explanation of what the phrase means: in Steve's presence, "reality is malleable. He can convince anyone of practically anything. It wears off when he's not around, but it makes it hard to have realistic schedules... It was dangerous to get caught in Steve's distortion field, but it was what led him to actually be able to change reality."

"He can deceive himself," Bill Atkinson said. "It allowed him to con people into believing his vision, because he has personally embraced and internalized it."[48]

The creation of the reality distortion field was a sophisticated form of lying. Why genuine computer scientists like Bud Tribble put up with it is one of life's mysteries. Not everyone did.

Arthur Rock—board member, early investor, and one of the founding venture capitalists of Silicon Valley—did not. He had (and still has) a firm grasp on reality, and no man-child could dislodge it.

Bill Gates did not. A true technologist himself, Gates admired Jobs's unmatched presentation skills but was not seduced by his technical castles in the air.

John Sculley's wife, Carol Lee Adams (known as Leezy), did not. She never liked Steve. When his relationship with her husband was collapsing, she tracked him down to a restaurant at lunchtime. "My normal instincts would have been to slug him, but I was perfectly controlled... Do you have any idea," she said to him, "what a privilege it has been even to know someone as fine as John Sculley? He has been a real friend to you, but you'll never know it until the day you're on your deathbed... When I look into your eyes, I see a bottomless pit, an empty hole, a dead zone... I feel sorry for you."[49] (Years later, Leezy's anger would turn toward Sculley. He had an affair with a woman he met at Apple, and Leezy and he were divorced in 2011. Four years later she sued him for hiding assets during the divorce settlement.)[50]

Andy Grove, CEO of Intel during its glory years in the 1990s, did not. When Grove was diagnosed with prostate cancer, he faced facts unvarnished. Steve was not able to do the same.

Steve really could con himself. But he could not con cancer. He was diagnosed with a rare form of pancreatic cancer in October of 2003. The finding was an "incidentaloma." That is, doctors found it when they were looking for something else. "To the horror of his friends and wife, Jobs decided not to have surgery to remove the tumor..." He chose alternative medicine, which unsurprisingly proved completely ineffective. According to Andy Grove, "Steve talked to me when he was trying to cure himself by eating horseshit and horseshit roots, and I told him he was crazy."[51]

Even if Steve had had surgery the day after the diagnosis, the cancer might have killed him. But the weight of expert opinion is that he had a chance to beat it.[52] Alternative treatments, on the other hand, were a death sentence.

"Reality is unforgiving," said Arthur Levinson, an Apple board member, chairman of the board of Genentech, and a knowledgeable individual in this field. As another expert said, Steve "essentially committed suicide."[53]

In this, the climactic decision of his life, Steve had outgrown the usefulness of his personality. His death from a form of cancer that he had the fantastic luck of catching at a very early stage illustrates the view of the ancient Greeks that "character is fate."[54]

CHAPTER 2

WHAT IS CHARISMA?

The word *charisma* **has its roots in ancient times, when it signified the "gift of grace."** It is used in the Bible, and until the twentieth century it was confined to the context of religion. Today, it is employed widely. What does it mean?

Alas, that is a difficult question. Rakesh Khurana, dean of Harvard College and an authority on this subject, has written that charisma "is as difficult to define as 'love' or 'art.' ...Few personality traits," he observes, "are more subjectively perceived and resistant to precision."[1]

We can begin with the dictionary, according to which charisma is "compelling attractiveness or charm that can inspire devotion in others."[2] This definition obscures as much as it reveals. Attractive to whom? Inspired to do what?

The German sociologist Max Weber did more than anyone else to import the word into common parlance. Here is the key passage: "The term 'charisma' will be applied to a certain quality of an individual personality by virtue of which he is considered extraordinary and treated as endowed with supernatural, superhuman, or at least specifically exceptional powers or qualities. These are such as not to be accessible to the ordinary person, but are regarded as of divine origin or as exemplary, and on the basis of them the individual concerned is treated as a 'leader.'"[3] Thirty years ago, organizational scholar Alan Bryman described this as "one of the most heavily quoted passages in the social sciences."[4]

To Weber, charisma suggested four characteristics. First is the gift of grace. Second, the charismatic individual had followers. Third, these followers assumed what might be called new selves. They were "born again." Fourth, individuals endowed with charisma had to prove themselves through miracles. This definition is not quite satisfactory. Anthropologist Clifford Geertz observed that "there are multiple themes in Weber's concept of charisma... almost all of them... more stated than developed." A historian of the term has observed that charisma "retains a mysterious, elusive quality."[5]

There has been a major academic effort to render charisma a more scientific concept. One of the leading figures in this effort has been Professor John Antonakis at the University of Lausanne in Switzerland, who has worked with numerous colleagues to tame the definitional beast. He has mastered the literature of charisma, which is large and growing larger quickly. He and his colleagues have written that *transformational leadership* is a phrase that is not useful because it is tautological. Furthermore, "We omit using the word 'vision' in the definition, because vision is really quite a vague notion, which in any case stems from using symbolic means of communication that are useful for triggering a mental image and hence a vision." The definition that Antonakis and his colleagues offer is: charisma is a values-based, symbolic, and emotion-laden leader signaling.[6]

This definition is also not quite satisfactory. By using *signaling*, it consigns us to another definitional thicket. Indeed, in a paper published a number of years before this one, Antonakis and other colleagues used somewhat different language for their definition: "We... define charisma as symbolic leader influence rooted in emotional and ideological foundations."[7]

Missing from both definitions is attention to the relationship between charismatic people and the culture they create. Trust is an essential component of this relationship. So is communication. It is difficult to think of a charismatic leader who has not been an outstanding communicator.

More serious is the decision to omit vision from the definition. Vision is a central characteristic of individuals the world considers charismatic. The essence of the talent—indeed, the magic—of the charismatic business leader is to see not what is—we all can do that—but what might be. My approach to the definition of the slippery concept that is charisma is unapologetically inductive. We will discover what charisma is by seeing how people viewed as charismatic act and what they have accomplished.

That said, Professor Antonakis's work is thought-provoking and useful. From a comprehensive literature review, he has distilled thirteen elements that scholars have used to define charisma.[8]

None of the charismatic individuals I have studied pass all of the tests, but all pass some of them. Some of the items on this list can be taught. Indeed, they have been taught since Aristotle explained more than two thousand years ago that the art of persuasion entails ethos (loosely, the credibility of the person attempting to persuade), pathos (equally loosely, the ability to see the world through the eyes of those one is trying to persuade), and logos (loosely once again, the logical reasoning of the argument of the persuader).

The ability to teach charismatic traits is useful, but it is also dangerous. You can teach someone to seem charismatic. But you cannot teach someone to be charismatic. Think of a historical figure that we would all agree possessed charisma. In American political history, we can agree that Washington and Lincoln qualify. They possessed and employed some of the traits, such as vision and persuasiveness, discussed above.

You can teach the form but not the substance. One can't create a Washington or Lincoln to order. The fact that these men were both charismatic and yet so different from one another illustrates the difficulty of generalizing about charisma. Each truly charismatic individual that we will learn about in this book was unique. We will let them be our teachers. We can learn from them how the charismatic leader's style differs from leaders who are not charismatic.

What we cannot offer is a recipe. An essential aspect of charisma is our inability to capture it fully. To homogenize the "mysterious, elusive quality" of charismatic leadership would be to rob it of the mercurial, creative nature that makes it so interesting.

Alan Bryman writes that "in the concept of charisma we find a seductive but irritatingly intangible way of discussing leadership."[9] Charisma is indeed seductive and intangible, but one should not be irritated by those qualities. Get used to the fact that there will never be a definition of the word that is scientifically satisfying. When discussing charisma, we have to be at home with ambiguity rather than irritated by it. To quote a remark made in another context, "It is a riddle that… will remain forever unresolved."[10]

In his discussion of hard-core pornography, Supreme Court Justice Potter Stewart offered a formulation which became quite well-known: "I know it when I see it."[11] You will find that to be equally true of charisma. You will know it when you see it. When an article about Elon Musk described him as a man who has "managed to sell the world on his capacity to achieve objectives so lofty that from the mouth of anyone else, they'd be called fantasies,"[12] that is an illustration of charisma in action. The charismatic individual makes something sound possible that the rest of us would dismiss out of hand.

No other business leader in modern times has been described as charismatic more often than Steve Jobs. He is the touchstone to which all other leaders—certainly in high technology—are compared. What was charismatic about Jobs?

Jobs cofounded Apple and then saved it when it was in deep trouble. Michael Dell famously observed (in a statement he insists was taken out of context), "What would I do [if I were running Apple]? I'd shut it down and give the money back to the shareholders."[13] Instead of doing that, Jobs made it possible for Apple to become, at least for a time, the most valuable company in the world and America's first company with a market capitalization in excess of two trillion dollars. Both Jobs and Apple were "born again."

How did Jobs succeed in doing what someone as smart as Dell thought impossible? His first advertising campaign upon his return to the company gives us a clue. The headline was "Think Different." I can tell you from personal experience that those words remain deeply meaningful at the company. What "Think Different" means at Apple is that you must liberate yourself from the way opportunities and problems are approached by others. You must disenthrall yourself from conventional wisdom.

Here is one small example. Steve Ballmer, who followed Bill Gates as CEO of Microsoft and is a multibillionaire, said that a smartphone had to have a physical keyboard to succeed.[14] In 2007, Apple introduced the iPhone. It became the most important consumer product of the twenty-first century so far, and it has no physical keyboard. Its creators "thought different." A miracle. Which is an important component of charisma—a word that has never fully lost its religious roots.

Every company has a leader, a chief executive officer who makes the final decision about issues at hand. Most CEOs are not charismatic. Those few individuals endowed with charisma are first and foremost visionaries. They strive not for "continuous improvement" but rather to reconceptualize a whole way of doing business and in the process, in a phrase often heard in technology companies, "to make a dent in the universe."

Here is what historian and journalist Randall E. Stross has to say about Jobs and charisma: Jobs's charisma derived "from a perceived connection to the overarching questions of human existence. Jobs was not engaged in the business of selling breakfast cereal or bathroom faucets; he was not even focused on the pursuit of profits, per se. Others could pursue the mundane. He was after the much larger quarry of *changing the world*, rescuing computer users from the existing prison of mediocrity, making a dent in the universe, carrying out revolution, claiming an enduring place in history; it was the extraordinary scope of his ambition that was the ultimate source of his appeal."[15]

Stross also observes that "Steve Jobs is persuasive only because we have our own needs that mesh with his. As a society, we are desperate for the heroic figure, and if Steve Jobs wields powers of persuasion with few equals, the credit or blame... should also fall upon the audience."[16]

The vision of the charismatic leader stretches belief right up to, but not over, the breaking point. When the vision violates that breaking point, it hurtles into madness. It is difficult for those of us who have driven automobiles powered by internal combustion engines to imagine a world of self-driving cars powered by batteries. That is where the industry is headed, even though it is a simple matter to list what not long ago were considered impossible obstacles to arrive at that goal. The charismatic businessperson is quite aware of these obstacles. But he or she climbs an imaginary ladder to see over those problems to the achievement of the vision.

Charismatic business leaders are magnetic. This trait is a necessity because they must attract a team of surpassingly talented people to transform their vision into a reality. It is the team that must attack and defeat the obstacles in the way of the achievement of the vision. The charismatic visionary cannot do it alone.

Charisma is an invaluable asset in the quest for fundamental innovation. The charismatic leader wants to change the world. Innovation on this scale is hard to comprehend. Charisma is a vital tool for the leader to sell the vision to those he or she needs to make dreams come true.

Here is my own set of seven characteristics that define charisma. These have emerged in the course of writing this book.

1. Charisma entails ambition, aggression, and the urge to dominate.

2. People may be born with the potential to become charismatic, but unless that potential is developed, it will wither on the vine. Charisma must be both born and made.

3. Charisma is not digital—on or off, zero or one. It is possible to have some charisma, or charisma in some parts of one's life but not others.

4. Charisma is a precarious way to lead. Failure to make magic is always just around the corner, and failure puts charisma at risk. Style is important, but it is no substitute for results.

5. Because of the previous point, charismatic leaders are often paranoid.

6. Vision is essential to the charismatic leader.

7. In today's media age, charisma is a very important attribute of leading at scale. This is a notable change from the 1950s, when media was much less important in the business world for personality creation.[17]

In the years following World War II, there was not much charisma in American business. That is because there was precious little innovation. How different was the 1956 Chevrolet from the 1955 version? Not very. General Motors did not have a charismatic CEO at the time. It did not need one. This was the era of *The Man in the Gray Flannel Suit*.

In the period from roughly 1975 to 1995, innovation was forced upon American business leaders because of stagflation at home, new global competition, and the sudden appearance of activist investors able to fight traditional managers for control of American corporations. Some names from this era, such as that of junk-bond king Michael Milken, may be familiar to you.

From 1995, in August of which Microsoft introduced Windows 95 and Netscape had its initial public offering, to the present, we have been living in what may be the most innovative era in the history of business. Innovation is greatly facilitated by charisma. The names of America's charismatic business leaders during this period are known to almost everybody. When Jeff Bezos made a surprise visit to a Washington, DC, high school, one of the students did not recognize him. That student asked the student next to him, "Who's Jeff Bezos?" And it was that question that made news.[18]

Charisma attracts attention. It expands our sense of the possible. And it is exciting.

CHAPTER 3

AMERICAN BUSINESS LEADERS IN THE POSTWAR WORLD: GENERAL MOTORS AS A CASE STUDY

Sunday, September 2, 1945, marked the official end of World War II. On that day, representatives of the Japanese government and military signed the instrument of surrender aboard the USS *Missouri*, anchored with other warships in Tokyo Bay. The *Missouri* was a gigantic engine of destruction. Its main battery consisted of nine sixteen-inch guns, which were capable of firing 2,700 pound armor-piercing shells twenty miles.[1] It was accompanied that day by the American third fleet.

Think about the psychological impact of this ship and of the fleet in Tokyo Bay. Imagine for a moment how you (if you are an American) would feel seeing a Japanese warship with similar armaments anchored in New York Harbor. This was VJ Day, Victory over Japan Day. (VE Day, Victory in Europe Day, had taken place on May 8, with the formal surrender of Germany to the Allied forces in Berlin.)

As massive and imposing as the *Missouri* and its accompanying ships were on that September day, something took place that was even more impressive, more terrifying. As Douglas MacArthur's final words were spoken at the surrender ceremony, the flyover took place. Journalist Theodore H. White was on the deck of the *Missouri* on the day of the surrender. Forty years later, this is how he remembered the event:

"At this point happened the episode that stands out sharpest among the memories of that day—the flyover. As [General Douglas] MacArthur intoned, 'These proceedings are closed,' we heard a drone and looked up. It is difficult to recall now... how very good we were in those days. Four hundred B-29's had taken off from Guam and Saipan hours before to arrive over the Missouri at this precise minute of climax. They stretched across the rim of the horizon, and their heavy droning almost instantly harmonized with a softer buzzing as 1,500 fleet aircraft from our flattops joined them."

The aircraft flew very low, circling the ships. They could fly low because there was nothing to stop them. Then they "disappeared across the sky" to Yokohama and Tokyo, two cities they had virtually obliterated.[2]

The B-29 was a gigantic, four-engine heavy bomber almost a hundred feet long, which boasted a wingspan of 141 feet and had a range of over 5,500 miles. On the night of March 9/10, 279 B-29s conducted the Great Tokyo Air Raid, destroying most of the eastern part of the city. Between eighty thousand and one hundred thousand Japanese, predominantly civilians, were killed. The Americans lost fourteen aircraft and ninety-six airmen. Japan was helpless.

But the B-29 will always be remembered as the only aircraft to drop a nuclear weapon on a city. Hiroshima was the target of an atomic bomb on August 6. Three days later, it was Naga-saki. The firepower of the USS *Missouri*, impressive though it was, could not compare to nuclear weaponry. For the first time in the history of the planet Earth, human beings had in their hands a tool of species destruction. And the United States was the sole possessor of this tool at the war's conclusion.

On February 17, 1941, Henry R. Luce, the founder of Time/Life, prophesied that this was destined to be the "American Century."[3] On the deck of the *Missouri* four and a half years later, it certainly looked like Luce was right. America's leadership was economic as well as military. Japan and Germany were occupied by the nations they fought. The So-viet Union had been devastated by the war, suffering more casualties than any other country. France had been occupied by Germany for almost half a decade. Britain was thoroughly spent, with its industries in shambles and its once-great em-pire falling to pieces.

Now consider the United States. Not one battle had been fought on our soil, nor had any of our factories or cities been bombed.[4] The nation suffered over 405,000 military deaths. The Soviet Union lost more than twenty million combatants. Unlike other nations, very few American civilians lost their lives during the war.

Joseph Stalin is said to have remarked that Britain gave the world time, America gave money, the Soviet Union gave blood. Whether or not he actually made this statement, there is a lot of truth to it. At the close of 1940, Franklin D. Roos-evelt described the United States as the "arsenal of democra-cy."[5] Economically, the war was enormously beneficial to the United States. The 1930s were the grimmest decade in the twentieth century for American business. The Great Depression saw the collapse of the US GDP and, most devastating, the skyrocketing of unemployment. As late as 1938, the unemployment rate was a staggering 19 percent. In 1944, it was 1.2 percent.[6]

Looking toward the end of the war, the United States was gripped by nothing less than a "depression psychosis."[7] Wars the United States fought had almost always been followed by economic contractions. This was true after World War I, when the economy slumped sharply from 1919 to 1921. The fear during World War II was heightened by a "stark new fact": this war followed the nation's worst depression. Why wouldn't America fall back into a depression when the war was over and military spending collapsed (the arsenal of democracy having served its purpose) and millions of soldiers returned to civilian life? A Gallup poll in January of 1945 asked, "After the war, do you think everyone who wants a job will be able to get one?" Unsurprisingly, 68 percent of the respondents answered "No."[8]

Yet this time it really was different. The federal government innovatively pursued economic measures to prevent the rise of unemployment and release the pent-up demand that had been building during the war. For example, the GI Bill of Rights, which was enacted into law in 1944, made it possible for a million discharged soldiers to attend college and for another million to open their own businesses. The Treasury and the Federal Reserve ensured that ex-servicemen and their families could sell billions of dollars of US bonds purchased during the war at full face value.

Government expenditures did decline sharply from 1945 to 1946, but this decline was met by rising disposable income, consumption, and investment. The result was a postwar

boom with unemployment hardly rising at all. This constituted a great environment in which to do business.[9] As early
as 1943, Thomas J. Watson Sr., CEO of IBM, observed that
"This war is changing everything."[10] He was right.

By 1950, almost 40 percent of global economic activity
took place in the United States. Look at the signature product
of the first half of the twentieth century—the automobile.
In 1950, 85 percent of the automobiles manufactured in the
world were produced in this country. As late as 1960, more
than 70 percent of the sales of the world's two hundred largest firms were booked by American corporations. Over three-
fifths of those two hundred firms were headquartered in the
United States.[11]

At the center of the arsenal of democracy was General
Motors. The production of automobiles in the United States
ceased shortly after Pearl Harbor. General Motors convert-
ed its plants to the manufacture of war matériel such as
aircraft, tanks, trucks, and engines of all kinds. Seven and
nine-tenths percent of all military contracts during World
War II were filled by General Motors, compared to the second
largest contractor's 4.1 percent.[12]

Charles E. Wilson was the president and CEO of General
Motors from 1941 to 1953. Wilson's career was typical for
young men working for big companies during these years: he
got a job at Remy in 1919. This was an Indiana-based start-up
that produced electrical equipment for the military during
World War I and was absorbed by General Motors in 1919.
Step by step, he worked his way up to the top.

Wilson was nominated to become secretary of defense
by President-elect Dwight D. Eisenhower in January 1953. A
remark he made at his Senate Armed Services confirmation

hearing became quite well-known. Asked if he could make a decision that was in the national interest but not in the interests of GM, Wilson responded, "Yes, sir, I could."

Wilson should have stopped there, but he continued by making a statement that was to follow him for the rest of his years. "I cannot conceive [of such a decision] because for years I thought what was good for our country was good for General Motors and vice versa. The difference did not exist. Our company is too big. It goes with the welfare of the country. Our contribution to the nation is considerable."[13]

This statement was mangled by horrified liberals as "What's good for General Motors is good for the country." Wilson corrected this misquotation endlessly but eventually learned to live with it. Given GM's contribution to the war effort, his point of view was understandable, if poorly expressed.

Wilson's successor as the president and CEO of General Motors was Harlow H. Curtice. He held that position from 1953 to 1958. Probably no one reading this sentence will recognize the name Harlow H. Curtice. If you had walked by a newsstand (do such things still exist?) on January 2, 1956, however, you would have seen his smiling face on the cover of *Time* magazine. *Time* announced that Curtice was its choice for 1955 "Man of the Year." ("Man of the Year" did not become "Person of the Year" until 1999.)

Curtice was selected because he was the eleventh president of the largest company in the largest industry in the world. There was one move in particular that *Time* spotlighted. When a gloomy mood was reportedly settling over businessmen who were expecting a slowdown in the economy early in 1954, "Curtice stood up before 500 of the nation's top... industrialists and gave his own pronouncement on the future." GM would spend a billion dollars to expand its plants for the increase in sales it was forecasting. "Screamed the headlines," according to *Time*, "GM BETS BILLION: NO SLUMP."[14] General Motors, with sales of $13 billion, twice the size of the second-largest company, which was Standard Oil of New Jersey, was the keystone of the Detroit–Pittsburgh economy that dominated the American business landscape in the mid-1950s. It had the money to spend.

Curtice was the quintessential corporate statesman. He was an organization man from head to toe, having joined GM in 1914 at the age of twenty, directly after graduating from Ferris Business College (at the time a two-year college—today Ferris State University). He started as a bookkeeper for the AC Spark Plug division of General Motors and worked his way up to division controller, then to the Buick division, and after that to a corporate vice presidency.

Curtice commuted by corporate plane from his home in Flint, where he spent his weekends, to Detroit, where he lived in a nine-room suite in the General Motors building. What was Flint like when Curtice lived there in 1955? According to the article, "There is a job in Flint for virtually anyone who wants one. Of a workforce of 135,400, some 86,700 are employed by GM." There was a car for every 2.8 persons, as opposed to 3.7 nationwide. Almost 80 percent of the residents owned their own homes, and 80 percent of those homes had televisions. According to the president of the city's largest department store, "People have got money. They feel safe."

What was Curtice's life like in 1955? It doesn't sound all that bad. "In many ways he lives a life that is beyond the comprehension of most of his car owners. Platoons of subordinates jump when he twitches. Garages filled with gleaming limousines and beaming chauffeurs stand ready to transport him wherever he desires. A private 18-plane air force of multi-engined, red, white, and blue airplanes is at his disposal. Private secretaries and public-relations men take care of bothersome detail, see to it that Cadillacs, hotel suites, restaurant tables and theater seats are there when and where he wants them. High-salaried assistants smooth his path, greet him wherever he arrives, order his drinks, fetch his newspapers."

Curtice didn't work for nothing. Salary plus bonus came to $800,000 a year. GM's eighty-three thousand hourly employees averaged $109 a week, "with some skilled old-timers at the forge plants earning $10,000 a year."

"The rough process of elimination," we are informed, "absolutely prevents a phony from getting that job [i.e., Curtice's]." Another observation from the article is worth noting: "No GM president could ever be a dictator even if he had the inclination because the unwritten constitution of GM has its full quota of checks and balances. Big decisions at the top are made in committee and the president must sell the top committees... on his policies before he can execute them... The GM constitution reserves considerable power to the semisovereign, ever competitive divisions." And finally, "Beneath all the glitter, Curtice is regarded by friends as essentially still the small-town boy who came out of Petrieville, Michigan."[15]

The article speaks of competition, but the truth is there really wasn't much. General Motors controlled half the domestic automobile market. Ford and Chrysler, the other two members of what back in the day were known as the "Big Three," knew their place. And foreign firms played no role at all. Imports accounted for 0.71 percent of the American market in 1955. GM's biggest worry was not another automobile company but rather the threat posed by the antitrust division of the Justice Department.

The difference between Curtice's life (his dates are August 15, 1893, to November 3, 1962) and career and, say, Elon Musk's and the difference between Curtice's GM and Steve Jobs's Apple speak volumes about how the business world has changed in the course of the past decades.

Curtice may have been intelligent. He certainly put in long hours. He was known to work from seven in the morning until eight at night each weekday.[16] But no one would call him charismatic. Steve Jobs concluded his graduation speech at Stanford by saying, "Stay hungry. Stay foolish." It is unimaginable that Curtice would have offered such advice.

If Curtice seemed somewhat self-satisfied in the *Time* article, that attitude is not without reason. Nineteen fifty-five was a record-breaking year for the automobile industry—7,169,908 units were sold in the United States, an increase of almost 30 percent from the previous year.[17] GM's market share was 51 percent. Sales were $12,443,277,420 and profits $1,189,477,082, an increase of 26.7 percent and 47.6 percent, respectively, from 1954.[18] GM became the first company to make more than a billion dollars in a single year. Return on invested capital was a fantastic 50 percent.[19]

General Motors was founded by William Durant in 1908. He lost control of the company during the sharp business downturn following World War I. It was bought out of virtual bankruptcy by Pierre S. Dupont and the company his family controlled. He served as CEO until 1923, when he turned GM over to Alfred P. Sloan Jr. Sloan served as president until 1937 and as chairman of the board until 1956.

Alfred P. Sloan Jr. (May 25, 1875–February 19, 1966) was the great man of General Motors and among the most important American businesspeople in the twentieth century. He was the architect of GM, designing a system of divisions that is credited with making possible the combination of decentralized decision making with centralized control. His autobiography, *My Years with General Motors*, was widely praised.[20] Sloan's approach to business exercised a powerful influence over Wilson, Curtice, and others who succeeded them. For them, Sloan defined what the business world was and the role GM was destined to play.

Sloan's autobiography itself is remarkably impersonal. In a 472-page book, his father and siblings are mentioned in two paragraphs. His wife is not mentioned at all. The best description of Sloan is provided by historian Irving Bernstein:

"Sloan was extremely intelligent, tough-minded, and a master of complex organization [which is fortunate, because the organizational structure he created for General Motors was incredibly complicated]. His decisive quality was intensity, evident in the slender frame, the thin face, the expressive eyes, the constant movement of hands and feet, and the listening with the special attentiveness of the partially deaf... His manner with people was formal, even remote. He 'dreaded' the American business practice of entertaining a prospective buyer. 'I liked working with that customer,' he wrote, 'but playing with him was another matter.' ...He was... totally absorbed by the challenge of running GM, dedicated, as he put it, 'perhaps to a fault.' He was childless, uninterested in books or art, considered golf and other sports a waste of time, did not smoke, and rarely drank. He had one consuming interest: Business. His recipe for success was 'work hard... There is no short cut.' An associate likened him to a roller bearing: 'self-lubricating, smooth, eliminates friction, and carries the load.'"[21]

How did Sloan define business, in which he had such a "consuming interest"? In his autobiography, he explained, "The measure of the worth of a business enterprise... is not merely growth in sales or assets but return on the shareholders' investment, since it is their capital that is being risked and it is in their interests first of all that the corporation is supposed to be run..."[22] The results in 1955 must have pleased him. Famed economist Milton Friedman could not have put it more succinctly.[23]

It should be emphasized that when Sloan writes of shareholders, he is not thinking about the *green mailers* and *activist investors*. He has in mind people like himself and his colleague Charles F. Kettering, the head of research at General Motors, who would never have entertained the thought of working for another company and who both owned large blocks of stock that they held for decades. He is also thinking of the Dupont family and company, which saved General Motors from bankruptcy back in 1920. GM had a thirty-two-member board of directors in 1955, very large by today's standards. Five of the directors were directly associated with Dupont, which became GM's largest stockholder when it invested the then-staggering sum of $50 million in the company between 1917 and 1919. Dupont only sold when it was forced to do so by the Supreme Court in 1957 for antitrust reasons.[24]

Business author Peter Drucker, who knew Sloan, wrote in an introduction to Sloan's autobiography, "Leadership is not 'charisma.'"[25] Indeed, Sloan was not a charismatic man. His successors were even less so. Men like Wilson and

Curtice exemplified lives devoted to the organization. They were skillful and hardworking. But they were limited in their definition of the role of the CEO.

These limitations extend beyond the obvious restriction of their responsibilities to shareholder returns to the exclusion of other stakeholders. It is hard to imagine that they would appear onstage before a global audience to extoll the virtues of a new product. The keynotes of Steve Jobs were prepared meticulously and executed flawlessly. Nothing comparable took place at GM in these years. Despite the size of GM, its CEOs did not view themselves as public figures. Nor did the public view them as such. For example, Charles E. Wilson received about ten times more attention in the *New York Times* in 1953 as secretary of defense than in 1950 as president of GM.[26]

According to *Time*'s article on Curtice, General Motors had 514,000 employees in 119 plants in sixty-five cities in nineteen states. These hundreds of thousands of workers may not have held a lot of shares in the company. But obviously they were making an investment in it through their labor. Where did they fit in?

The United Automobile Workers succeeded in organizing the industrial workers of General Motors as a result of a forty-four-day strike that began in Flint, Michigan, on December 29, 1936. In his autobiography, Sloan simply observed that "I have no desire to revive the bitter controversies that arose over these early encounters with labor organizations."[27] With good reason. GM handled itself very badly, earning the undying enmity of many of its workers.

By the mid-1950s, a pattern had developed in which the United Automobile Workers union (UAW) pushed for higher wages, which the company granted while maintaining its financial returns by raising prices. This was a manageable arrangement until the automobile industry became globally competitive.

If you are looking for charisma in the American automobile industry in 1955, the UAW union is a better place to find it than corporate management. Walter Reuther was the head of the union at the time. He survived beatings and two assassination attempts to turn the UAW into what was perhaps the wealthiest and most powerful labor organization in the world in 1955.

Among the other stakeholders of General Motors in 1955 were, of course, the consumers. It is not hard to argue that the company should have been treating its customers better—especially in the realm of safety—than it was. There were 36,688 motor vehicle fatalities in the United States in 1955. In those days, safety was an afterthought for GM. The industry convinced itself that, in a phrase attributed to Lee Iacocca in 1972 about the Pinto, "safety doesn't sell." Ford marketed safety features in 1956 models ("You'll be safer in a '56 Ford!" according to an advertisement), but they did not result in greater sales.[28]

GM broke no new ground in this area. Indeed, when Ralph Nader published his exposé *Unsafe at Any Speed* in 1965, General Motors tapped his phone and hired prostitutes to lure him into compromising situations.[29] It was Nader, not the president of GM at the time, James Roche, who led the charge for automobile safety. The interests of the nation and of GM were not as congruent when it came to this literally vital issue as Charles Wilson asserted they were.

"General Motors must always lead," said Curtice. That was certainly true in terms of market share and profitability during his tenure as president of the company from 1953 to 1958. But in other areas, it was quite untrue.

No one suspected it at the time, but 1955 was the apogee of the American automobile industry. Sales slumped sharply in 1956, and in the recession year of 1958, the last of Curtice's forty-four years as an executive at GM, 4,654,514 units were sold. Not until 1963 did the industry's sales exceed 1955 levels, and by then import penetration reached 5.11 percent. This trend continued until the United States placed import restrictions on Japanese automobiles in the 1980s. By that time, Japan had become the largest car-producing nation in the world, a position the US had held since the introduction of the Model T Ford in 1908. In 2018, foreign manufacturers produced more cars and trucks in the United States than were produced by what used to be called the "Big Three."[30]

General Motors itself filed for bankruptcy on June 1, 2009. The company sold off nameplates, shuttered plants, fired a quarter of its workforce, and terminated thousands of dealers. GM was reborn as the General Motors Company LLC. This rebirth was made possible by a $51 billion bailout from the US Treasury.

One can hardly blame Curtice for the collapse of the domestic industry and the bankruptcy of the company over half a century after his tenure as CEO. But one can see in him symptoms of what eventually leads to a company's demise. By way of stark contrast, Andy Grove, CEO of Intel during its glory years from 1987 to 1998 and an exceptionally charismatic man, used to say that "only the paranoid survive." He published a book by that title in 1996, which became a best seller and is still worth reading.[31] It is precisely this paranoia, a hallmark of the charismatic personality—the fear of the unknown unknowns that may get you—that was absent from Curtice, from GM, and from the whole domestic automobile industry in the 1950s.

GM began its existence as a challenger to an incumbent, Henry Ford and his Ford Motor Company, which did nothing less than put America on wheels. According to Sloan, the automobile industry was in the 1920s in the midst of change as radical as any since the introduction of the Model T in 1908. "[L]uckily for us," wrote Sloan, "because as a challenger to the then established position of Ford, we were favored by change. We had no stake in the old ways of the automobile business; for us change meant opportunity."[32]

By the 1950s, nobody at GM could imagine that other entrepreneurs might be looking at it just the way Sloan was looking at Ford in the 1920s. But they were, especially executives at Toyota, which was bound and determined to attack the industry globally and specifically in the heart of what in Japan was known in the 1950s as the "automobile kingdom."[33] "The old master had failed to master change," Sloan wrote, referring to Henry Ford. "Don't ask me why." But we know why. Ford had fallen into a competency trap and become myopic. Jim Collins, well-known student of business leadership, explains that "[t]o go from good to great requires transcending the curse of competence."[34] This is something neither the "old master" nor his successors at Ford were able to do.

There are lessons to be learned from the history of the automobile industry. However, it took imagination as well as a touch of paranoia to learn them, and those were traits that Curtice, with his undoubted virtues, did not possess.

An important symptom of a problem in a company is when necessary evils start being regarded as positive goods.

("It's not a bug, it's a feature.") The annual model change, for example, was adopted at General Motors with considerable reluctance. Sloan said in 1923 that "while the bringing out of yearly models results in many disadvantages and, for that reason, we are all against yearly models, I don't see just what can be done about it."[35]

Ford had not introduced yearly models up to this time. For two decades, between 1908 when the Model T was introduced, to 1927, when it was discontinued, the Model T was the only car Ford produced. According to Sloan, "There is a legend cultivated by sentimentalists that Mr. Ford left behind a great car expressive of the pure concept of cheap, basic transportation. The fact is that he left behind a car that no longer offered the best buy, even as raw, basic transportation."[36]

No one in the industry during the 1920s and 1930s argued against the idea that the automobile should improve as a product. However, there was a good deal of controversy about the relationship between change and improvement, between style and substance. It was not at all a settled matter that a new model brought out annually as opposed to a policy of continuous improvement was the best way to create better cars. Speaking of the annual model change, Sloan said that the strain on Fisher Body "in bringing out all these dies at one time is something terrific..."[37]

Nevertheless, the fall of the Model T in 1927 cast a long shadow. The policy of what came to be known by the 1950s as "planned obsolescence" was adopted by GM, Chrysler, and, eventually, by Ford as well. A major problem that Ford faced toward the end of the life of the Model T was that it could not compete with its own used cars. Planned obsolescence solved that problem, but it caused others.

The annual model change cost a fortune. According to one calculation, it was costing the industry about $5 billion a year in the latter half of the 1950s.[38] This added more than 25 percent to the purchase price of the average car. Was it worth it? Curtice said that "it is my considered opinion that the annual model change has been the most important single factor responsible for the growth and vitality of our industry."[39] What Sloan adopted with reluctance because he did not see any choice, Curtice celebrated as the key to the growth of the whole industry.

Real change, such as the creation of the Toyota production system, overwhelmed the American industry following the oil shocks of 1973 and 1979 and the stagflation of the late 1970s. It would have taken charismatic leadership to have shaken the American industry loose from the torpor into which it had sunk. Neither Curtice nor his successors could supply it.

As far as Curtice himself is concerned, not much is known about him. No biography of him has been written, and it is a safe bet that none will be. He seems to have been a decent family man with a head for details who inspired loyalty on the part of his subordinates at the company. He was a competent trustee and administrator of a resource-rich company.[40] No one ever called him charismatic. With its numberless committees and checks and balances, the GM of Curtice's time was more like a government than a business. Has anyone ever encountered a charismatic committee? One suspects that if Charles E. Wilson, Curtice's predecessor, had not become secretary of defense but had remained as GM CEO for a couple more years, and if his successor, Frederic G. Donner, had begun his tenure as CEO a few years earlier, and

Curtice therefore had never held the position, the history of the company and of the industry would not have been very different. As noted above, the job had a man rather than the man having a job. *Time*'s headline for its article about him is "First Among Equals." Curtice was the CEO, but it is the role that mattered.

Curtice retired from GM on August 31, 1958, two weeks after his sixty-fifth birthday, having devoted forty-four years of his life to the company. He remained on the board until his death at the age of sixty-nine on November 3, 1962. Curtice's death prompted a two-column obituary on page 88 of the *New York Times*. His life as recounted therein could not have gone better, with the exception of one incident that strikes a startlingly discordant note.[41]

Curtice enjoyed hunting. In November 1959, he and a close friend, Harry W. Anderson, a retired vice president at GM, and two other friends went duck hunting on St. Anne Island, an exclusive, seven-thousand-acre preserve on the Canadian side of Lake St. Clair. (Detroit is on the American side of the lake.) On November 18, Curtice accidentally shot and killed Anderson.[42]

Decades later, Anderson's widow, Veda, recalled Curtice's visit to her home to pay his condolences. "He was so distraught. It was really something. He hardly knew how to walk, how to talk. It was so difficult for him, and it was such a sad thing for him. In fact, he died... with a broken heart. He just didn't snap out of it."[43]

Curtice exemplified the organization man. He was competent, paid his dues, and was honest. In a growing company in a dominant economy, that is what it took to move up. This tragic ending should not have been in the script. But even a man who plays by the rules may have to deal with the cosmic randomness of life.

THE BUSINESS EXECUTIVE OF THE 1950s IN FICTION:
THE MAN IN THE GRAY FLANNEL SUIT

In 1955, the year Harlow Curtice became *Time's* Man of the Year and Steve Jobs was born, Sloan Wilson published his first novel, *The Man in the Gray Flannel Suit*.[1] The book became a bestseller and was made into a movie starring Gregory Peck in 1956, which was the year William H. Whyte published *The Organization Man* (which we'll cover in the next chapter).

As a novel, *The Man in the Gray Flannel Suit* is quite forgettable. The movie version is dreadful. But the story resonated with the public, and the novel is a noteworthy document of its time. It is to novels what *The Organization Man* is to journalism.

The novel was translated into twenty-six languages and banned in the Soviet Union. Tailors wanted to fit Wilson with gray flannel suits for free, and businessmen who had worn them since prep school started to go to work in sports clothes to prove their freedom of spirit. Journalist David Halberstam called it "one of the most influential novels of the fifties." "[I]t hit a vital nerve," he wrote.[2]

The novel is set in 1953. The protagonist is Tom Rath, a nice enough person with a nice family composed of a wife and three children. He lives in the fictional town of South Bay, Connecticut, located near Westport, and commutes by train to New York City, where he works at a nonprofit foundation.

The story is set in motion when Rath gets word of a job opening at UBS, the fictional United Broadcasting System, which might make it possible for him to earn $10,000 annually rather than the $7,000 he was making at the foundation.

Rath gets the job and finds himself the personal assistant of the CEO of UBS, Ralph Hopkins. We live through the political machinations with which he deals, and those take up most of the novel.

We also learn that Rath was a captain in the army during World War II, a paratrooper. He killed seventeen men, at least one with his own hands. Among those seventeen was his best friend, whose death he caused in a friendly-fire incident. While in the service, he had a forty-nine-day affair with a young Italian girl. Orders compelled him to leave her soon after learning that she was pregnant.

What strikes the reader is the contrast between the intensity of Rath's wartime experiences and the inanity of his peacetime life. There are periods when he sits at his desk at UBS with nothing to do.

What is even more striking is what an empty person Rath is, and the same can be said of his wife. Wilson wrote of his protagonist, "Underneath the bland exterior which the business world demanded of him, Tom Rath was of course a very angry man. When I named him 'Rath' I thought I might be criticized for making this too obvious… but Tom's manners in the book were so good that very few people picked this up."[3]

I confess to being one of the readers that failed to "pick this up." Following D. H. Lawrence's dictum to "[n]ever [trust] the artist. Trust the tale[,]"[4] Rath is presented not as angry but as empty. Wilson does not understand him.

Even during the war, when his life was at times very much at risk, Rath betrays no hint of what the war is about and no particular dislike—certainly no hatred—for the enemy. He does not fight out of a sense of patriotism. He joined the army because that is what Harvard graduates like him were doing then.

In civilian life, Rath does not want a career, he wants a job. If the job is to please his boss, that is fine. Rath is not inspirational. He is not aspirational. The thought of following this man into a real battle or a corporate battle is terrifying. Rath is, in a word, a conformist. So is his wife. They define the opposite of charisma. They are simply boring.

What about the big boss, Ralph Hopkins, CEO of UBS? What are we to make of him? He seems like a rather nice fellow, unfailingly polite. He is, by the standards of the times, rich—with a salary of $200,000 a year and assets of about $5 million. It is mentioned more than once that he is short of stature, not more than "five feet three or four." Tom was expecting someone "seven feet tall" prior to their first meeting.

Facing the classic trade-off between love and power, Hopkins chooses the latter. His spoiled, insufferable eighteen-year-old daughter marries a worthless playboy twice her age. His wife is depressed, and the gulf separating the two of them is wide. Hopkins is a workaholic and doesn't have time for such matters. We are told that Hopkins is fifty years old, but the reader pictures him as at least ten years older. He is compelled to live the life he lives. He is without free will.

Although one assumes that UBS is a big company, the other executives we encounter do very little work. They are flunkies. Job One is managing Hopkins without his knowing he is being managed. They deal with him very much the way Harlow Curtice is dealt with ("Platoons of subordinates jump when he twitches").

For all his worldly success, Hopkins is a stranger to happiness. Toward the end of the novel, he says to Rath, "Somebody has to do the big jobs! ...This world was built by men like me! To really do a job, you have to live it, body and soul! You people who just give half your mind to do your work are riding on our backs!"[5] In the movie's screenplay, this parting declaration is slightly altered to make the point crystal clear: "...body and soul, who lift it up regardless of anybody or anything else. Without men like me, there wouldn't be any big successful businesses. My mistake was in being one of those men."[6] Each of us has his cross to bear, but Hopkins finds his especially heavy. "Success" is indeed a "bitch-goddess" to him.[7]

He is a victim, not a man to be envied or emulated. A less charismatic character one will rarely encounter. Perhaps it is lonely at the top. But this lonely? I have met CEOs who did not like their jobs. But not many.

THE BUSINESS EXECUTIVE OF THE 1950s IN FACT: *THE ORGANIZATION MAN*

William H. Whyte published *The Organization Man* in 1956, and, as a columnist correctly observed, "Whyte's [organization] man rapidly became confused with the hero of a popular novel, Sloan Wilson's *The Man in the Gray Flannel Suit*."[1] The confusion is understandable. Tom Rath, the man in the gray flannel suit, is the fictional depiction of the modal person about whom Whyte reports in *The Organization Man*. If anything, the confusion is unfair to Whyte, who is a more astute observer than Wilson.

Neither Whyte nor Wilson doubts the hegemony of the large corporation in American life during the 1950s. The question they both pose is: How does the individual deal with this institutional reality?

The demands of the corporation are clear in Whyte's book. The organization presents itself as benevolent. It will pay you well enough so that you will live better than your parents did. It will take care of you.

The price of this benevolence is invisible at first but anything other than trivial. In the organization, your goal is to conform to the mediocrity it demands. Remember: "No geniuses here; just a bunch of average Americans working together." Average is the goal. The goal is achieved through conformity to the dictates of the organization and of the committees through which the organization polices itself. The price of belonging is your individuality. Whatever makes you different, whatever makes you special, must be left at the threshold of the organization. The organization kills you with kindness. "It is easy," Whyte writes, "to fight obvious tyranny; it is not easy to fight benevolence..."[2] It is the velvet glove, not the iron fist. But the glove is tight.

Whyte was born into an upper-middle-class family in suburban Philadelphia, attended prep school, and graduated from Princeton in 1939. He served in the Marine Corps from 1941 to 1945, worked for *Fortune* as a writer and as an assistant managing editor from 1946 to 1958, and was an independent author for the remainder of his career.

Between Princeton and the marines, Whyte got a job with the Vick Chemical Company, now owned by Procter & Gamble. His description of Vick's training program is worth the price of the book. The approach of Vick to business was the opposite of what Whyte chronicles after the war.

The training was intensely practical. Whyte and his classmates spent most of their time "memorizing list prices, sales spiels, counters to objections, and the prices and techniques... of Vick's most troublesome competitors." "What management philosophy we did get," Whyte explains, "was brief and to the point."[3] The company president, Mr. H. S. Richardson, took the class of new recruits up to the Cloud Club on top of the Chrysler Building. All thirty-eight recruits came. It was taken for granted that only six or seven would be invited back a second time.

Richardson posed the following problem to the group: You have been buying cartons for your product for years from one supplier. This supplier has proven perfectly satisfactory and has become so specialized that your business is the only account he has. One fine day, another supplier tells you he will deliver the same boxes less expensively. What do you do?

The trainees squirmed. How much money would we save? Could the traditional supplier meet the new low price? Richardson was unimpressed. The decision is easy. The new man gets the contract. You have to decide whether you want to be a businessman or not. If you do, the answer is simple and straightforward.

After this lesson in naked Darwinism, the trainees were sent out into the field. There the rubber met the road. It was the Parris Island of business. Whyte was assigned eastern Kentucky. He rose early and went to sleep late in run-down lodging houses. The waking hours were not that nice, either.

"Our assignment was to persuade the dealer [i.e., the proprietor of a general store] to take a year's supply at once, or, preferably, more than a year's supply, so he would have no money or shelf space left for other brands. After the sale, or no sale, we would turn to market research and note down the amount sold by 'chiseling' competitors (i.e., competitors; there was no acknowledgment on our report blank of any other kind)."[4] The trainee would next seize an opportunity to squirt some Vatronol (this was a decongestant designed to prevent or shorten the common cold) up the dealer's nose. In addition, the trainee plastered signs all over the store and on every barn door and fence post he could find leading to and from it.

This was not easy work. Whyte found himself feeling sorry for the storekeepers on whom he was assigned to push product. He found himself feeling sorry for himself, working twelve-hour days selling to people who didn't want to buy and filling out forms day and night. Worst of all, he didn't succeed in selling much of anything.

"The company sent its head training supervisor to see if anything could be salvaged." The problem, the supervisor told Whyte after observing his technique, was his state of mind. "Fella, you will never sell anybody anything until you learn one simple thing. The man on the other side of the counter is the enemy." And that is how Vick taught its trainees to treat everybody: as the enemy. Believe me, this is not what they teach at Harvard Business School. The goal was to move merchandise and plaster the countryside with signs. Pure and simple. Show no mercy. That is what the trainees learned in this "cram course in reality."[5]

After serving briefly in the Vick Marine Corps, Whyte joined the United States Marine Corps, became an officer, and saw action in Guadalcanal. The action he saw was murderous. He killed men. Friends of his were killed. He saw bravery and stupidity not only on the enemy's side but on his own as well.

This was a genuine "cram course in reality." This enemy was not a store proprietor. He was a real soldier with real weapons who could and did kill your friends and certainly could have, in the randomness of battle, killed you. Whyte lived in reality the wartime experience of the fictional Tom Rath.

Whyte contracted malaria on Guadalcanal and returned to the United States after the campaign. He spent the remainder of the war at the United States Marine Corps Staff and Command School, lecturing and writing on the qualities of the Japanese soldier. His writing is astute and clinical, and the self-pity he experienced in the hills of eastern Kentucky as a "drummer" for Vick is nowhere in evidence.

Whyte grew up on Guadalcanal. An interesting quality of his writing is its tone, approaching, at times, empathy for the enemy. For example, "Enemy morale: Low. Members of outposts probably physically weak and suffering from hunger, and probably very unhappy about the whole thing."[6] Whyte's articles in the *Marine Corps Gazette* brought him to the attention of *Fortune*.

Whyte's experience first with Vick and then with the infinitely more enveloping experience of the Guadalcanal campaign must have shaped his attitude toward corporate America as he perceived it after the war. In Guadalcanal, especially serving as Whyte did as an intelligence officer, it was worth your life to develop a very firm grasp on reality. "You have to watch every clump of bushes for snipers and machine guns. You also have to listen to the birds and distinguish between the real McCoy and the phony birdcalls the Japs use."[7]

———

One work of fiction; one work of nonfiction. Commentators in the 1950s saw them as zeroing in on a signature aspect of the times. At the core of the lives of the people discussed, there was emptiness. No sense of mission. No spiritual life. No chance for heroism. No opportunity to stand out.

It was a world characterized by what one scholar labeled "repressive tolerance."[8] As long as you played by the rules and played the game between the lines, you would be taken care of by the corporation. The price of security was mediocrity. Fit in. Let others make decisions for you. Shun individuality.

Some people found this environment comfortable in its undemanding nature. Others found it stifling.

CHAPTER 5

EDWIN H. LAND: THE CHARISMATIC BUSINESS LEADER BEFORE HIS TIME

Edwin Herbert Land was born in Bridgeport, Connecticut, on May 7, 1909. He was a genuine individualist, an impact player, and a born revolutionary in technology. He was not included in *Time*'s Gallery of Corporate Leaders, which accompanied the article on Man of the Year Harlow Curtice. *Time* did put Land on the cover of its June 26, 1972, issue, taking a picture with an SX-70 camera—the greatest technical, if not financial, creation of Polaroid, the company he cofounded and ran.[1] A few months later, on October 27, 1972, Land was featured on the cover of *Life* magazine. Just above him on the cover is the headline "A Genius and His MAGIC CAMERA."[2] No amount of advertising dollars could buy publicity like this. The original code name for the SX-70 was "Aladdin."[3] It was appropriate—Land and Polaroid did indeed deal in magic.

Land's parents were of Eastern European Jewish descent. His father owned a scrap metal yard. The family was apparently reasonably prosperous. Shortly after World War I,

Land's father moved the family and the business to Norwich, Connecticut, which became the family's home from then on. The Land family's life was "stable and conventional," according to one biographer.[4] The description is intriguing, because Land was the least conventional of businesspeople. In 1964, he said, "No person could possibly be original in one area unless he were possessed of the emotional and social stability that comes from fixed attitudes in all areas other than the one in which he is being original..."[5] Land married Helen Terre Maislen in 1929. The marriage lasted until his death sixty-two years later.

Land viewed himself as a scientist, but he was a scientist with "the rare ability to transform brilliant technical ideas into commercial successes."[6] From youth, and indeed from childhood, he developed an interest in light. Also from an early age, he came to believe that great inventions—inventions that challenged the imagination of the inventor and that improved people's lives—were tied up with business enterprise. This point of view helps explain why Land did not go into the academy, in which he certainly would have thrived, and why he did not make a living by selling his creations to large, established businesses as a consultant. He wanted to control the commercial fate of his technical creations.

Land's idea was to invent the future by creating products people did not know they wanted. His goal was to solve problems others did not know existed. The products that solved these problems had to be uncompromising, to stand out not only for their functionality but for their beauty. For him, aesthetics and enterprise were inextricably intertwined. "I am first of all an artistic person," he said later in life. "I'm interested in love and affection and sharing and making beauty part of everyday life... I'm lucky enough to... earn my living by contributing to a warmer and richer world... And if I use all my scientific, professional abilities in doing that, I think that makes for a good life."[7] One business historian entitled his chapter on Land "The Philosopher Scientist..." The rest of the chapter title is "...with Some Account of His *Doppelgänger*, Steve Jobs."[8] In this case, the comparison is apt. On Land's Wikipedia page, we see: "Influenced: Steve Jobs."[9]

"Not only was [Land] one of the great inventors of our time," Jobs said in 1985, "but, more importantly, he saw the intersection of art and science and business and built an organization to reflect that... The man is a national treasure."[10] When Jobs visited Land at his Rowland Institute (a research organization that Land created), Tom Hughes, who knew both men, said that Jobs showed an emotional side Hughes had not seen previously. "It was sort of a father-son reunion. Steve was so clearly in admiration of Dr. Land and taken with every word he had to share. It was a very touching moment in time."[11]

Jobs once said that "It is in Apple's DNA that technology alone is not enough—it's technology married with liberal arts, married with the humanities, that yields the results that make our hearts sing."[12] Although Land was a brilliant self-taught scientist and inventor and had his name on 533 patents (Thomas Edison had 1,093), he had an extraordinarily rich artistic side. That is a valuable asset if one aims to transform the world of photography. His most famous invention was instant photography, the purpose of which, he said, was "essentially aesthetic."[13]

Land graduated from the Norwich Free Academy in 1926. In his high school years there, he learned more than the school had to teach. His physics instructor said Land "was already working at a level where I couldn't help him."[14] Next it was on to Harvard, where Land studied chemistry for a year before leaving to go to New York City. It was there that he invented the first inexpensive filter for polarizing (removing the glare from) light.

In the fall of 1929, Land returned to Harvard. He was married on November 10. That weekend he lost almost $10,000 because of the stock market plunge that began on October 29. The loss of what was then quite a large amount of money did not faze the newlyweds.[15]

One of his physics instructors at Harvard, George Wheelwright III, was so impressed with Land's intellect and his drive that he suggested they go into business together. This they did in the summer of 1932, founding the Land-Wheelwright Laboratory. For the second time, Land dropped out of Harvard. The depth of the worst depression in American history was not a good time to start a business, but the two were undaunted. They believed there was a market for lenses in the automobile industry that could polarize light in order to solve the problem of glare from headlights. With a myopia that increased with time, the automobile industry was not interested. There was, however, a market for polarized lenses among sunglass manufacturers and also during the first 3-D motion picture craze. The company did more than survive. It began to establish a reputation as an innovator, and Land began to attract some publicity. A new name was needed. They chose Polaroid in 1937, and the partnership was turned into a corporation. This is the year that is referred to as the founding of the company, not 1932.

Wheelwright left the company that year. Land lived life at a torrid pace. Wheelwright simply could not keep up. He was disappointed "that I didn't accomplish what I intended to for him." To this observation, a mutual friend hit upon a truth. "Look, George—a man like Land—if you get one act out of the show... you have all you can expect. You've had it, and so have I."[16] Wheelwright and Land parted painfully but on good terms. Their parting illustrates a truth about charismatic people. They often create a persona that resists lasting intimacy with the people with whom they work. For more than the next four decades, Polaroid really was the lengthened shadow of a single man.

The company survived during World War II as a military contractor for devices such as night-viewing goggles. The breakthrough insight with which Land and Polaroid will forever be associated took place in 1943. Land and his family were on vacation in New Mexico. He took a picture of his three-year-old daughter, Jennifer. Like father, like daughter. Jennifer wanted to see the picture immediately. Why couldn't she? Anyone who has ever seen a darkroom could have given a dozen reasons. But for Land, that question meant it was time to think.

"There was about an inch of snow," he later recalled, "and the wonderful sunshine and you could walk with no coat. And so, I went for a walk, haunted by my daughter's question, stimulated by the dangerously invigorating plateau air of Santa Fe. And during the course of that walk the question kept coming, 'Why not? Why not make a camera that gave a picture right away?'

"I think we all solve problems in one way only, namely in terms of our own personality, experience, and background. Prior to that day, I had been working with my colleagues on a number of photographic processes—in particular one call Vectograph, which makes images in terms of vectorial inequality, three-dimensional images. We had been making those for military purposes, and in the course... of doing that had learned a great deal about the image-making...

"Strangely, by the end of that walk, the solution to the problem had been pretty well formulated."[17] New Mexico's state motto is "The Land of Enchantment." Edwin Land would have found that appropriate.

The camera and the world of photography were the perfect place for Land to devote his attention. They contained within them both limitless technological challenges as well as opportunities to make an aesthetic statement.

People have drawn pictures since before history began. This activity unites us with one another, and it differentiates us from animals. They don't draw; we do.

Pictures are a powerful weapon against an adversary that every human being faces. Life comes to an end. We all die. But a photograph stops time. Imagine the happiest day of your life. If you have a picture of it, look at it. You can relive it in some sense even though the time in which it took place has passed. In 1972, Land recalled the following episode from his childhood. "The world around the child is shifting and fleeting and unreliable and hazardous. It cannot be retained; it is constantly slipping away. To a child, a photograph gives a permanent thing that is both outside himself and part of himself. He gets a new kind of security from every picture he takes. I remember the first picture that I developed as a child. It was a picture of our French poodle. The dog really was unavailable to me. He was always running away; there were things he had to do at night as he roamed through the countryside. Then there was a picture I took of him. There I had him. He couldn't get away."[18] One of Land's associates once described him as having "the exuberance of a small child."[19] In addition to his ability to concentrate fully for hours on end, there was an inviting playfulness lurking nearby.

Many volumes have been written about photography since its invention, and some of the most creative artists in the world have chosen to express themselves through it. A camera is not merely a toy, nor is it only an instrument of magical technology, although it combines both toy-like and magical properties. Like other great media of artistic expression, a photograph can touch people of different backgrounds, cultures, and languages. This is not just another product. It permits the photographer to make a statement about the human condition.[20]

Land said in 1987, "My motto is very personal and may not fit anyone else or any other company. It is: Don't do anything that someone else can do. Don't undertake a project unless it is manifestly important and nearly impossible."[21] Instant photography qualified. According to the American Chemical Society write-up on the occasion of the dedication at the MIT Museum on August 13, 2015, "The instant photography system Land imagined was a radical departure from traditional film processing… Land's system required a new kind of camera and film, a system that would compress all the components of a darkroom into a single film unit, to be processed in under a minute after being ejected from the camera… [T]he System would allow users to evaluate and share images moments after they had been taken, a transformational change from traditional photography."

Land demonstrated instant photography for the first time on February 21, 1947, at a meeting in New York City of the Optical Society of America. He knew how to introduce a product. "Using a modified 8x10 camera, Land took a picture of his face. He then pulled the negative sheet out of the camera, joined it with a sheet of photo paper, and began the development process by feeding the whole thing through a processor... Then he set a timer, and told the crowd, '50 seconds.' When [the timer] went off, he revealed a fully-developed photo of his face. The crowd gasped, and instant photography was born." The verdict of journalists was that the device was "revolutionary." Figuring out how to manufacture the camera took a year. [22]

The first Polaroid camera sold directly to consumers was marketed at Jordan Marsh, a well-known Boston department store, the day after Thanksgiving in 1948. It was the Model 95 with Type 40 film and, truth be told, it was not one of the world's great cameras. The ideal was "a compact, one-step color picture machine." The reality was "Large, heavy (five pounds), and... expensive ($89.95), it required manual setting of shutter speed and lens opening, needed considerable practice to get passable results... and turned out pictures printed in sepia tones reminiscent of a bygone era."[23] Land bet the company on this device. And when you bet the company, you only have to lose once.

No one knew how the camera would do. Needless to say, no focus groups had been conducted. The camera sold out in minutes. "The scene was so hectic... that one customer was [accidentally] sold a nonworking model."[24]

With instant photography, however imperfectly realized, Land and Polaroid had struck the mother lode. "As Land had predicted, the new camera found its own unchallenged market niche. It catered to Americans' love of gadgetry, their craving for instant gratification, and their orientation toward things visual, a penchant long nurtured by movies, newsreels, picture magazines, and… soon to include television. It also unleashed a whole new cottage industry, home pornography, permitting the libidinous to realize their fantasies without fear of exposure by prurient druggists or tale-bearing film developers."[25]

In the following years, Polaroid kept bringing out new and improved cameras. It is striking how many cameras there were. Polaroid had no fear of SKU creep. Quality kept improving as prices fell. The company was not reticent about invading the low-price market. For all the many comparisons to Apple, the two companies are quite unlike in this regard. Apple sells products at premium prices. When Polaroid decided to invade the mass market, it introduced in 1965 its Model 20 "Swinger," retailing at $19.95.

This was the camera for the Pepsi Generation. "The lightweight (22 ounces), fixed-focus Swinger was intended to be easy to use. You looked into the viewfinder, turned a red knob, clicked the shutter as soon as you saw the word 'YES' and then zipped off your finished black-and-white picture (there were eight to a pack of film) in 10 to 15 seconds, after which you had to apply a chemical coating. Equipped with a 'built-in flash gun,' the product sold so quickly that Polaroid had to ration its supply to camera stores."[26]

The Swinger was the fastest-selling camera the company ever produced. In Swinger ads on YouTube, young people frolic on the beach with their cameras. Ali MacGraw is one of the models. A journalist at the time praised the "catchy jingle."[27] Be warned. The jingle is terrible. Mute the sound.

In 1947, the year Land dramatically introduced instant photography, Polaroid posted sales of $1.5 million and a loss of almost a million dollars. A decade later, when the company was listed on the New York Stock Exchange, sales were $48.043 million and profits $5.355 million. A decade after that, in 1967, sales were $374.4 million and profits $57.4 million. In 1968, $402 million and $58.9 million. In 1969, $469.6 million and $63.1 million. Polaroid became one of the "nifty fifty," a darling of Wall Street. By 1972, the company enjoyed a price/earnings ratio of 93.5 as its stock soared above $140 a share.[28]

Polaroid cameras, for all their success, still had some stark deficiencies. In the words of a journalist in 1970, "[T]he Land camera was—and still is—everything a camera for a mass market should not be. It is too big, too expensive, and too difficult to use. A quick sequence of photographs is impossible. A Land camera user leaves a trail of refuse. Additional prints and enlargements are difficult to obtain. The film seems expensive. And despite elegant innovations that delight the technically minded, it forgives few errors."[29]

All this was true. The solution was going to be the SX-70. This was another "bet the company" product. It taxed Polaroid to the very limit. Land liked to say that "Virtue and a good product are invincible."[30] Another one of his sayings was that what they don't teach you at Harvard Business School is that "[I]f anything is worth doing, it's worth doing to excess."[31] The SX-70 was a great product, when it worked as Land conceived it—which was not as often as was necessary. It would test these propositions. Could one individual be an entrepreneur, a visionary, a basic scientist, a technologist, and a marketer? Land was all these things, but the strain and tension involved in bringing the SX-70 to life were so great that they opened up fissures in the corporation, which widened with time. Polaroid never really recovered from the trauma of giving birth to this product.

George Eastman purchased his first camera on November 13, 1877. It cost him $49.58. The lessons he bought to learn how to use it set him back another $5, for a total cost of $54.58. You had to know a lot to be able to take a photograph in 1877. Here is a description of Eastman's starting kit: "The heavy camera itself, together with a tripod, plus plates, paper, boxes for storing negatives, and a tent that could be set up as a dark room, [and] also the furnishings of a small chemistry laboratory—nitrate of silver, acetate soda, chlorides of gold, sodium, and iron, collodion, varnish, alcohol, litmus paper, hydrometer, graduate, evaporating dish, funnel, bristle brush, scales and weights, and washing pans."

Twenty-three years later, in 1900, the Eastman Kodak Company brought out the Brownie. This was the product that made mass-market photography possible. It cost one dollar, plus fifteen cents for the film. The advertisement for it was one of the great slogans in history: "You press the button and we do the rest."[32]

Polaroid's cameras were not nearly as complex as the first one Eastman bought. But they were not simple to use. The instruction manual for the Swinger went on for page after page, and like all instruction manuals, it is facedown-in-the-soup boring to read. What would be the penalty if you did not master the instructions? As the manual itself warned, "[I]f you don't follow the instructions, you're heading for trouble."[33] Needless to say, this warning is not mentioned in the advertisements. For all the comparisons between Jobs and Land, we should note that Apple sells almost all its products without manuals.

The SX-70 was the camera Land had wanted to bring out since he gave birth to instant photography decades previously. This was going to be Polaroid's version of the Brownie. You push the button. The camera does the rest.

The SX-70 was introduced to the world on April 25, 1972. The company had been working on it since the mid-1960s and had spent a half a billion dollars developing it.[34] That day, thousands of shareholders, market analysts, Polaroid employees, and reporters gathered at the Polaroid campus in Needham, a suburb of Boston, to see Land take the stage, remove the SX-70 from his jacket pocket (it weighed a mere twenty-two ounces), light his pipe, and proceed with what the *New York Times* called a "one man show." "Photography," according to the *Times*, "will never be the same after today."[35]

Here is a description from Peter C. Wensberg, a Polaroid marketing vice president, of the magnitude of the project the company undertook: "The camera was to include revolutionary optics and a complete set of photonic controls, some of which had not yet been invented. Three Polaroid factories were being built simultaneously... Each required process machinery that was yet to be conceived, built, and installed... Many of the most important manufacturing issues had not been solved, since the specifications of the camera and film were still changing. The SX-70 program was so complex and so extended the boundaries of half a dozen technologies that those who worked on it had difficulty in stretching their faith and their optimism beyond the piece of the whole on which their own energies were concentrated. Land was virtually the only person in the company who knew in detail all the difficulties that had to be surmounted. The rest of us could only guess."[36]

Think of what Wensberg wrote. Those involved in the SX-70 had to "stretch their faith." Why did people stretch their faith? Because they had in Land a charismatic leader. He had defied the odds and proved the doubters wrong time and again. Surely, this adventure would be no exception.

As far as the marketing and selling of the camera were concerned, the rule was: only the best. Perhaps the greatest actor of the twentieth century, Laurence Olivier, made a sixty-second commercial for it. He was paid a quarter of a million dollars to do so, and his contract stipulated that the commercial not be shown in Britain. It was the only commercial he ever made.[37]

Land was dreaming big dreams. "My fantasy is that it'll be as widely used as the telephone." This time, Land's reach exceeded his grasp. The SX-70 was nine months late to the market, achieving national distribution in September of 1973. When it arrived, it was beset by numberless problems. By mid-1974, a share of Polaroid stock sold for fourteen dollars. This was a staggering overreaction. The book value of the company's assets was over nineteen dollars a share. Suddenly, a company that was once worth $4.5 billion was worth $450 million. Land, his wife, and their charities lost about $600 million before the stock bounced back somewhat.[38] So much for the alignment of management compensation with shareholder value through using stock to provide an incentive to management.

The SX-70 turned out to be a technological triumph but only a moderately successful commercial product. The effort to create it derailed the company. Something of Land's magic was lost. Here is the conclusion of one expert on the product: "SX-70 was a huge gamble that eventually paid off, but bloodily and later than expected, damaging Land's credibility with... managers, with investors, and even with those members of the board of directors who had known him longest. With investors hurt and the status of a glamour investment gone, the company could no longer recruit fresh capital from the stock market, as it had done thrice to create war chests for the next technical adventure ...[At length] Polaroid got the hang of this revolution, without collapsing."[39] Damning with faint praise. As Max Weber observed about charismatic individuals, when they lose their ability to deliver miracles, they lose their charisma as well.

In January 1975, Land appointed William J. McCune to be president of Polaroid. Until that time, Land had been everything—president, chairman of the board, chief executive officer, chief technology officer, chief everything else—and a major shareholder. McCune was fifty-nine years old and had been with Polaroid since 1939. Land was sixty-five and made this move at the urging of, and under pressure from, the board. Polaroid earnings in 1974 ($28.4 million) were well below those of 1973 ($51.8 million). Something had to be done, and this was it. Land remained chairman of the board and chief executive officer. He was not finished with adventures on the technological frontier.

Polavision was an instant home movie system, which was Land's next great love. He introduced the idea to the press in 1977. When the time came for Q&A, one person asked, "What about the bottom line?" Land responded that Polaroid's mission was "to build, in industry, domains that haven't existed before. That helps the economy and brings beauty, but makes it profitable, too. I beseech you to put an end to the phony nonsense of industrial structure. It turns off young people.

'The only thing that matters is the bottom line'? What a presumptuous thing to say. The bottom line is in heaven. The real business of business is building things."[40]

Now it was Land's turn to learn that reality is unforgiving. Polavision was a failure—the most complete failure of Land's career. Polaroid announced a $68 million write-off in September of 1979.

This was also the end for Land at Polaroid. His greatest strengths—his genius, his tenacity, his optimism, his relentlessness, his stubbornness—had slowly during the 1970s become his greatest weaknesses. He had become more isolated within the company. Finally, in 1979, the board asked him to step down. He could have fought this decision. He owned a lot of shares of the company. But for reasons that are lost to history, this man, a fighter his whole life, decided that it was time to go. He severed his connection with the firm as an executive, and in 1982 and 1985, he ended his connection with it financially by selling the four million shares of stock he held. An era had come to an end.

What can one say about Polaroid after Land? "Dr. Land is a genius, and much of the creativity of the company came from his perceptions and convictions about things," William McCune, Land's successor as Polaroid's CEO, told the *New York Times* in 1983, a year after Land resigned as chairman. "We obviously do not have a genius of that caliber in the company anymore."[41] That was quite true, and it is more than a little surprising that McCune made this admission publicly. Neither under him nor his successors did Polaroid produce a truly exciting product. The company spent a lot of money exploring electronics but did not know what to do with whatever it learned. Crippled more than anything else by a failure of imagination, Polaroid was left behind by the digital revolution and declared bankruptcy in 2001. Land became a pure researcher at the Rowland Institute, his creation, until his death on March 1, 1991.

Whatever an organization man was, Land was not. The company worked for the man, not the other way around. He satisfied himself—a characteristic of the charismatic personality. In the terminology of sociologist David Riesman's classic, *The Lonely Crowd: A Study of the Changing American Character*, Land was "inner directed" rather than "other directed." His "control equipment" was the gyroscope, not radar.[42]

Inner directed is in no sense a synonym for selfish. By giving the world instant photography, Land gave the world a capability that he believed would enrich people's lives. He felt that he had a better chance of achieving this goal than anyone else. Remember, he said that you should do what only you could. Challenge yourself. Push yourself.

To live this life, you must be an autodidact. No one can teach you how to do what has never been done before. A darkroom used for developing photographs is a complicated place where a complicated process is undertaken. The idea that you could put all this complexity into a handheld device was breathtaking. It is both unsurprising and charming that the idea was first suggested to Land by his three-year-old daughter, Jennifer. All she knew was what she wanted. She did not know how difficult it would be to satisfy her desire. She was too young to have had her imagination educated out of her. In the charismatic businessperson, you will often encounter a childlike optimism in the face of challenges.

Land was a mission-driven man who was fascinated by light his whole life. He made a great deal of money during the course of his career, but he was not money-motivated. He did not believe in market research because he was engaged in creating products people did not know they wanted. One of his executives said, "I learned from Dr. Land... that 'the ideal business is composed of managers and dreamers, and it is the responsibility of the former to protect the latter.'"[43]

PART II

1975 TO 1995:
THE TRANSITIONAL ERA

The United States in 1975 was a very different country from what it had been a half decade earlier. The swinging '60s had morphed into the sobering '70s. The Vietnam War, in which the nation had been involved since at least the Kennedy administration and arguably since the Eisenhower administration, finally came to an end in April of 1975 when President Gerald Ford declared that it was over. America's defeat was complete and unmitigated.

President Richard Nixon, the "New Nixon" who reappeared on the national scene in the late 1960s, won a close election against Hubert Humphrey in 1968 and was overwhelmingly reelected to a second term in 1972, winning every state in the union except Massachusetts (and the District of Columbia), thus burying his opponent George McGovern.

It turned out that the new Nixon was not that different from the old one. His involvement in the cover-up of the Watergate break-in turned his second administration into a slow-motion train wreck. At length, even the Republican Party turned against him, and he was the first president forced to resign, which he did in the face of certain impeachment and conviction, on August 9, 1974. The evening before he left office, Nixon delivered a surreal speech in which he said, "[A]lways remember, others may hate you, but those who hate you don't win unless you hate them, and then you destroy yourself." Unwittingly, Nixon solved the riddle of his whole career. His hatred of those who hated him destroyed him.[1]

People of an age to follow such things will never forget this drama. For the first time in American history, an American president, the nation's chief executive officer, was forced to resign because of his fear of those he perceived to be his "enemies" and because of the transparent lies he could not keep himself from telling.

Vietnam and Watergate. Those words should be written as one. The nation's attitude toward its leaders would never be the same. People began putting bumper stickers on their cars that declared in red letters, "Question Authority." One did not see such things in the 1950s, and the authority meant to be questioned was not only political.

America's place on the global business scene was deteriorating during the 1970s. Japan and Europe were climbing back onto their feet after the devastation of World War II. The United States no longer had the "free world" all to itself.

Imports of automobiles, which you may recall were 0.71 percent in 1955, accounted for 18.2 percent of American domestic sales in 1975. Half of these cars were from Japan, where Toyota pioneered a new production system that delivered high-quality, fuel-efficient vehicles.[2]

Fuel efficiency mattered more than ever before in the history of the automobile industry. In 1968, the State Department informed foreign governments that American oil production was approaching its limits. Two years later, domestic oil production peaked. By early 1974, the end of the era of cheap oil had arrived. The Arab oil embargo with the support of other OPEC members successfully pushed the price of oil up by a factor of eight compared to five years earlier.[3]

Oil was the oxygen of the industrial economy that America had known for a century. Not only automobiles but all manufacturing in addition to heating oil, lubricants, and a host of other activities were affected. Here is one example: majestic but aging buildings on northern college campuses had been constructed without regard to heating costs, which suddenly mattered a great deal.

Americans were living in a new world. A world of lines at gas stations and Sunday gas station closings. A world of lengthy winter breaks for schools where winter was severe. When the United States lost control of oil, it lost control, to an important degree, of its destiny.

In this time of trouble, the nation was asking: Where have all the leaders gone? In the four chapters that follow, we will look at three business leaders—Lee Iacocca, Mary Kay Ash, and Sam Walton. How did they answer this question? In the fourth chapter we will also look at an important trend: the rise of the influence of the investor in business administration. In this era, the professional manager had to take the investor into account to a greater extent than previously. The hostile takeover, rare in the preceding years, became much more common.

CHAPTER 6

RESILIENCE:
THE LEE IACOCCA STORY

In 1964, a historian of American culture named Henry Nash Smith published an essay entitled "The Search for a Capitalist Hero: Businessmen in American Fiction." Search though he did, Professor Smith couldn't find any. "The search for a capitalist hero has... led to no viable results, and there is little indication that it will be more successful in the future. For the stereotypes used by the popular novelists cannot sustain a character of real imaginative substance, and serious writers seem unable to take an interest in a system of values based on economic assumptions."[1] Had someone written an article by the same title precisely twenty years later and had the article dealt with capitalist heroes in fact rather than in fiction, finding one would not have been difficult. It would have been Lee Iacocca.

Born in Allentown, Pennsylvania, to Italian immigrant parents on October 15, 1924 (he died on July 2, 2019, at his home in Bel Air, California), Iacocca spent his whole business career, spanning half a century from 1946, in the automobile industry. What would have made him number one on a list of capitalist heroes was saving Chrysler, at the time the nation's tenth largest corporation, from bankruptcy.

Cementing his selection would have been the publication of *Iacocca: An Autobiography* in 1984.[2] To the surprise of many, this became the best-selling nonfiction hardcover book of 1984 and 1985. Indeed, this book has been quite a phenomenon. It was released on October 15, 1984, and rocketed to the top of the best-seller list in a week. Two months later, the publisher of the paperback version printed the millionth copy.[3] This was the biggest-selling business autobiography up to the time of its publication.

Iacocca had, in the midst of the Chrysler crisis, testified publicly before Congress. Even more important, he was featured in the television advertisements for the "new" Chrysler Corporation. He managed to persuade Congress to pass what was colloquially known as the Chrysler bailout bill. President Jimmy Carter signed into law what was formally known as the Chrysler Corporation Loan Guarantee Act of 1979 on January 7, 1980.[4] This act authorized the federal government to guarantee $1.5 billion in loans to Chrysler conditional upon the company's generating $2 billion from interested parties such as suppliers, dealers, and labor unions. Loans guaranteed under the act would have to be repaid in full by December 31, 1990.[5]

This was not the first corporate bailout in US history, but it was the largest, and it was very controversial. Without it, Chrysler, which had been living from hand to mouth for months, would have gone bankrupt. The business world offers no challenge more daunting than turning a failing company around. In the fall of 1979, this was Iacocca's assignment. The phrase was not used at the time, but Chrysler was adjudged to be too big to fail. Chrysler paid the Treasury back in full in 1983, seven years early, which did not hurt the sales of *Iacocca* the following year.

How did Chrysler find itself in the position of having to go to the federal government hat in hand for funds in 1979? How did Lee Iacocca find himself the man doing the asking? Let's approach this second question first and do so by taking a look at his book.

Commenting on his autobiography, Iacocca writes, "Nobody was more surprised than I was when this book jumped to the top of the best-seller list... After all, this is just a story about a kid from a good immigrant family who studied hard and worked hard, who had some big successes and big disappointments, and who made out fine in the end because of the simple values he learned from his parents and teachers, and because he had the good luck to live in America."[6] This is a surprisingly humble self-presentation.

Iacocca graduated from Allentown High School in 1942. Four years earlier, he had been stricken with rheumatic fever, spent half a year in bed, and lost forty pounds. Even though he had fully recovered by 1941, the army classified him as 4F, which meant he was physically unfit for service. This was an "enormous disappointment" to him. He wanted to fight. "Being burdened with a medical deferment during the war seemed like a disgrace, and I began to think of myself as a second-class citizen." The result was that "I buried my head in my books." He was a good student.

Iacocca enrolled in Lehigh University, a first-rate school a couple of miles from Allentown. With the exception of freshman physics, in which he got a D, he excelled at Lehigh, graduating with high honors as an industrial engineering major. Next was a postgraduate fellowship at Princeton, where he studied politics and plastics(!).

In August 1946, Iacocca began his career in the automobile industry with a job as a "student engineer" at Ford. He soon decided that he did not want a career in engineering. "I was eager to be where the real action was—marketing or sales. I liked working with people more than machines."

In his early days at the company, Iacocca describes himself as "bashful and awkward," with "no natural talent" as a salesman. Hard to believe, but those are his words. With one brief setback, he began his upward climb at the company. "[I]t wasn't prestige or power I wanted. It was money." He was still young when he said this of himself. Soon he would want all three.

With the accession of Henry Ford II to the pinnacle of the company in 1945 and his hiring of a team of talented executives, the Ford Motor Company was reorganized and reborn. In 1950, Ford surpassed Chrysler in unit sales to become the nation's second-largest automobile producer, as it had been prior to the decade-long decline under the aged Henry Ford I—albeit quite a distant second to General Motors, which dominated the industry.

Iacocca's career flourished at a company that was on an upward trajectory. Success as an assistant sales manager in the Philadelphia region brought him to the attention of Ford's leadership in Dearborn, Michigan. On November 10, 1960, he became vice president and general manager of the Ford Division, the biggest division in a very large company. "My years as general manager of the Ford Division were the happiest period of my life," according to his autobiography. "...I couldn't wait to get to work in the morning. At night I didn't want to leave."

In 1964, Ford introduced the Mustang, for which Iacocca has always taken the credit. The car was what in the retail world is known as a "door buster." "During the first weekend it was on sale, an unprecedented four million people visited Ford dealerships. The car's public reception [exceeded] our wildest hopes." It is hard to communicate the euphoria this kind of public enthusiasm for your product generates in a company.

The Mustang's success—profits of $1.1 billion in its first two years—was an important boost to Iacocca's career. In January 1965, he was promoted to vice president of Ford's car and truck group. His new office was in the Glass House, the home of the top executives of the company. "I was finally one of the big boys, part of that select group of officers who ate lunch every day with Henry Ford." Two years later, he became an executive vice president of the corporation. "By 1968," he writes, "I was the odds-on favorite to become the next president of the Ford Motor Company." However, "fate intervened."

Fate took the form of Semon "Bunkie" Knudsen. Henry Ford II, the chairman of the board and chief executive officer of the company, was the man who made these decisions, and he hired Knudsen when he was passed over for the presidency of General Motors. Knudsen's father, William, had worked for Ford from 1911 to 1921. He was the production manager at the company, making what at the time was the stupendous salary of $50,000 a year with a 15 percent bonus. But he found Henry Ford I impossible to work for, so he quit.

It did not take long for Knudsen to wind up at General Motors. He was put in charge of the Chevrolet division, which lost $8.7 million in 1921 and which some in the company were advising be shut down. In 1922, with Knudsen in charge, the division made $11.3 million.[7] Along with these profits came promotions. Knudsen became executive vice president in 1933 and president in 1937. His presidency was cut short only when Franklin D. Roosevelt asked him to come to Washington to be co-director of the Office of Production Management.

I have asked the reader to indulge me in this digression for two reasons. First, the story illustrates that the Ford Motor Company has always lost top executive talent because of the idiosyncrasies and sometimes the idiocy of the Ford family. Second, the story shows how ingrown the world of the Detroit automakers was at this time.

Bunkie Knudsen, Iacocca says, "was always suspicious of me. He assumed that I had been after the presidency before he came and that I was still gunning for it after he arrived. He was right on both counts." That last sentence is unquestionably true. But Iacocca follows it with "Fortunately, we were both too busy to spend much time on office politics." According to one source, Iacocca "waged a guerilla campaign under the rubric of 'making life miserable for the son of a bitch.' It was the sort of thing he was best at."[8] Which account is the truth? From available narratives, it seems unlikely that Iacocca could not make time for office politics. Critics branded him a "Machiavellian huckster."[9]

Henry Ford II was delighted at hiring Knudsen. He regarded it as a coup, a view shared by the press. "About fifty-six years ago," Ford said at the press conference with Knudsen announcing the hiring on February 7, 1968, "a man named Knudsen became associated with a man named Ford in a young automobile company. Their relationship became one of the legends of this industry. The senior Knudsen eventually parted company with my grandfather and joined General Motors where he became president. Today the flow of history is reversed."[10]

Bunkie Knudsen was a talented man, and he might have grown into a successful president of Ford, but he never had a chance. Henry Ford himself had a long track record of getting rid of those closest to him in the company. Iacocca and his team had their knives out, too. And other top people in the company did not like the idea of an outsider parachuting into the office next to Ford's.

Knudsen never really understood the environment in which he found himself at Ford. He inadvertently offended people. In addition, "there was the charisma factor. While Iacocca was an excellent speaker and an inspirational leader, Knudsen, a product of the GM system with its deemphasis on self-promotion, was a step backward even from the colorless Arjay Miller…"[11] (Miller, who had joined Ford in 1946, became president of the company in 1963 and was unceremoniously pushed aside to make room for Knudsen.)

Knudsen was out on September 3, 1969. His firing was handled with a maximum of clumsiness. The quip that made the rounds at the company was that Henry Ford I said that history is bunk. Now, Bunkie is history. Henry Ford II briefly established a three-man office of the president. Then, on December 10, 1970, Iacocca writes, "I finally got what I was waiting for: the presidency of Ford."[12]

Ford had 432,000 employees and a $3.5 billion payroll. In North America, its annual output of cars and trucks was 2.5 million and 750,000 respectively. Overseas, Ford built another 1.5 million vehicles. Sales in 1970 were $14.9 billion. Profits, $515 million. It sounds more like an empire than a company. Said Iacocca, "I loved my job... To me, it was sheer excitement." At first.

Like all previous presidents of Ford since 1945, Iacocca got into arguments with Henry Ford II. In his autobiography, he is put in the position of having to attack Ford despite the fact that he owed his career—the wealth, the power, and the prestige—to him.

At first, everything was great. "If Henry was the king, I was the crown prince. And there was no question that the king liked me... All of us who constituted top management... lived the good life in the royal court. We were part of something beyond first class—royal class, perhaps... White coated waiters were on call throughout the day." The top executives ate lunch together in what could have passed for "one of the country's finest restaurants. Dover sole was flown over from England on a daily basis. We enjoyed the finest fruits, no matter what the season. Fancy chocolates, exotic flowers— you name it, we had it."

Slowly but inexorably, the bloom faded from those exotic flowers. Here is Iacocca's explanation. Henry Ford II was "superficial... a sucker for appearances." He "believed" in the "arbitrary use of power." He "never had to work for anything in his life." He was "a little paranoid about some things" such as keeping written records. "He was even worse after Watergate." Iacocca made a deal to buy engines from Honda, which Henry vetoed because "No car with my name on the hood is going to have a Jap engine inside." He had "never been accountable to anyone." He never "[spent] a penny of his own money," charging everything to the company. He "was always a playboy... the ultimate chauvinist, who believed that women were put on earth only for the pleasure of men." He was a racist. In a word, he was "evil."

This was just the beginning. "In 1975, Henry Ford started his month-by-month premeditated plan to destroy me... He turned animal."

"That was when I should have quit." But he didn't. Why not?

Here are his reasons. He hoped that things would somehow get better. He had spent his whole professional life at Ford and "couldn't imagine working anywhere else." He felt he "was far more important [to the company] than Henry." Since Ford was publicly held, he thought his importance might save him. We finally get to the ground truth when Iacocca declares bluntly, "I was... greedy. I enjoyed being president. I liked [the] perks, the special parking place, the private bathroom, the white coated waiters." He was making about a million dollars a year, which was more than the CEO of General Motors. He liked that, too.

Finally, after three years worthy of any soap opera, Iacocca was forced to resign. The official date was October 15, 1978, his fifty-fourth birthday. The reason Henry Ford gave was, "Well, sometimes you just don't like somebody."

"Look at me," Iacocca said to Ford in what he realized would be the final time the two men would speak. "Your timing stinks. We've just made a billion eight for the second year in a row. That's three and a half billion in the past two years. But mark my words, Henry. You may never see a billion eight again. And do you know why? Because you don't know how the fuck we made it in the first place!" The depth of the wound inflicted by being fired cannot be overstated. Iacocca's hatred for Henry Ford was complete. He could not let go of it.

It would not be surprising if he cherished his anger until the day he died.

What was the real reason Ford fired Iacocca? Ford told the truth when he said that sometimes you don't like a person. There was a great deal behind this statement. The late 1970s were a chaotic period in Ford's personal life. He began having angina attacks, and his cardiac problems grew only more serious. He discovered he was mortal. His second marriage collapsed. His relations with his family were frayed to the breaking point.

As for the company, it was enduring a spate of dreadful publicity. Ford was being sued because the Pinto, which was at least as much Iacocca's car as the Mustang, had proven unsafe. It was costing lives and generating lawsuits. A host of other matters were making the company look sleazy.

In the midst of all this, Iacocca, once Henry Ford's fair-haired boy, was emerging unscathed. He upstaged Ford at a conference of Wall Street analysts. Iacocca himself suspected this was trouble. He writes, "When Henry got up to speak at that meeting [of analysts], he was well into his cups. He actually started to babble about how the company was unraveling." The company's chief financial officer said to Iacocca, "Try to save the day for us, or we'll all look like idiots." Iacocca did speak, which, as he said, "may have been the beginning of the end for me." Iacocca had developed a swelled head. He felt the company could not do without him but could do very well without his boss. He grossly underestimated Henry's power. He also underestimated the ability of the man whom Henry had already spotted to be his successor, Philip Caldwell.

Henry, who had always—to put it kindly—been erratic in his treatment of others, had had all he wanted to take from what he viewed as this Italian immigrant interloper. So he did to Iacocca what he did to so many others: he got rid of him. For decades, backstabbing had been a way of life at Ford. The 1970s were no exception.

When Henry Ford II died on September 29, 1987, Iacocca issued a statement. "Our industry and all American business has lost a true leader. His vision and hard work transformed Ford into a great company... Henry Ford and I were friends and colleagues for a lot longer than we were adversaries, and my sympathy goes to his family and friends."[13] Did he write this? Did he mean it? One has one's doubts. Iacocca certainly was not one to bury the hatchet. He was a charismatic leader in a gray-flannel-suit company with a boss whose name was on the door.

If Iacocca had retired at this point—he was fifty-four and had plenty of money—he would not make it onto a list of "capitalist heroes." He would be classified along with Ernest Breech, Arjay Miller, and other top Ford executives since World War II who are of interest only to historians of the industry. It is because of the next chapter in his life—as CEO of Chrysler—that he stands out. And in his next job, Lido Anthony Iacocca would not be penalized for his charisma.

July 13, 1978, was Iacocca's last day in his palatial office in the Glass House. He still had three more months at Ford, during which he could look for a new job. His new office was in a warehouse, a few miles away from the Glass House. "For me, this was Siberia. It was exile to the farthest corner of the kingdom." The warehouse was ugly, unadorned, and depressing beyond words. Someone had tipped off the media that Iacocca would be there that morning. A television reporter "shoved a microphone in my face and asked: 'How do you feel, coming to this warehouse after eight years at the top?'" How is one supposed to answer such a question? Iacocca was mute. When he was out of television range, he said, "I feel like shit."[14]

"This final humiliation was worse than being fired. It was enough to make me want to kill... Henry Ford or myself. [Neither] were real possibilities, but I did start to drink a little more—and shake a lot." Being warehoused he simply could not abide. "The private pain I could have endured. But the deliberate public humiliation was too much for me."

Iacocca's next stop was Chrysler. And it was Chrysler that made him, to use his own word, a "hero." But Iacocca begins his discussion of his saga at Chrysler by saying, "If I had the slightest idea of what lay ahead for me when I joined up with Chrysler, I wouldn't have gone over there for all the money in the world." The task of turning Chrysler around was that hard.

On the other hand, we don't know how seriously to take Iacocca's declaration. His task was unquestionably difficult. But what is more satisfying than doing something that you feel is profoundly worthwhile, that only you can do, and that triumphantly proves that the firing—by which Iacocca was so deeply wounded—was undeserved?

Feelers from Chrysler began almost immediately after it became known that Iacocca had been kicked out of Ford. Iacocca wanted to know how bad things were at the company. The CEO, John J. Riccardo, laid the situation out for him. The biggest immediate problem Iacocca faced was not that people were being untruthful but rather that even top management "didn't have a very good idea of what was going on. They knew Chrysler was bleeding. What they didn't realize... was that it was hemorrhaging."[15]

It became apparent that if the federal Treasury were to come to Chrysler's aid, the company needed to reinvent itself, to be reborn, in the eyes of the public. Chrysler's public affairs officer told Riccardo that "Congress and the country weren't going to act until we staged a morality play. And I told him how he'd been cast: Riccardo takes on himself all the sins of commission and omission, we drive him into the woods and the company is pure again."[16]

Iacocca did have one demand that was nonnegotiable. He wanted "to be my own man... It wasn't just my experience with Henry, although that was part of it... I needed a completely free hand to be able to turn the company around." Physically exhausted, Riccardo not only agreed, he resigned early. Iacocca became what he wanted to be, "numero uno," on November 2, 1978.[17] On the same day he joined the company, Chrysler announced its third-quarter results. It lost almost $160 million, the worst quarter in its history. The stock that day was up three-eighths. By a slim margin, Wall Street was betting that in the contest between brilliant management and a company with bad economics, management would come out on top. The traders were putting their money on Iacocca.

"Why does a guy want to be president?" Iacocca asked rhetorically. "Does he enjoy it? Maybe, but it can make him old and tired. So why does he work so hard? So he can say: 'Hey, I made it to the top. I have accomplished something.'"

Iacocca anticipated that Chrysler would be back on its feet in a couple of years. "But the opposite happened. Everything collapsed. We had the Iranian crisis, and then we had the energy crisis. In 1978, nobody could have imagined that by the next spring there would be havoc in Iran and the price of gas would suddenly double. Then... came the biggest recession in fifty years." This was one of those moments when Iacocca "came close to drowning."

It is remarkable, indeed it is amazing, how little Iacocca knew about Chrysler when he became CEO. During his years at Ford, he "barely knew that Chrysler existed." All eyes were always on General Motors. In his first day in his new position, Iacocca wasn't even certain where Chrysler was and had to ask directions. He knew the company was floundering. But he did not know how badly. And he did not know why. He was to pay the price for this lack of due diligence.

Soon enough, Iacocca "stumbled upon my first major revelation: Chrysler didn't really function like a company at all." The most basic organizational structures and functions that every large company requires to operate properly were absent. The practices of management that had been developed on the railroads in the United States all the way back in the 1850s and that were advanced and sharpened by Alfred P. Sloan Jr. at General Motors in the 1920s were either ignored or unknown. No matter which, they weren't practiced.

There were "thirty-five vice-presidents, each with his own turf. There was no real committee setup, no cement in the organizational chart, no system of meetings to get people talking to each other. I couldn't believe, for example, that the guy running the engineering department wasn't in constant touch with his counterpart in manufacturing... I took one look at that system and I almost threw up."

What was the result of this organizational chaos? You could see it by visiting the Michigan State Fairgrounds. There were at one point in 1979 a hundred thousand cars there and in other large fields as well. These cars were finished goods inventory for which there were no dealer orders. There they were, just baking in the sun, slowly deteriorating, plaintively waiting to be wanted by somebody. They had been manufactured just to keep the plants running. Iacocca was "horrified," and rightly so. Six hundred million dollars in finished goods inventory and a company that was short on cash. Lots of product. No one to buy it.

This was bad, but there was more bad news. Chrysler had not been selling cars to the rental companies Hertz and Avis. It had been leasing them. Every six months, the rental car companies returned the used cars to Chrysler. The company got rid of them at auctions. "Chrysler was running the world's largest leasing company... Sixty thousand used cars were about the last thing we needed."

A few months after he came to Chrysler, "something hit [Iacocca] like a ton of bricks. We were running out of cash... This was probably the greatest jolt... in my business career." He was shocked at the company's lack of financial controls. Without them, how could he make the decisions so vital to the company's survival? Throughout the company, "people were scared and despondent. Nobody was doing anything right." Iacocca eventually fired thirty-three of Chrysler's thirty-five vice presidents. They had been ruined by working at the company.

All this became apparent in 1978, which was not that bad a year for the domestic automobile industry overall. General Motors and Ford posted record sales and profits. Struggling Chrysler sold fewer than half the cars that Ford did. Chrysler's market share dropped from 12.2 percent to 11.1 percent in one year. Its cars were old and boring and of poor quality. Customer reaction was not surprising. The question was:

How do you get the first-class talent necessary to right this sinking ship? Of all the challenges Iacocca faced, this was the biggest, because as everyone in business or any other endeavor knows, without the right people, you are helpless.

When Iacocca was at Ford, he tracked the careers of hundreds of executives there. His first requirement in his effort to fix Chrysler was to get hold of someone who could establish a financial system that generated the information vital to making the right decisions. He did, and the man he hired, Gerald Greenwald, brought others along with him. Soon Greenwald was to become the number two man at Chrysler.

Another key player was Hal Sperlich. "Hal is so talented," Iacocca writes, "that it's difficult to praise him too highly. He may be the best car man in Detroit." Henry Ford forced Iacocca to fire Sperlich in 1977 because he rubbed him the wrong way. Sperlich went to Chrysler. He helped Iacocca unleash the "dynamic young talent [dormant in the company]... I'm talking about people with fire in their eyes. You can practically tell they're good just by looking at them." Iacocca got rid of top management, these people's bosses, and promoted them. Imagine what his arrival on the scene meant to them.

Dealer relations were another part of the enterprise that had to be turned around. The ill will was without bounds. Iacocca found another Ford alumnus and brought him to Chrysler's headquarters to deal with this dilemma. He turned out to be just the man for the job.

Product quality was an enormous problem. Doing something about quality control was vital. Iacocca put together a four-man team to deal with that issue. To handle the sorry state of supplier relations, Iacocca recruited another Ford executive.

For all these people, young and old, Iacocca's arrival heralded a rebirth. The young were being recognized and given responsibilities they could only have dreamed of. The veterans were being asked to use the talent they had accumulated over years to save a failing but iconic American company. Their talent was vital, and it was needed now! "It was more than a challenge," Iacocca writes, "it was an adventure."

Chrysler was on the move. But just as there was a glimmer of hope on the horizon, disaster struck. The Iranian Revolution led to skyrocketing gasoline prices. The sales of large cars collapsed. Then came a major recession, which saw unit volume drop by half.

For Chrysler, this was a crisis. Plants had to be closed. Divisions had to be sold off. Anything to raise cash. Overseas operations were disposed of. Chrysler was now strictly a North American company. Even the beloved tank division had to be divested. That sale raised almost $350 million, and Chrysler needed every penny to keep its suppliers shipping to it. "All of the measures we took to keep Chrysler alive were difficult. But none was more difficult than the mass firings." Thousands of blue-collar and white-collar workers were let go. "The firings were just tragic, and there's no way to pretend otherwise." "Ideologically," Iacocca writes, "I've always been a free-enterpriser, a believer in the survival of the fittest." But even more, he was a believer in the survival of himself. So he decided to ask the government for financial assistance. "[T]here was no other choice except bankruptcy. And bankruptcy was no choice at all." Government aid was to come in the form of loan guarantees. Such guarantees were not unprecedented. When Iacocca pointed that out, it "wasn't what people wanted to hear." But once he made his mind up that help from the federal government was a necessity, Iacocca was relentless, brash, and "in-your-face" about it.

"From the very start, the prospect of government-backed loans for Chrysler was opposed by just about everybody." Leading the opposition were the CEOs of General Motors and Citicorp, the National Association of Manufacturers, and the Business Roundtable. Even some of Chrysler's major suppliers opposed it.

In his autobiography, Iacocca makes some rather confusing observations about going to the government. On the one hand, Chrysler was a captive "of an outmoded ideology." On the other hand, "Free-enterprise capitalism is the best economic system the world has ever seen... All things being equal it's the only way to go." But what happens when things are not equal?

Chrysler, Iacocca complained, was the victim of a long list of inequalities. High on this list were the Japanese, who were striking at the whole domestic automobile industry, hurting Chrysler, the weakest player, the most. The cost per car of burdensome American government regulations was another inequality. These regulations were more damaging to Chrysler than to the competition because it produced fewer cars. What Iacocca does not say but what very much needs saying is that "things" are never "equal." What does that brute fact do to his rationalizations?

In the midst of the maelstrom, Iacocca did not engage in philosophical disputes. He wanted money from Congress. And in his blunt, unvarnished way, he said it was in the interest of Congress to give him what he asked for. If Chrysler went bankrupt, the Treasury estimated that the six hundred thousand jobs lost would cost the country $2.7 billion in unemployment insurance and welfare payments in the first year alone. Thus, Iacocca testified to Congress, "You guys have a choice. Do you want to pay the $2.7 billion now, or do you want to guarantee loans of half that amount with a good chance of getting it all back?"

Bankruptcy is, of course, quite legal in the United States. Many other companies had gone that route. Why didn't Chrysler take that option? Declare bankruptcy but continue operating.

Iacocca insisted that bankruptcy was uniquely unsuitable for an automobile company. "Just the whisper of bankruptcy would shut off the cash flow to the company." No one would buy a car with the warranty, replacement parts, and resale value all suddenly in question.

Going to Congress was tough. Really tough. Iacocca said he felt more like a defendant than a witness. His inquisitors were out to punish him and the company he represented. "And punished we were. During the Congressional hearings, we were held up before the entire world as living examples of everything that was wrong with American industry. We were humiliated on the editorial pages for not having the decency to give up and die gracefully. We were the object of scorn by the nation's cartoonists, who couldn't wait to paint us into the grave. Our wives and kids were the butt of jokes in shopping malls and schools. It was a far higher price to pay than just closing the doors and walking away. It was personal. It was pointed. And it was painful."

Chrysler fought back not only with Iacocca's remarkable strength during the hearings but with advertisements advocating its cause. Iacocca signed the advertisements published in numerous newspapers and magazines. He felt he needed to say, "I'm here, I'm real, and I'm responsible for this company. And to show that I mean it, I'm signing on the dotted line."

Iacocca was not all alone. He had allies. He had dealers and unions on his side as well as key politicians such as Speaker of the House Tip O'Neill. Most important, President Jimmy Carter was planning on running for a second term in 1980. He certainly did not want to see a bankrupt Chrysler. And it is not unimportant that he was a Democrat. "There's no question in my mind," Iacocca writes, "that if there had been a Republican administration in 1979, Chrysler wouldn't be around."

Iacocca paid himself a salary of one dollar in 1980. This was just one of a number of important gestures to show that he was personally making sacrifices. "Leadership means setting an example." The leader's every word and every act are scrutinized. As the "general in the war to save Chrysler," he was going to ask his troops to make a lot of sacrifices. One false step—one bank account in the Cayman Islands—and the troops would mutiny. The unions, the employees, the dealers, the suppliers, and the banks (which were the most difficult)... they were all going to have to take a haircut. Since the speed of the boss is the speed of the gang, Iacocca, metaphorically, shaved his head.

All the deals—the banks were the last—finally closed "to resounding cheers" at 12:26 p.m. on June 24, 1980. Steve Miller, the company's chief financial officer, whom Gerald Greenwald had hired, walked into an office of the Manufacturers Hanover Trust Company "and filled out a deposit slip, just like any other depositor." The amount was $486,750,000. "At long last," Iacocca writes exultantly, "the New Chrysler Corporation was in business to stay."

For all the bad luck Iacocca had to contend with, there was one stroke of good luck, which was vital. Hal Sperlich had been working on the "K-car" since coming to Chrysler in 1977. If Iacocca could buy enough time to bring the K-car to market, the company might have a fighting chance to survive. Fuel efficient. Front-wheel drive. The K-car was positioned as "an American alternative." Advertisements were designed in red, white, and blue. "We also pointed out that the K-car was roomy enough to hold 'six Americans'—a little shot at our Japanese competitors." Iacocca was not alone singing its praises. The Dodge Aries and the Chrysler Reliant, both K-cars, were chosen as "cars of the year" by *Motor Trend* magazine.

Nineteen eighty was a financial bloodbath for Chrysler—$1.7 billion in losses on $9.2 billion in sales, down from $12 billion the previous year. The K-cars were introduced in October of 1980. For a variety of reasons, some Chrysler's fault, others not, they got off to a slower-than-expected start. "Throughout 1981, our survival was never more than a week-by-week proposition." The K-cars eventually got straightened out and started selling. Nevertheless, "our losses were still staggering—$478.5 million for the year." November was the low point—a million dollars away from disaster.

From a financial point of view, the turnaround began, though on a shaky basis, in 1982. Sales dropped slightly, from $10.8 billion the previous year to $10 billion. However, in a tribute to Chrysler's cost-cutting, the company posted a profit of $170 million.

It was the next year, 1983, that Iacocca was convinced the company had really come back. Sales climbed to $13.2 billion. Profits soared to $700 million. Chrysler issued twenty-six million new shares of stock in the spring. The offering was priced at $16.625. Soon the price more than doubled. Iacocca decided to pay off the federal loan in full. He made the announcement at the National Press Club on July 13, 1983, "by an eerie coincidence exactly five years to the day since Henry Ford fired me." That event was never far from Iacocca's mind. Here is what he said: "This is the day that makes the last three miserable years all seem worthwhile. We at Chrysler borrow money the old-fashioned way. We pay it back." Vindication!

There is one aspect of the story of Iacocca at Chrysler that we have not yet explored but that deserves our attention. An automobile is a passionate product. For most customers, it is the most expensive branded product they ever buy. Advertising speaks directly to the customer, and it played a key role in Chrysler's survival. What was the strategy?

On March 1, 1979, Iacocca called a press conference in New York City to announce that Chrysler was pulling its business from the two advertising agencies it had been using, Young & Rubicam and BBD&O. They were replaced by Kenyon & Eckhardt. All three of these agencies were tier-one companies. But Iacocca had worked with Kenyon & Eckhardt when he was president of Ford. The other two agencies "were perfectly okay," but Iacocca did not have the time "to teach them my philosophy." Kenyon & Eckhardt offered "familiar professionals who knew me so well that when I gave half an order, they already knew what the other half would be." This $150 million decision, which Iacocca himself called "ruthless," was meant to show the business world that "we weren't afraid to take... bold steps." This was the biggest account switch in the history of advertising.

Previous agencies had tried to persuade Iacocca to make television advertisements. He refused, feeling that a CEO in an advertisement was "on an ego trip." But Kenyon & Eckhardt succeeded where its predecessors had failed, and suddenly Lee Iacocca was pitching Chrysler's cars on television in advertisement after advertisement.

The most famous line was the tagline in the early commercials. "If you can find a better car—buy it." Iacocca's pitch was decisive and direct. He thought up that tagline himself. It was a bold claim of superiority. This is precisely the same approach used by Walter P. Chrysler himself when in print advertisements in 1932 he urged people in the market for a car to "Look at All Three"—that is, Plymouth as well as Chevrolet and Ford. This was pure hard sell. The author of that advertisement believed "essentially it was the sportsmanship of this appeal and the forthright tone... that captured the public's imagination."[18] The same may well be true of the Iacocca ads.

The advertisements, in Iacocca's view, were "an essential part of Chrysler's recovery." He was a bit uncomfortable with the "feeling that I'm going to be remembered only for my TV commercials."[19] There is a good chance that he will be proven right on both counts.

How, at the end of his eventful life, are we to regard Iacocca in the context of charismatic business leadership?

He satisfies many of our criteria. He was a strong man who could take a punch without being knocked out. One cannot overstate the impact on him of being fired from Ford. At Chrysler, he was down more than once but never out. He gathered around him an extraordinary team of executives who had safer futures at other companies. Trusting him, supporting him, in a relationship that was mutual, Iacocca and his team achieved more than they had any right to believe they could.

No other contemporary automobile industry executive could have done what Iacocca did. Certainly not Harlow Curtice. Iacocca's combination of deep knowledge of the industry, decisiveness, courage, strength of character, and power as a communicator was unique.

Iacocca is the only businessperson I have encountered who has actually written about charisma. Here is what he says in *Where Have All The Leaders Gone?*: "A leader should have charisma. I'm not talking about being flashy. Charisma is the quality that makes people want to follow you. It's the ability to inspire. People follow a leader because they trust him."[20] Everyone has his or her own definition of this word. Iacocca's is very good. By his own criteria, he qualifies.

However, it is also true that there are a couple of pieces missing. Perhaps most important, Iacocca came to believe his own press notices and to revel in what Jim Collins called his "rock star status." Sadly, Iacocca had trouble leaving center stage and letting go of the perks of executive kingship. In Collins's view, he became all about himself rather than about Chrysler. His "brilliant turnaround" of the early 1980s was not sustained, and Chrysler failed to become an enduring great company. Indeed, it should be noted that Collins is no fan of charisma, which he feels, "can be as much a liability as an asset" because it motivates people to please you by "filter[ing] the brutal facts from you." He prescribes "conscious attention" to overcoming these liabilities. Collins is equally suspicious of "vision."[21]

Iacocca was a fighter, but he was fighting to restore a past that could not endure. It is intriguing that two decades after he saved Chrysler, he became interested in electric vehicles. In 1998, he co-founded EV Global Motors. "This is the changing of the guard," Iacocca, then 73, said. "In the new millennium, for young people it's going to be an electric world."[22] He was more right than he knew. Tesla was founded five years later.

He was obsessed with Japanese trade practices. Many of his complaints were not unreasonable. However, he never seems to have appreciated—at any rate, he does not write about—the revolution constituted by the Toyota production system. Toyota marketed better automobiles than its American competitors because it had a better way of manufacturing them. In this general realm, possibly the most revolutionary move Iacocca made was to ask Douglas Fraser, president of the United Automobile Workers, to join Chrysler's board. Fraser served from 1980 to 1984. Dramatic though this gesture was, it is not the same as systemic change. As Iacocca said, at Ford nobody looked at Chrysler. Everyone looked at GM. The top executives should also have been looking at Toyota. But all of Detroit was self-blinded when it came to foreign competition.

Unlike Edwin Land, Iacocca, though trained as an engineer, was not a technologist. He concentrated on sales and marketing, where he thought the real action lay. In this he was not alone. The domestic automobile industry as a whole complained endlessly about Japanese trade practices without serious investigation into what the Toyota production system meant for the future.

When Iacocca lists his accomplishments, he includes the Mustang, Ford's profitability during his presidency, and turning Chrysler around. All impressive, and the skills required for these achievements should not be underestimated. In Chrysler's salvation, you see all his charismatic attributes on display. The completeness of his commitment to the goal. His willingness to cast aside ideas about competition and free enterprise when the government offered the only hope of survival. His ability to tell a convincing story that Chrysler's survival was better for the country than its bankruptcy would have been. His leadership not only of Chrysler's stakeholders but even the doubting Congress. His superb ability as a communicator.

But in his case, his charisma was deployed for goals that were all comfortably within the realm of "normal science." Iacocca writes, "There can't be a Silicon Valley without a Detroit." But that is not true. The next paradigm shift in the automobile industry will be the use of electricity rather than the internal combustion engine as motive power for the vehicle. Batteries, not gasoline, are the future. The leading company in that effort is Tesla, a start-up headquartered not in Detroit but in Palo Alto, California, in the heart of Silicon Valley. As one historian has written, "There may have been a 'New Chrysler,' but there were not new Chrysler ways of running its operations."[23]

On April 30, 2009, Chrysler filed for bankruptcy (as did General Motors on June 1, 2009). The world hasn't come to an end as a result. The federal government rode to the rescue once again. Said Iacocca, "This is a sad day for me. It pains me to see my old company, which has meant so much to America, on the ropes. But Chrysler has been in trouble before, and we got through it, and I believe they can do it again."[24] The United States still has an automobile industry centered in the Midwest. But it will never again be what it once was.

The difference between Silicon Valley and Detroit is symbolized by the difference in two commercials. One, the Apple 1984 Super Bowl advertisement. Unique. The other, Lee Iacocca's hard-sell advertisement. The best of the old style.

CHAPTER 7

"ALL THINGS NOT TRUMP": SAM WALTON, MERCHANT

Walmart's headquarters are located in Bentonville in the northwest corner of Arkansas, just south of Missouri, east of Oklahoma, and southeast of Kansas. All three states are within an easy drive. "Bentonville appealed to me," Sam Walton said, "because I could hunt quail seasons in all four states." (This quotation, like many others in this chapter, comes courtesy of Walton with Huey, *Made in America*.)[1] It is not at all surprising that Jeff Bezos "Imbibed [this] book thoroughly" and gave it to others in the early days of Amazon.[2]

Those in the know will tell you that there is nothing like the quail hunting in the Rio Grande Valley of South Texas. Walton bought some property down there. "A rustic little cluster of trailer homes out in the middle of South Texas nowhere. This isn't the quail hunting of rich southern gentry, the kind with white-coated servants and engraved Belgian shotguns and matched mules in silver harness hitched to mahogany dog wagons. Sam calls that variety 'South Georgia quail hunting,' and he's tried it, but it isn't really him. In case the ambiente [*sic*] of Campo Chapote [the name Walton gave his ranch] hasn't sunk in yet, it is, to put it simply: 'All Things Not Trump.'"[3]

Those four quoted words are as good a brief description of Sam Walton as you are likely to find. Before we explore how he deployed charisma to become the greatest retailer of the twentieth century and the richest man in the United States, it will be useful to make some comments about retailing.

Walk into a retail store. Choose any one. What do you see?

If you selected a large clothing store (Macy's, Kohl's, JCPenney) in a shopping mall, even if the mall is doing well— as fewer and fewer are these days—and you visited at, say, two o'clock on a Tuesday afternoon, you are likely to see product hanging on display fixtures and a lot more piled high on tables. You are likely to encounter few other customers. And if you want a salesperson to help you, you will probably have to send out a search party to find one.

If you are lucky enough to locate a salesperson, there is a good chance that he or she will be in a conversation. But not with another customer. With another salesperson. If you have the temerity to interrupt the conversation and ask for help finding an item, you probably will not be met with rudeness. Worse—you will be met with indifference. The salesperson you buttonhole will more likely than not have no idea where what you want might be. If by some miracle you can locate the product category in which you are interested, the salesperson you find will be unable to help you decide what to buy. He or she will know nothing about the store's stock in trade.

Discounters are worse. They occupy the least interesting segment of the retail world. Their merchandise consists of staples. From small-ticket items such as health and beauty aids all the way up to household appliances and automobile accessories, discounters sell what people need to make it through the day. The selection you will encounter in these product categories is unimaginative. Discounters stock the most well-known brands for a couple of reasons. First, the sole appeal of the store is price, and well-known brands are widely available so prices can easily be compared. Second, in pursuit of the low cost structure that is essential to discount store operations, sales help must be kept to a minimum.

The salespeople employed will receive the minimum wage, if that. Many of the employees will be part-timers so the store does not have to pay benefits. With no training and no motivation, such salespeople are not in a position to explain why one brand of a product might be better than another. The products have to sell themselves. Indeed, most of the employees you encounter at the big discount stores are not there to help you select merchandise. They are there to stock the shelves. Equally important, they are there to keep an eye on you to make sure you don't shoplift. Shrinkage (as theft is often called in retailing) has devastated more than one discounter because the margins they operate on are so thin.

Everything about these stores must be as cheap as possible. Rent, fixtures, restrooms—everything. Discount store customers are shopping to procure goods at the lowest price. They are not out for entertainment or excitement.

Discount store customers are usually bargain hunters. Most look for the cheapest goods by necessity. A few by inclination. But they won't be loyal to the store unless the store is loyal to them. These people are transacting business, not building relationships. Some of them have more time than money, and as soon as they locate an item at a lower price than yours, they are out the door.[4]

Discount retailing is the last place in the business world where one would expect to find a charismatic leader. It is boring but also nerve-racking. Discount retailers hire—at least when they start out—people of limited natural ability or, if such ability be present, it is more often than not unrecognized and therefore undeveloped. Sam Walton revolutionized discount retailing because he was a charismatic leader. What does that mean in this case?

One of the key characteristics of the charismatic leader is vision, and Walton was the leading visionary in his industry. He understood, as no one had before, that small towns could support big stores if the goods in those stores were sufficiently low-priced. Customers will travel for miles and stock-up shop if the items you are selling are such bargains that the trip is worthwhile.

Walton was a fanatic about buying merchandise at the lowest possible prices and passing the savings along to his customers. A classic business school question is: What business are we really in? Walton's answer was succinct and easily communicable to every one of the 380,000 employees, known as associates, who worked for Walmart on the day of his death (April 5, 1992). We are the purchasing agents for our customers.[5]

Everyone in business knows that the time to make a change is when you don't have to. The reason is that when you are forced into a change, time is working against you, and your options are limited. If you elect to make a change when business is good, you have time to experiment. You can dictate the pace of your own initiatives. You are in control of your destiny.

If everybody knows this, why do so few people act upon it? Because when business is good, it is easy to believe that it will continue to go well indefinitely. Change is hard, even under the best of circumstances. In 1960, Walton was "the largest variety store operator in the United States." But he understood that "the business itself seemed a little limited." He was right.

Walton was convinced that discounting was the wave of the future in retailing. Changing from a variety store operator to a discounter would be a big step. Moreover, Walton could see that discounters came and went with remarkable speed. In 1992, Walton noted that seventy-six of the top one hundred discounters in 1976 had gone out of business. Seventy-six in just sixteen years. If discounting was such a great idea, why did all these "bright stars" turn out to be bright stars only "for a moment"?

Walton's answer to his own question was, "It all boils down to not taking care of the customers, not minding their stores, not having folks in the stores with good attitudes, and that was because they never really even tried to take care of their own people. If you want people in the stores to take care of the customers, you have to make sure you're taking care of the people in the stores."

In addition to vision, the charismatic leader has a special relationship, approaching the mystical, with his followers— those "people in the stores." Sam Walton, this fabulously wealthy man, interacted with his associates as an equal. Not only was he at ease with them, they were at ease with him. He genuinely respected them, and they knew it. He paid them the greatest compliment a leader can pay a follower: he listened to them, and more than once he took their advice.

They were all building Walmart together. To an extent, every charismatic leader is created by his followers. Because of Walton's authentic common touch, he created followers who created his charisma.

You will not find many executives opposed to a motivated workforce. You will also not find many who could equal Walton in the art of motivation. How did he do it? How did he create a workforce that treated the customers better than they were treated at other stores? Indeed, the customers were treated better than they expected.

Walton knew the business better than anybody else, and everyone in the company realized that. In the words of one store manager in the early days, "Sam had us send our sales reports in every week, and along with this we had to send in a Best Selling Item. I mean we *had to*... [A]nd if you reported that nothing was selling well, Mr. Walton would not be happy. He would think you weren't studying your merchandise, and in that case he'd come study it for you." Nobody, but nobody, wanted Mr. Walton to study your merchandise for you.

Despite his encyclopedic knowledge of every one of his stores, Walton remained modest. "[T]hat feeling of awe is overcome by a sort of kinship. He is a master at erasing that 'larger-than-life' feeling that people have for him." He was always open to suggestions. The testimony on this point is universal. He listened because, as he endlessly emphasized, you can learn from anybody.

Here is an example: "an hourly associate in our traffic department... got to wondering why we were shipping all the fixtures we bought for our warehouses by common carrier. She figured out a program to backhaul those things on our own trucks and saved us over a half million dollars... So we brought her in, recognized her good thinking, and gave her a cash award."

The people-greeter innovation came about in a similar way, according to a Walmart executive. "Back in 1980, Mr. Walton and I went into the Walmart in Crowley, Louisiana. The first thing we saw as we opened the door was this older gentleman standing there. The man didn't know me, and he didn't see Sam, but he said, 'Hi! How are ya? Glad you're here. If there is anything I can tell you about our store, just let me know.'" This kind of a greeting is the last thing a discount store shopper would expect. But one can see how it would be most welcome.

"Neither Sam nor I," this executive continues, "had ever seen such a thing, so we started talking to him... [H]e explained that he had a dual purpose: to make people feel good about coming in, and to make sure people weren't walking back out the entrance with merchandise they hadn't paid for... The store... had had trouble with shoplifting, and its manager was an old-time merchant... who knew how to take care of his inventory. He didn't want to intimidate the honest customers by posting a guard at the door, but he wanted to leave a clear message that if you came in and stole, someone was there who would see it."

Walton's leadership style was simple to describe but hard to enact. Everyone uses the same words, such as *empowerment*, *motivation*, and so on. Walton's achievement was in making those words—which can quickly generate the opposite of their intention if they are honored more in the breech than in the observance—real.

Walton accomplished this goal in a number of ways. He was an exceptionally "high-touch" executive. "I got my fifteen-year pin from him personally," said one district office trainer. Do you think that meant a lot to her? He seems to have been able to be everywhere at once. His omnipresence was made possible in part by the airplanes Walmart used. By 1992, the company had twelve planes, only one of which was a jet. Every Monday morning, that fleet took off from Bentonville to the four corners of the Walmart domain. There was no other choice. From small town to small town, Walton and his top executives were able to see store after store in a way that economized on time. Not only was he thus able to visit stores, he could also get a pretty good idea about appealing sites for new store locations from the air.

Walton was a regular at the break room for Walmart's truckers, often showing up at four in the morning with some doughnuts. "He grilled them. 'What are you seeing at the stores?' 'How do people act there?' 'Is it getting better?'" "When you're out on the highway and you pass by a Walmart truck," Walton said, "you can bet your bottom dollar that the guy behind the wheel is a true professional. He's not just driving a truck. He's dedicated to servicing those stores, and he knows he's an ambassador of Walmart and everything we stand for out on the road. I'll just say it: we have the best damned truck drivers in America..." How many other CEOs would do this?

Under Walton, Walmart developed a unique culture in which everybody had a chance to contribute. It is very hard for a culture to scale, but as long as Walton was running the company, it did. "These days," he said, "the real challenge for managers in a business like ours is to become what we call servant leaders. And when they do, the team—the manager and the associates—can accomplish anything."

This last quotation is critical to understanding Walton's emergence as a charismatic figure. Thanks to his dedication, focus, praise (when it was deserved), discipline, and willingness to permit the associates to experiment, the people who worked for Walmart achieved far more than they thought possible.

Sam Walton underpromised and overdelivered for his team. Here is the testimony of another trucker: "I went to work for Mr. Walton in 1972, when he only had sixteen tractors on the road. The first month, I went to a drivers' safety meeting, and he always came to those. [Omnipresence at work once again.] ...I'll never forget, he said, 'If you'll just stay with me for twenty years, I guarantee you'll have $100,000 in profit sharing.' I thought, 'Big deal. Bob Clark will never see that kind of money in his life.' I was worrying about what I was making right then. Well, last time I checked, I had $707,000 in profit sharing..." Of such stuff is charisma created.

Sam Walton did not spring fully blown from the head of Zeus. It took time for him to become the man that he did. Let us do some history now to see what experiences shaped him.

Samuel Moore Walton was born on March 28, 1918, in a farmhouse near Kingfisher, Oklahoma. His only sibling, James L. "Bud" Walton, was born on December 20, 1921. Their parents, Thomas Gibson Walton and the former Nannia Lee Lawrence, were married in 1917 and were twenty-six and nineteen years of age respectively when Sam was born.

Kingfisher is forty-five miles northwest of Oklahoma City, which is another way of saying that it was in the middle of nowhere at the time of Walton's birth. Its population in 1920 was 2,446. It is still a small town, with 4,633 residents in 2010. According to Wikipedia, its only tourist attraction is the Chisholm Trail Museum.[6] This was precisely the kind of small, isolated, easily overlooked settlement that would serve as the foundation of Walton's retail empire.

Not much is known about Walton's parents. His father first worked for his uncle in the farm loan business. He left that to go into farming himself. The 1920s were tough years for farmers in Oklahoma, although not nearly as bad as the Depression decade was to be. Tom Walton did not prosper as a farmer. Fortunately, he had a half brother, Jesse Walton, whose Walton Mortgage Company represented the Metropolitan Life Insurance company in Springfield, Missouri. Jesse hired Tom. Springfield, which styles itself the Queen City of the Ozarks, had a population of 57,527 in 1930. It was the first town that the mature Sam Walton remembered. He began his schooling there.

The family was not in Springfield for long. Jesse dispatched Tom to Marshall, Missouri, population 8,103 in 1930, about 150 miles north of Springfield. Soon thereafter, Tom decided to try farming again, and once again that didn't work out. Jesse rehired Tom, sending him to Shelbina, Missouri, one hundred miles from Marshall. Yet another small town, with a 1930 population of 1,826. The next stop was Columbia, midway between Kansas City and St. Louis. Columbia is the home of the main campus of the University of Missouri, from which Sam graduated in 1940, becoming the first member of his family to earn a college degree. The year Sam graduated, the population of Columbia was 18,399.

Here are some of the observations that Sam has left us about his father: "Dad never had the kind of ambition or confidence to build much of a business on his own... [He] became the guy who had to service... old farm loans, most of which were in default... [He] had to repossess hundreds of farms from wonderful people whose families had owned the land forever. I traveled with him some, and it was tragic, and really hard on Dad, too—but he tried to do it in a way that left those farmers with as much of their self-respect as he could. All of this must have made an impression on me as a kid, although I don't ever remember saying anything to myself like, 'I'll never be poor.'"[7]

We can take him at his word about that last sentence. Doubtless, he never uttered an analog to Scarlett O'Hara's "I'll never be hungry again." On the other hand, what we infer from this brief discussion of his father is that his father was the model of what he did not want to be.

Walton's father does not seem to have been a major factor in Walton's creation of himself, with two exceptions. The first was the single point upon which his parents agreed: "One thing my mother and dad shared completely was their approach to money: they just didn't spend it." The second exception was the fact that Tom and Nan Walton did not get along. They were a mismatch, "always at odds." They stayed together for their children, but once their children were grown, they lived apart. "I swore early on that if I ever had a family, I would never expose it to [their] kind of squabbling." "The simple truth is that Mother and Dad were two of the most quarrelsome people who ever lived together."

Walton and his brother, Bud, give us to believe that their mother was a more important influence than their father. Bud said, "Sam has a lot of our mother's characteristics." Walton wrote that "Mother must have been a pretty special motivator, because I took her seriously when she told me I should always try to be the best at whatever I took on." This is certainly good advice. It is a fair bet that more than one mother has thus advised her son. What matters more than that she said it is that he "took her seriously." Nan Walton died in 1950 of cancer. She was fifty-two. "One of the great sadnesses in my life," Walton wrote, is that his mother died so young. Tom Walton lived to be ninety-two, well into the era of Walmart's greatness. Indeed, two years before he died, he made a few remarks at the grand opening of the Walmart in Kingfisher.

The greatest desire motivating Walton from earliest youth was neither money nor fame. It was winning. The desire to win was innate in the man. It sounds as if his mother reinforced that desire rather than creating it. Walton "always pursued everything [he] was interested in with a true passion—some would say obsession—to win." He always "set extremely high personal goals."

"Even when I was a little kid... I remember being ambitious. I was a class officer several years. I played football and baseball and basketball with the other kids, and I swam in the summers. I was so competitive that when I started Boy Scouts... I made a bet with the other guys about which one of us would be the first... Eagle." When Walton was thirteen, he became the youngest Eagle Scout in the history of the state of Missouri.

Team sports began for Walton in fifth grade. By the time he got to Hickman High School in Columbia, he found himself drafted for the basketball team even though he was only five feet nine inches tall. "I liked running the team, I guess." Hickman's basketball team was undefeated and won the state championship. He played quarterback on the high school football team and linebacker on defense. The football team also went undefeated and won the state championship.

"[I]n my whole life I never played in a losing football game... It taught me to expect to win... It never occurred to me that I might lose; to me, it was almost as if I had a right to win. Thinking like that often seems to turn into sort of a self-fulfilling prophecy." He explained that his main athletic talent "was probably the same as my best talent as a retailer—I was a good motivator."

Early in life, Walton realized that you can't be a leader without followers—you can't be a winner in an important endeavor without a team. He became a student of team building. Like so many other activities to which he devoted himself, no one was better at it.

Walton's high school career was marked by making the honor roll—which he did by hard work; he did not consider himself to be a naturally good student—participating in numerous clubs, and being voted "Most Versatile Boy." The next step was the University of Missouri, conveniently located in the town, Columbia, in which he was living.

Walton immediately decided that he "wanted to be president of the university student body. I learned early on that one of the secrets to campus leadership was the simplest thing of all: speak to people coming down the sidewalk before they speak to you. I did that in college... I would always look ahead and speak to the person coming toward me. If I knew them, I would call them by name, but even if I didn't I would still speak to them. Before long, I probably knew more students than anybody in the university, and they recognized me and considered me their friend. I ran for every office that came along. I was elected president of the senior men's honor society... and officer in my fraternity, and president of the senior class. I was captain and president of Scabbard and Blade, the elite military organization of ROTC." He also ran a Sunday Bible class and earned a good deal of money in 1939 and 1940 through paper routes, some of which he subcontracted, in his spare time.

Walton graduated from the University of Missouri on May 31, 1940, and took a job as a management trainee at a JCPenney store in Des Moines, Iowa, for seventy-five dollars a month. From the beginning, he loved retailing. He was a born salesman, a natural with customers. The climax of the experience was meeting James Cash Penney himself, who taught him how to tie a ribbon around a box using as little ribbon as possible.

After Pearl Harbor, Walton expected to join the army. Because of ROTC at the University of Missouri, he was already a second lieutenant in the army reserve. However, when he took his physical to join the regular army, he was shocked to learn that he had a heart defect that could lead to arrhythmias. He was cleared for limited duty only and did not leave the United States during the war. He did leave Penney and drifted south to Oklahoma, where he got a job in a munitions plant in Pryor, not far from Tulsa. Finding no lodging there, he took a room in nearby Claremore. "I wish I could recount a valiant military career—like my brother, Bud... but my service stint was really fairly ordinary time spent as a lieutenant and then as a captain... supervising security at aircraft plants and POW camps..."

It was in Claremore that Walton met the woman who was to be his life partner, Helen Alice Robson. She proved to be an extraordinary individual. She was the valedictorian of her high school class and a graduate of the University of Oklahoma, where she majored in finance. She was very bright and strong-willed as well as attractive. They were married on February 14 (Valentine's Day), 1943. They had four children from 1944 to 1949.

After the war, Sam was interested in the possibility of going into the department store business in St. Louis. But Helen "spoke up and laid down the law." She said, "I'll go with you any place you want so long as you don't ask me to live in a big city. Ten thousand people is enough for me."

In the spring of 1942, Walton met his future father-in-law. Leland Stanford Robson became his mentor. Listening to him, Walton said, "was an education in itself. He influenced me a great deal. He was a great salesman, one of the most persuasive individuals I have ever met. And I am sure his success as a trader and a businessman, his knowledge of finance and the law, and his philosophy had a big effect on me. My competitive nature was such that I saw his success and admired it. I didn't envy it. I admired it. I said to myself: maybe I will be as successful as he is someday." Robson was involved in innumerable endeavors and was successful in all of them. He knew how to conduct himself in the world of affairs, and he took Walton under his wing. Walton could not have asked for a better coach and adviser. Robson played the part that his father never could have. He was quite a remarkable man, but he would be overlooked by history had his daughter not married an even more remarkable man.

In addition to finding the woman with whom he would spend his life, Walton found out two other important things while he was serving in the army. One was that he wanted to go into retailing. The second was that he wanted to be in business for himself. At war's end, he was prepared to see how far his ambition would take him.

Sam and Helen Walton settled in Newport, Arkansas, late in the summer of 1945. This little town had a population of 4,301 in 1940 and 6,254 in 1950. It is about eighty miles northwest of Memphis and ninety miles northeast of Little Rock. Both Sam and Helen admired her father, but neither wanted to see Sam mature in the shadow of L. S. Since Helen ruled out big cities, Newport was the choice.

Arkansas in 1945 was a poor state and a small state in terms of population and in the process of getting smaller. As a historian of the state put it, "Unless one owned land or a business, those who left Arkansas to help fight World War II or for a well-paying defense job had little economic reason to return to the state..."[8]

Walton approached Butler Brothers, a large wholesaler that also had a franchise chain of five-and-ten-cent variety stores named Ben Franklin, and asked to become a franchisee. Butler Brothers responded that it had a store for him in Newport. Walton grabbed it. He was twenty-seven years old when he opened his five-thousand-square-foot Ben Franklin "in the heart of town, looking out on the railroad tracks" on September 1, 1945, the day before the formal surrender of Japan, which brought an end to World War II.

"I've always believed in goals," said Sam, "so I set myself one: I wanted my little Newport store to be the best, most profitable variety store in Arkansas within five years."[9] (One must pause to reflect how small this ambition is compared to what Walton eventually achieved.) The price for this franchise was not small. Walton paid Butler Brothers a cover charge of $25,000. This equals more than $350,000 in 2020. Walton and his wife contributed $5,000, which they had managed to save. The remaining $20,000 came in the form of a loan from

Helen's father, who always backed Sam financially as well as with business advice.

In a state in a city in a store that was primitive by contemporary standards in most other places in America, Sam Walton launched his career in retailing. "[T]hings weren't working out at all" for the previous owner. Under his management the preceding year, the store had done $72,000 in business. Across the street there was another variety store, part of the long-forgotten Sterling chain, which did $150,000, slightly over twice Walton's store's volume. Walton later recalled, "I was the sucker Butler Brothers sent to save [the store]." Walton's Ben Franklin had a very long way to go to measure up to his ambitions.

Millions of small stores failed during the course of the twentieth century in the United States. There were about 1.7 million retail establishments in the country in 1945. Why wouldn't this one be among the many that didn't make it? Surely, any analyst of the situation in 1945 would have found in Walton a good candidate for failure. As he himself put it, "For all of my confidence, I hadn't had a day's experience in running a variety store..." In fact, he had not had a day's experience in running a business of any kind. He paid a price for this inexperience and excessive enthusiasm before his store even opened. He had selected the wrong store and paid too much for it. "Only after we closed the deal, of course, did I learn the store was a real dog." The rent was 5 percent of sales. This sounded fine to Walton, but after signing the lease, he discovered that this "was the highest rent anybody'd ever heard of in the variety store business. No one paid 5 percent of sales for rent." There were more problems with the deal Walton made, serious problems, which would take him a half decade to discover.

Standing in the way of Walton reaching his goal was Butler Brothers itself. Butler Brothers operated a network of warehouses that carried thousands of items in inventory. Their franchisees were obliged to purchase 80 percent of their goods from those warehouses. Since Butler Brothers priced their goods high, the franchisees were not in a position to offer their customers bargains.

"At the beginning," Walton writes, "I went along and ran my store by their book because I didn't know any better." But Walton always "thought different." Soon he started "experimenting—that's just the way I am and have always been." He didn't want to absorb the high markups from Butler Brothers. He wanted to buy direct from manufacturers. Most of them did not want to sell to him because they did not want to run afoul of Butler Brothers. "Every now and then, though," said Sam, "I would find one who would cross over and do it my way."

This was the beginning of practices that would come to define Walmart. "I was always looking for offbeat suppliers or sources. I started driving over to Tennessee to some fellows I found who would give me special buys at prices way below what Ben Franklin [i.e., Butler Brothers] was charging me. One I remember was Wright Merchandising Co. in Union City, which would sell to small businesses like mine at good wholesale prices. I'd work in the store all day, then take off around closing and drive that windy road over to the Mississippi River ferry at Cottonwood Point, Missouri, and then into Tennessee with an old homemade trailer hitched to my car. I'd stuff that car and trailer with whatever I could get good deals on—usually on soft lines: ladies' panties and nylons, men's shirts—and I'd bring them back, price them low, and just blow that stuff out the store."

Butler Brothers didn't like Walton's freelancing, but that didn't stop him. "Somehow or another" he got in touch with a manufacturer's agent in New York City named Harry Weiner. His Weiner Buying Services at 505 Seventh Avenue would sell to Walton, taking 5 percent for himself as opposed to the 25 percent that Butler Brothers took.

"I'll never forget one of Harry's deals, one of the best items I ever had and an early lesson in pricing. It first got me thinking in the direction of what eventually became the foundation of Walmart's philosophy. If you're interested in 'how Walmart did it,' this is one story you've got to sit up and pay close attention to. Harry was selling ladies' panties—two-barred, tricot satin panties with an elastic waist—for $2.00 a dozen. We'd been buying similar panties from Ben Franklin for $2.50 a dozen and selling them at three pair for one dollar. Well, at Harry's price of $2.00, we could put them out at four for $1.00 and make a great promotion for our store."

The "simple lesson [Walton] learned" was that if he bought an item for eighty cents and marked it up to a dollar, he would sell three times as many units than if he marked it up to $1.20. "Simple enough," Walton keeps repeating. Which leaves us with a question. If this is so simple, why have so many discounters failed? Walton couldn't push his simple formula as far as he wanted because of the Butler Brothers contract, but "I stretched that contract every way I could."

Butler Brothers was mollified to some extent because of the performance of Walton's store. Between the low prices he offered and his flair for promotion—a popcorn machine and an ice cream machine in front of the store—sales surged. In his first full year of ownership, sales of his Ben Franklin store reached $105,000. The next year $140,000. The year after that $175,000, surpassing the volume of his rival John Dunham's Sterling store. After thirty months in business, Walton was able to repay his father-in-law's loan in full. And in his fifth year, Walton did $250,000 in business and made a profit of between $30,000 and $40,000. He was the leading variety store operator in Arkansas.

Walton learned retailing from the ground up. If he wanted to obtain product more cheaply than he could from his standard supplier, he would drive around the countryside himself and find someone with whom he could do business. If the best supplier was in New York City, he located him. He understood that nothing could beat the appeal of low price. But he also understood that a little fun, such as popcorn and ice cream machines, could attract a lot of attention.

Not only had Walton built a successful business in Newport, he had invested a lot of himself in the town. He was an active member of the Rotary Club, a member of the board of deacons of the Presbyterian Church ("even though I was a Methodist, it worked out real well"), and he became the president of the Chamber of Commerce. Equally important, Helen loved the town. Three of her four children were born during those five years. "We had built a life there," she recalled in 1992. "I still have good friends from those days." And then, in a heartbeat, they lost everything.

The problem was that there was no renewal clause in the store lease. Options to renew were standard features of leases such as the one Walton had originally entered into. But his landlord, Mr. P. K. Holmes, did not include that clause in Walton's lease, and Walton did not think to ask for its inclusion.

A good case can be made that Holmes should have renewed the lease. Sales of that Ben Franklin had soared from

$72,000 to a quarter of a million dollars. Since the rent was 5 percent of sales, Holmes's income from the store increased from $3,600 to $12,500, for a total of $8,900. He received this bounty for doing nothing whatever himself, and there was no reason to believe that Walton's success would not continue. Eighty-nine hundred dollars in 1950 is the equivalent of over $97,000 in 2021. But Holmes refused to renew the lease because he wanted to give that Ben Franklin to his son, and he could see how well it was doing.

Walton recalled this as "the low point of my life... I felt sick to my stomach. I couldn't believe it was happening to me. It was really like a nightmare. I had built the best variety store in the whole region and worked hard in the community—done everything right—and now I was being kicked out of town. It didn't seem fair. I blamed myself for getting suckered into such an awful lease, and I was furious at the landlord. Helen, just settling in with a brand-new family of four, was heartsick at the prospect of leaving Newport. But that's what we were going to do." He had "done everything right," and his reward was being "kicked out of town."

If this story sounds familiar, it is because it is. Something similar happened to Lee Iacocca at Ford. He felt he also had "done everything right," and his reward was to be run out of Ford. Something similar also happened to George Eastman, the founder of Kodak. He had worked his way up to first assistant bookkeeper at the Rochester Savings Bank in 1880. The following year Eastman's immediate superior left the bank, and he expected to receive the promotion that he felt he had earned and for which he felt he was qualified. But he was passed over in favor of a relative of one of the bank's directors. "It wasn't fair. It wasn't right; it was against every principle of justice," Eastman told the *New York Times* many years later.[10]

There are commonalities in these three stories. The protagonist is denied what he deserves. His reaction is anger. He has suffered a defeat, but he is not a defeated man. In all three cases, and in many others, successful people feel that the world is a fair place that will reward their efforts. When something unfair or unjust happens to them, it is a result of some cosmic mistake that will be corrected in time by even greater efforts on their own part.

For Walton, the next stop was Bentonville, and it was difficult to tell oneself a happy story about Bentonville in 1950. The best thing Helen Walton had to say about it was that it had a railroad track. "I couldn't believe this was where we were going to live," Helen said.[11]

The store Walton leased was a step down from Newport. The year before he leased it—and this time his father-in-law negotiated a ninety-nine-year lease—it posted a mere $32,000 in sales. Bentonville was half the size of Newport, but it had three variety stores. Most people would be dreadfully discouraged by this turn of events. But for Walton, "It didn't matter that much, because I had big plans."

Walton's big plans bore fruit. In the next fifteen years, he became the largest independent variety store operator in the nation. And just as he reached the top of his industry, he decided to change his approach to retailing fundamentally.

Retailing was changing, and not in the direction in which he was having success. As Walton said, "The volume was so little per store that it really didn't amount to that much. In 1960 we were only doing $1.4 million in fifteen stores... I began looking around hard for whatever new idea would break us over into something with a little better pay-off for all our efforts."

The answer was Walmart. Walmart No. 1 was opened in Rogers, Arkansas, on July 2, 1962. The store was sixteen thousand square feet in size and sold everything from boys' apparel to books to automobile supplies. Not until August of 1964 was Walmart No. 2 opened. "Once we opened Rogers," remarked Walton, "we sat there and held our breath for two years." He had that luxury because he was making a change when he didn't have to.

When it became clear that Walmart was going to succeed, Walton began to open more stores very quickly and also to exit the variety store business. In 1991, Walmart surpassed Sears as the nation's largest retailer. On March 17, 1992, President George H. W. Bush and First Lady Barbara Bush flew to Bentonville to present Walton with the Presidential Medal of Freedom. Less than three weeks later, on April 5, Walton died of multiple myeloma. The year of his death, Walmart ran 1,928 stores and posted sales of $43.9 billion and profits of $1.6 billion. "Sometimes," Walton said when it was clear that Walmart was a runaway sensation, "even I have trouble believing it."

The linchpin of Walmart's astonishing success was Sam Walton's creation of a unique culture—a culture that never would have developed without his charisma. If ever a man in American business history can be credited with inspiring ordinary people to do extraordinary things, it is Walton. As one Walmart executive put it, "[T]o Sam, the people in the stores—the managers and the associates—are the kings. He loves them. And there's no doubt they feel they have an open door to him." The people he loved making heroes out of in turn loved making a hero out of him. This is the essence of the creation of charisma. There must be a mutuality of affect. Charisma flows in two directions.

Consider his acceptance of the Presidential Medal of Freedom. He knew he was dying, and he knew this would be the last public statement he would make. "We've had a lot of great leaders in this company, and the greatest thing is that we've got ideas from all 380,000 people in the company, and that's the best part. We are all working together... That's the secret. That's the key... We are proud of what we've accomplished. We think we've just begun."[12] Reconsider that last sentence. At the close of his own life, he was thinking of the future of the people he was leaving behind. And he kept using the first person plural.

Why was he so good at giving credit? What made praise from Walton so precious and so very special was that he knew the business so well that he knew when recognition was earned.

What Walton proves is that charisma can appear when and where you least expect it. Small town in Arkansas in 1945. Small (at first) retail stores. Sales promotions that were (at first) sloppy and disorganized. From variety stores to big discount operations where the competition was powerful and entrenched. Try to name a CEO of a Walmart competitor between 1962 when Walton founded Walmart and when Walton died thirty years later. Odds are you won't be able to do so unless you are a historian of the industry.

Walton led by example. He knew more about his company than anyone else. He knew more about each of his stores than the store managers. By 1980 if not before, he knew more about retailing than anybody else in the country. It is no secret that he was a great impromptu speaker. Nor is it a secret that he was a great motivator.

However, what really made Walton a gifted communicator was something else. He listened to you, and if you had a good idea, he would implement it and give you a bonus. The bonus money was nice, but the recognition was nicer. Communicating by listening can be more motivating than communicating by speaking. Here was the subject matter expert being publicly open-minded. How often does one encounter such a phenomenon?

Walton was great at avoiding the "larger-than-life" persona that his employees (or associates, as he dubbed them) might have developed for him. But as Benjamin Franklin wrote in *Poor Richard's Almanack*, "Fly pleasures, and they will follow you."[13] In the same sense, when a leader rejects the "larger-than-life" persona, that very rejection can have the opposite effect. You may believe that you're just like everybody else, but others will take that very belief as proof that you are not.

Walton was the genuine article. As one of his first employees said, "I always knew [Walmart] was going to be successful. The philosophy made sense, and you couldn't help but believe in the man."[14]

CHAPTER 8

COMPANY AND CRUSADE: THE STORY OF MARY KAY ASH

Mary Kay Ash was born Mary Kathlyn Wagner on May 12, 1918, in Hot Wells, Harris County, Texas, not far from Houston. Her father, Edward Alexander Wagner, had tuberculosis. When Mary Kay was seven years old, her father returned from the sanitarium. Three years of treatment there had arrested the progress of the illness but had not cured him. He was an invalid for the rest of his life. Mary Kay's older brother and sister were grown and gone from home when her father returned. Her mother, Lula Vember Hastings Wagner, was a trained nurse but found a job as a restaurant manager in Houston. She left home at five in the morning and returned at nine at night, often not seeing Mary Kay the whole day.

Thus at the age of seven, Mary Kay not only had to take care of herself, she was her father's cook and principal caregiver. The family scraped by with little money, but a strong bond developed between mother and daughter. Her mother was her principal motivator. She carried her words—"You can do it!"—with her always.[1]

Mary Kay graduated from high school, but there was no money to send her to college. In 1935, at the age of seventeen, she married a gas station attendant who was also a local musician, with a band called the Hawaiian Strummers, named Ben Rogers. The couple had three children: Ben Jr., Marylyn, and Richard. Mary Kay supported the family through various door-to-door sales jobs. In 1939, she got a selling job with Stanley Home Products.

Her husband served in the army during the war. By the time he enlisted, the marriage was already shaky. When he returned, he said he was having an affair and wanted a divorce. In Mary Kay's words, "It was the lowest point of my life. I had developed a sense of worth for my abilities as a wife and mother, and yet on that day I felt like a complete and total failure. Nothing had ever struck me so hard."[2]

Ben Rogers disappeared completely. Apparently there was no alimony or child support. It appears that neither Mary Kay nor her children ever saw him again. She had complete responsibility for the four of them, so she needed "a good-paying job with flexible hours."[3]

Mary Kay already knew that she liked to sell. She had sold everything from Girl Scout cookies to encyclopedias. Direct sales provided the opportunity she needed, so Stanley Home Products Company was a good fit. Founded by Frank S. Beveridge, a former Fuller Brush salesman, in 1932, Stanley made house cleaning products and sold them directly to customers through an innovative method, the "party plan."[4]

As a Stanley distributor, Mary Kay invited friends and acquaintances to her home for what purported to be a party.

A pleasant atmosphere was created by playing parlor games, the serving of refreshments by the hostess, and a surprise gift. Woven into the evening was the exhibition of products the hostess was selling. Guests could sample them, and the hostess would answer questions about them.

The party plan "skillfully blurred" a business transaction with a friendly evening.[5] It was the genuine soft sell. Not only that, a hostess was able to soft sell to a room full of people rather than one at a time.

Not long after she began, Mary Kay attended a Stanley regional sales convention in Dallas. There she saw a "Queen of Sales" selected and honored. For Mary Kay, "Recognition was as vital... as money."[6] She resolved to be the Queen of Sales the next year. She asked the newly crowned queen to put on a home party for her. The queen obliged, and Mary Kay took nineteen pages of notes at the event.

Thereafter, Mary Kay "boldly approached" Beveridge and told him she was going to be the queen next year. "He took my hand in both of his, looked me square in the eye, and after a moment said solemnly: 'Somehow I think you will!'" Her reaction: "Those few words literally changed my life." It hardly needs saying that she achieved her goal.[7]

Her career took her to several other direct sales companies. At one, the World Gift Company, she became a member of the board of directors. In her twenty-five years in direct sales, she made a good deal of money—enough to retire comfortably in 1963. However, she felt there was unfinished business in her life, and that concerned the treatment of working women.

In her quarter century in direct sales, she had seen "countless capable individuals" exploited because they were women working in a man's world. She herself was a case in point. "One company paid me $25,000 a year to be their national training director, but in truth, I was acting as their national *sales manager*—and for a salary much less than the job was worth. Then there were the times when I would be asked to take a man out on the road to train him, and after six months of training, he would be brought back to Dallas [where Mary Kay had moved from Houston], made my superior, and given twice my salary! It happened more than once."[8] The disrespect enraged her.

She did not remain retired for long. Almost immediately, she decided to put together a list of factors that described her "dream company." Not long after she began the list, she decided to found the company she was describing herself. So on September 13, 1963, Mary Kay Cosmetics was born.

The birth of the company was not without drama and tragedy. Mary Kay began by purchasing the formulas for cosmetics that she had personally used for about a decade but were not well-known to the general public. "I knew that the products were special," she said.[9] She was in for a dime, in for a dollar, investing "my life savings into the chance of a lifetime." She had plenty of connections in the world of sales and recruited a number of salespeople.[10]

In July of 1963, she married for the second time. Her new husband was George Hallenbeck, a chemist who had some knowledge of how to run a business. The plan was for her to train the salespeople while her husband managed her dream company. "My objective was to give women the opportunity to do anything they were smart enough to do... [T]o me, 'P&L' meant much more than profit and loss; it meant *people* and *love*."[11]

On August 13, she and her husband were having breakfast and he was going over the economics of the business while she was listening "with half an ear." At that moment, her husband of one month suffered a fatal heart attack.[12]

Her two sons and her daughter came to Dallas from Houston for the funeral. After the ceremony, the four met together to discuss what should be done with Mary Kay's company. Both her lawyer and her accountant had already advised her to abandon the project and to recoup whatever funds she could. Her accountant told her there were "not enough cents in the dollar" for the commission schedule she was proposing to establish. Her lawyer did some research to find out the number of cosmetics companies that had gone bankrupt that year. He told her, "Mary Kay, you have no experience in the cosmetics business, and you are a grandmother. Don't throw your life savings away!" Her children disagreed, telling her what her mother had always told her when she was caring for her father or in other difficult times: "You can do it!" Mary Kay knew the "odds were against me, and I'll readily admit there were many things I didn't know..."[13] But this was not a woman easily discouraged.

Her youngest son, Richard, was a sales representative for Prudential. At the age of twenty, he was "making the incredible salary of $480 a month." She would need Richard's help to make the company a reality but felt she could only offer him $250 a month. He accepted immediately and moved from Houston to Dallas. Her elder son, Ben, was married with two children and was making $750 a month with a Houston welding company. He could not move immediately. However, he gave Mary Kay his bank book with its $4,500 balance. He said, "I think you could do anything in this world that you wanted to. Here's my savings. If it will help you in any way, I want you to have it."[14] Eight months later, he joined the company at the same salary Richard was receiving. Later, daughter Marylyn joined the company as the first Mary Kay director in Houston.

Here are Mary Kay's reflections: "It's just possible that... the boys had a little more confidence in the Mary Kay dream than Mary Kay did! ...But I had mistrusted God. I should have known that when God closes a door, He always opens a window. I might not have realized how much ability Richard had, but God did."[15]

Mary Kay was devoutly religious. References to God are omnipresent in her writing and also in her public speaking, of which she did an enormous amount. In her autobiography, she states, "I have found that everything seems to work out if you have your life in the proper perspective: God first, family second, and career third. I truly believe the growth of Mary Kay Cosmetics has come about because the first thing we did was to take God as our partner... I believe He has blessed us because our motivation is right. He knows I want women to become the beautiful creatures He created, and to use the wonderful God-given talents that lie within each of us."[16] Independent sales directors often asked Mary Kay to sign one-dollar bills to give as awards to their independent beauty consultants. When she did, she put "Matthew 25:14-30" next to her name. This is the parable of the talents.[17] On July 25, 1982, in a segment on Mary Kay and her company on *60 Minutes*, interviewer Morley Safer asked her, "Do you think in a sense you're using God?" She responded, "I hope not. I sincerely hope not. I hope He's using me."[18]

In addition to his writings on charisma, Max Weber wrote a seminal book entitled *The Protestant Ethic and the Spirit of Capitalism.*[19] Weber focused especially on the teachings of

John Calvin. Mary Kay was a Southern Baptist, and, unlike Calvinism, there was nothing ascetic about the religion she practiced. (John D. Rockefeller, who once said "God gave me my money,"[20] was also a Baptist. There was nothing ascetic about him, either.) Unlike orthodox Calvinists, such as the Puritans who founded Massachusetts in the seventeenth century, Mary Kay believed she knew God's thinking. She understood His plan. She could therefore do His will. Mary Kay's religious beliefs were indeed vital to her success.

In the world she created, God and Mammon got along quite well. As we have just seen, she referenced biblical passages on dollar bills. When the company became successful, which it did very quickly, Mary Kay began driving a pink Cadillac. For a time, she lived in a multimillion-dollar, thirty-room mansion with twenty-eight-foot-high ceilings, a Grecian pool, crystal chandeliers, and eleven bathrooms. You owe it to yourself to take a look at this house.[21]

A startling fact deserves our attention as we begin our discussion of Mary Kay's company. As she has written, "In 1963, I had no previous experience in the cosmetics industry..."[22] She chose to enter a highly competitive trade in which the products are profoundly personal and epitomize "high touch." What do cosmetics companies really sell? The classic answer is hope.[23] It was the process of selling more than the product that captured Mary Kay's imagination. Though she was a stranger to the industry, "[M]y forte," she explained, "was recruiting and training salespeople."[24] Her ability in that area was impressive.

Started on a shoestring, Mary Kay Cosmetics made a small profit on $34,000 in sales in its first three and a half months. In its first calendar year, sales were $198,000. The next calendar year they were $800,000.[25] Mary Kay used the "multilevel marketing" business model, so wholesale sales were what mattered. The company sold its products to "beauty consultants," who sold them to the end user.

Start-ups customarily lose money, sometimes for years, before showing a profit. Mary Kay Cosmetics never had an unprofitable year. When asked how she was able to do so well so quickly, she said, "The answer is I was middle-aged, had varicose veins and I didn't have time to fool around. Have you heard the definition of a woman's needs? From fourteen to forty, she needs good looks, from forty to sixty, she needs personality, and I'm here to tell you that after sixty, she needs cash."[26] She was unapologetic about her definition of "a woman's needs" and often repeated this formulation.

The term "multilevel marketing" was used above. What is it? Multilevel marketing is a distribution system in which independent sales consultants buy product from a company at wholesale prices and sell those products directly to consumers at retail prices, keeping the profit. Independent sales consultants are recruited to the company by other sales consultants who occupy the level above them. Each level of the sales organization collects a percentage of sales of the level below them. The woman at the top of this structure increases her income as the number of levels increases and the number of retail-level sales contractors grows.

Mary Kay Cosmetics sold the product to "beauty consultants." These people held house parties and sold to the consumer. They also recruited more beauty consultants to sell Mary Kay products.[27]

In 1981, for which we have statistics courtesy of a Harvard Business School case, there were half as many rungs on the ladder as in 2020. There were 143,060 beauty consultants at Mary Kay: 2,088 sales directors, 1,110 senior sales directors, and thirty-one national sales directors. The latter made between $100,000 and $200,000 a year. As one can see, the pyramid is steep. Thirty-one is about 1/4,615 of 143,060. And it is not an easy pyramid to climb. Everyone in the system was an independent entrepreneur. None of these people worked directly for Mary Kay Cosmetics. Neither did the beauty consultants work for the sales directors, nor the sales directors for the senior sales directors, nor the senior sales directors for the national sales directors, nor did anyone work for the company. However, there was a pot of gold at the peak of the pyramid. One woman, Doretha Dingler, made more than $10 million during her thirty-six years working with Mary Kay.[28]

Nobody could give anybody else an order. This is why other methods of motivation were vital and why practices that in mainstream corporate America would have been unthinkable were standard fare at Mary Kay.

Indeed, an interesting aspect of Mary Kay Cosmetics is how the company diverged from the trends of business in the United States. For decades, as American businesses grew large, they integrated mass production and mass distribution. Manufacturers of both consumer and industrial products developed their own sales forces, which they trained and managed. Salesmen (and at first they were all men) for Standard Oil, American Tobacco, H. J. Heinz, National Cash Register, and dozens of other companies were employees, not independent entrepreneurs. Sales force management became one of the great strengths of American corporations in global competition in the twentieth century. Sales managers could manage the income of salesmen through salaries, commissions, and the assignment of territories.

With this control came obligations that increased during the twentieth century. These obligations included a wide range of benefits, such as, for example, health care. Full-time employment cost the company money.

Mary Kay was spared all those expenses but at the sacrifice of the command and control management the alternative model offered. The home office could establish basic ground rules, but its span of control was limited. The sales force was composed of a set of businesspeople who conducted their businesses as they saw fit.

An example of a ground rule was the financial basis of the transactions between the company and its beauty consultants. The company operated on a cash basis, quite out of the ordinary for its time. "...[O]ur Consultants and Distributors pay in advance for every item of merchandise, and they pay with a cashier's check or money order. We accept no personal checks... No Mary Kay Consultant can run up a debt with our company, and as a result, we have few accounts receivable and no expense of collecting bad debts."[29] There was no financial leverage in the distribution system.

The company advised its consultants to run their businesses on the same basis. "We encourage each Consultant to take an order, deliver the product, and collect her money the day of the sales presentation."[30] Close the sale the moment it is made. The company could "encourage" but not "demand." That is the price it chose to pay in order to deal with independent entities rather than its own sales force.

Not every consultant who signed up with Mary Kay was happy with the experience. Mary Kay herself constantly repeated that the goal of her company was to provide an opportunity for women "to fully utilize their skills and talents."[31] When she launched her dream company, she "wasn't interested in the dollars-and-cents part of [the] business... my interest was in offering women opportunities that didn't exist anywhere else."[32] She wanted to create a world in which women were not dismissed because they were "just women." She wanted them to fulfill their destinies. These are high-minded and praiseworthy sentiments. How, then, are we to think of the fact that in the early 1980s, turnover of consultants was 80 percent? For every five consultants who signed on each year, four quit.

One way to look at this figure is to compare it to turnover in other direct selling organizations. At Tupperware, it was 100 percent. Avon's was 150 percent. When a Harvard Business School case study of Mary Kay Cosmetics was written in 1983, one question it considered was not why turnover at Mary Kay was so high but why it was so low.[33]

Nevertheless, this much churn does tell us a couple of things. One is that only a small minority of people who tried could internalize that "Mary Kay enthusiasm," a phrase from one of the company's songs. They couldn't "do it," Mary Kay's mother's belief notwithstanding.

The second lesson is that despite all the effort that the company did make, the truth is that selling is hard and direct selling à la Mary Kay, Tupperware, or Avon is very hard. It takes a lot of nerve to contact people you know socially and ask them to come to your home for a party that really isn't a party. You are going to face a lot of rejection. Unless, like Mary Kay herself, you are immune to the inevitable disappointments of interpersonal selling, this experience can wear you down. Rejection hurts.

Charisma helps.

Despite the difficulties, Mary Kay Cosmetics became a sensational success. Why? What held this company together through the slings and arrows of outrageous selling? The answer is the charisma of "our leader, our motivator, our inspiration, our first lady," Mary Kay. She implicitly said to all these independent actors words I have heard attributed to Evita Perón: "I was once like you. You can be like me." Conspicuous consumption was one of her tools. That mansion she lived in. Those pink Cadillacs. (GM had never produced Cadillacs in pink until Mary Kay wanted them. They officially named her color Mary Kay Pink.)

What product was Mary Kay really selling? We have already mentioned hope. Hope for what? For better looks. For a better life. And, because of the multilevel marketing system, for more money. Perhaps hope to be like Mary Kay, with the adulation in which she basked, the fortune she had, and the respect and attention of a world that would never dismiss her as "just a woman." Mary Kay's answer to the question of what her company was selling was "femininity."[34] One could make a case that what the company was really selling was Mary Kay. And no one could do that better than she herself. To see how she did it, a look at the company's annual convention, called Seminar, will be of help.

The first Seminar was held on the company's first anniversary. It was a "very modest" affair, to put it mildly, by later standards. The setting was a warehouse with Jell-O salad melting over paper plates in the hot Texas weather. The need to economize was real, and the event was rich only in enthusiasm. But it was very rich indeed in that.

By the 1980s, Seminar, "the most important event in the Mary Kay year,"[35] had grown into a multimillion-dollar extravaganza that has been called an Academy Awards, Miss America pageant, and Broadway opening all rolled up into one. Seminar had dazzling awards, competition, drama, and excitement. "It is a three-day spectacular... We go to all this expense and effort because... the desire for recognition is a powerful motivator... [T]he highlight of Seminar is Awards Night. No expense is spared as we strive for elaborate staging and glamour worthy of a Cecil B. DeMille production. The event culminates as our top performers are rewarded with the fabulous prizes that have made Mary Kay Cosmetics synonymous with luxury and glamour: diamond rings, full-length mink coats, pink Cadillacs and dream vacations... Seminar is the ultimate expression of a very simple concept—*praise people to success!*"[36] In the *60 Minutes* piece on the company, Morley Safer described Seminar as a "blatant, unapologetic tribute to Mary Kay and capitalism. Other corporate giants walk on stage. Mary Kay levitates."[37]

Safer's description is accurate. On Awards Night, the biggest night of the year, Mary Kay appears on a platform that is slowly elevated from under the stage while music is playing with lyrics extolling her. Nobody ever called her bashful. Thousands of Mary Kay consultants pay their own way to Dallas each year to benefit from this motivation themselves.

Charisma is needed when people do new things or when a new class or category of people do things already done. It took charisma for a woman, Mary Kay Ash, to build a billion-dollar company beginning in 1963.

Mary Kay became Mary Kay Ash when she married Melville (Mel) J. Ash on January 6, 1966. It was a rewarding union. He knew how to fit into her life, and she understood the importance of "his time." She loved him. He loved her.

She needed someone with whom to share her life. "It's no fun to come home and count your money by yourself."[38] She finally found the companion she needed in Mel.

"We loved Mel," Doretha Dingler has written, "and especially the fact that he adored Mary Kay. From the day that she and Mel had their first date, he gave her a gift every week for the rest of his life as a way of honoring that special occasion."[39] Mary Kay wrote that "Whenever I meet someone, I try to imagine him or her wearing an invisible sign that says: MAKE ME FEEL IMPORTANT!"[40] Her husband Mel spared no effort in making her feel important.

There was a problem. Mel smoked. How could Mary Kay, the master motivator, convince him to stop? For a decade, "I begged, cajoled, reasoned, and pleaded with him to stop." As with her consultants, she couldn't give him orders. He did try to stop many times but simply couldn't.

One evening, Mary Kay read a magazine article about the dangers of inhaling secondary smoke for nonsmokers who lived with captives of the habit. She said nothing about the article but turned the magazine over and left it on the coffee table, knowing that Mel's curiosity would be piqued.

Mel read the article, and "[b]ecause he loved me and cared about me," he checked into a clinic, and after spending five days there never touched another cigarette. It appears that we will do for others what we will not or cannot do for ourselves. After almost half a century of smoking, he quit completely. But it was too late. "[T]he damage had already been done." The couple had five more years together. Then Mel was diagnosed with lung cancer. He lived only seven weeks after the diagnosis. He died on July 7, 1980, at the age of seventy-five.[41]

The funeral was on a Tuesday afternoon. A meeting of seventy-five hundred consultants was scheduled for the following Friday in St. Louis. Mary Kay decided to go. "I knew that many women would be spending a good deal of money to travel to that conference, and I felt an obligation not to let them down. These meetings are supposed to be joyful, inspirational times, and so even though I was grief-stricken, I made certain that I generated a positive attitude for everyone present. I went out in front of that large audience, and I did my best to project the happiness I felt for them rather than the sorrow I felt for myself." Just prior to telling the story in her autobiography of the death of the only man she ever really loved, Mary Kay made the following observation. "You see—the funny thing about putting on a happy face is that if you do it again and again, pretty soon that happy face is here to stay. It becomes the real you."[42]

When evaluating Mary Kay as a charismatic capitalist and as a human being, you have to make a decision about this assertion. Do you believe it? Do you believe that Mary Kay believed it? This is a woman who was not a stranger to grief. Her divorce from her first husband was devastating. Her second husband died of a heart attack a month before she launched her company. Her third husband died of cancer. Her daughter, Marylyn, died of pneumonia in 1991. This is nothing more than a guess, but the fact that she experienced her share of disasters and nevertheless persisted always in putting on a happy face contributed to her charisma.

When Mary Kay wrote that "Life has many sad moments..." she spoke from experience. "[W]hen you lose a loved one, you must accept the knowledge that he or she is in a better place. Our grief, then, is really for ourselves."[43] She was, as we know, devoutly religious. Despite her unabashed praise of money—which was celebrated so bluntly and unapologetically by her consultants that they would fit right in on Wall Street—Mary Kay wrote, "When you get to the bottom line, it doesn't matter how much money you've made—how big your house is—or how many cars you own. For on that day when God calls you to accept your relationship with Jesus Christ, nothing else matters. Each of us will come to that day—and we must ask ourselves whether or not our lives have been meaningful."[44] This declaration showed that Mary Kay and Wall Street embodied very different approaches to life.

How would Mary Kay have responded to the question of whether that happy face you put on really does become the genuine you? She would have said that what made her life meaningful was contributing to the welfare of women in two ways. One was that through her company she provided them with professional opportunities that were denied them in a man's world. The second was that by providing products that boosted the self-esteem of the consumer, she was in the business of making women happier. She was certain that appearance did indeed become reality. Cosmetics were the perfect product for this woman.

Mary Kay Ash (1918–2001) and Sam Walton (1918–1992) were contemporaries. Hot Wells, Texas, her birthplace, is about five hundred miles south of Kingfisher, Oklahoma, where he was born. Her company was located in Dallas, his in Bentonville, separated by about 350 miles. Both were based in the western part of what in 1861 became the Confederacy.

Both were charismatic, and their charisma had certain common aspects. Both had an innate belief in themselves. Both dreamed big dreams. Both founded their own companies.

Both valued money, but both were mission driven. Money was the scorecard. Both believed that business was about making meaning. When Walton spoke for the final time in public on the occasion of being awarded the Presidential Medal of Freedom, he said, "We'll lower the cost of living for everyone."[45] Mary Kay constantly preached that she wanted women to be the beautiful people God created, and she also wanted to give women the opportunities denied them in the business world.

Mary Kay Cosmetics—completely unlike, say, Apple—was not a product-first company. As Doretha Dingler said, "For me, it was... never just about selling lipstick. It was about making a difference, seeing all the opportunities that women are fully capable of creating for themselves once they open their minds to seizing the opportunity and doing it. It was about becoming the kind of role model and mentor who can take insecure women by the hand and lead them where they need to go—and the kind of leader who can take them to a certain point, then step back and watch them soar."[46] Many of her acolytes would describe Mary Kay just this way.

There are also remarkable differences between Mary Kay and Sam Walton. In 1942, the great heavyweight champion boxer Joe Louis said of World War II that "[W]e will win because we're on God's side."[47] This is how Mary Kay felt about her company. She had few doubts because she believed herself to be an instrument of God's will. A belief in a living god that played an active role in human affairs was central to who she was. Nothing like this kind of religiosity can be found in Walton's biography (or in Edwin Land's, either). This is a fundamental difference.

Quite unlike Walton, Mary Kay made a practice of creating a "larger-than-life" persona. This she did, for example, by the way she managed her "levitation" onto the stage at the company's annual Seminar. Walton would never have done anything similar. She also did it in the way she created her lavish mansion.

Like Walton, there was a seeming omnipresence about Mary Kay. She was able to be everywhere at once. However, and this is very important, as close as she was to so many people in the company, there was still a separation that she maintained. "Mary Kay, as friendly and warmhearted as always, figured out how to keep the appropriate distance of leadership as she closely mentored those of us who were the original salesforce leaders. She encouraged us to pay close attention because she already knew what we were to find out: it's hard for leaders to become 'best friends' with those they lead."[48] It is an odd combination—this mixing of intimacy with the creation of an aura of specialness. Mary Kay succeeded in this endeavor, and that was an element of her charisma.

Indeed, a list of contrasts between these two unquestionably charismatic personalities—Mary Kay Ash and Sam Walton—would be longer than a list of similarities. This illustrates why it is difficult to generalize about charisma in a sentence. Stories of charismatic people working their magic are preferable.

In 1996, Mary Kay established a foundation that today is dedicated to fighting cancer and domestic violence. Soon after its establishment, she suffered a stroke. This stroke must have been to her what Beethoven's deafness was to him. She was a powerfully effective public speaker. However, she could speak no more. She continued to attend the annual Seminar but no longer could rally the troops as only she had the ability to do. According to one recollection, "At one of the meetings, miraculously she was somehow able to haltingly utter a few words. There was a silenced hush in the arena. It was the last time anyone was to hear that voice; the last time we were to hear from the champion of womankind who had poured so much into our lives. Mary Kay spoke clearly enough that everyone understood: 'You can do it.'"[49]

The most compelling evidence of Mary Kay's charisma comes from an unlikely source. Jackie Brown was a poor young girl from Arkansas who "had a consuming desire to overcome my past... and make money, a lot of money. It was as simple as that." She was working as a legal secretary in Dallas when she saw the original advertisement for recruits for Mary Kay Cosmetics in the *Dallas Morning News* in 1963.[50]

Brown was recruited, and Mary Kay took her under her wing. She taught Brown how to build a team ("Take a two-dollar gift, wrap it in a three-dollar package, and give it with a $100 worth of praise"[51]), how to sell, and how to deal with disappointment. Soon Brown became the top performer in a company that was growing very fast.

Slowly but steadily, from the time Mary Kay wanted to spike the punch at the first Seminar to make sure everyone had a great time, Brown began to lose confidence in her mentor. Eventually, she was convinced she was being cheated of her just financial rewards and left to found a competing company. According to a Mary Kay loyalist, the departure of Brown and a friend "broke Mary Kay's heart. She had loved those women and felt totally betrayed. But I'll never forget her marching down the hallways with her shoes off, determined not to let this new company do us in."[52]

The result was a protracted, harrowing, and altogether ugly battle between Mary Kay Cosmetics and BeautiControl (the name of Brown's new firm). Brown recounts all this in her memoirs.

Remarkably, Brown ends her recollections with the story of her last visit to Mary Kay. The year is unspecified. It must have been late in 1995 or early in 1996. She had heard Mary Kay's health was frail, "and on impulse I called her assistant and asked for an appointment to see her." The assistant called back right away to set up the meeting.

Brown said, "The reason I wanted to see her was to tell her that in my opinion she had done more to advance the economic status of women than any other person had in the twentieth century. I could tell she was touched, and from that point on, she was... the Mary Kay I remembered and loved. We talked for hours about the early years and how we had to do everything ourselves. We both remembered the exact food we had cooked for the first Seminar and the excitement we felt as the company began to grow."

"Can I ask you a question?" said Mary Kay. "Of course, anything," answered Jackie. "If you had to do it all over again, would you answer my newspaper ad?" Jackie responded, "In a heartbeat, Mary Kay. You showed me a way to accomplish my goals in life."[53] After what seemed like endless conflict, the relationship between these two women was restored.

Mary Kay never lost her magic.

CHAPTER 9

MANAGER VERSUS MONEY: THE RISE OF THE MARKET FOR CORPORATE CONTROL

The weakest link in the political economy of capitalism is, ironically, capital. The biggest threat to our well-being is not a failure of industry or of agriculture. It is a failure of the financial system. According to John Maynard Keynes, "Lenin is said to have declared that the best way to destroy the Capitalist System was to debauch the currency... Lenin," Keynes continues, "was certainly right. There is no subtler, no surer means of overturning the existing basis of society than to debauch the currency. The process engages all the hidden forces of economic law on the side of destruction, and does it in a manner which not one man in a million is able to diagnose."[1]

Keynes's comment is correct. Currency is created by "hidden forces," which only the most knowledgeable can "diagnose." Banks keep on their books only a fraction of the funds that would be necessary if all their depositors demanded all their deposits at once. When depositors do that, the "run" on the bank can create a panic that can quickly spread from the financial economy to the real economy. Your savings vanish. The result is that business freezes, as do your investments.

How can banks exist when everyone knows that they could not survive a run? Only help from the federal government or some other extraordinary assistance could bail them out of such a dilemma.

Banks can exist in spite of this because depositors do not believe there will be a run, at least not today. What is the proper ratio between the funds banks have out on loan and the reserves they keep in order to meet the demands of the daily vagaries of their business? You can get a lot of answers to this question. Experts will offer expert opinions. The truth is no one knows.

The mystery of finance is not limited to dollar bills. It extends to all kinds of financial instruments. A share of Apple stock at this writing sells for $124.61. That is because the price/earnings ratio is 28.01. If that ratio should fall to 8.41, that share of stock would be worth $61.31. Why is the price/earnings ratio what it is today? Because, to make a very long story short, that is what people think it should be. If they think that ratio should be different next week, it will be.

Everybody knows this. Why, then, do people buy Apple stock? Because they believe the price is reasonable and that it will go up. As with bank deposits, there is a lot of mystery here. The truth is no one knows whether Apple stock will go up or down next week or next year. The key word with all financial transactions is *believe*.

In an important book published in 1957, Bray Hammond, a former official at the Federal Reserve System, wrote the following about the revolution in thinking brought about by the development of financial instruments in the unsophisticated world of the early American republic: "The conventions of a monetary economy were coming swiftly into use and sweeping the unsophisticated off their feet. An economy in which barter had been important and financial transactions had been wholly subordinate to the exchange of goods was giving way to an economy concerned more and more with obligations, contracts, negotiable instruments, equities, and such invisible abstractions. Money per se was giving way to promises to pay money, most of which were never performed... but were canceled by bookkeepers in the increasingly frequent offset of liabilities and specie [hard money—gold or silver] was dissolving into obligations to pay specie in a volume greatly exceeding the total that existed... In the absence of enough experience, the point at which the proper use of a convention became an abuse was unperceived. If a promise was as good as a deed in some instances, it was unapparent why everything might not be left to promise... [If people] could owe five times what they could pay, why not a hundred?"[2] That last question is as pertinent today as it was many years ago.

Finance is the soft underbelly of the economy for the reasons cited above. It is intangible—nothing to touch, kick, and feel. It is inscrutable. And it is that part of the business world where suckers are welcome and those who would cheat them are plentiful.

The financial system depends on credit, a word derived from the Latin *credere*, to believe. Credit has rightly been called "money of the mind." It is there if you and others believe in it. Those who inspire belief can become very powerful in this domain. Charisma matters a lot in finance.

J. P. Morgan and Michael Milken were major change agents. Both were charismatic. That said, there were plenty of differences between them.

Morgan was the consummate establishment insider, son of a very successful international banker. Novelist E. L. Doctorow described him as "that classic American hero, a man born to extreme wealth who by dint of hard work and ruthlessness multiplies the family fortune till it is out of sight."[3]

In contrast, Milken was an outsider. Born in Encino, California, on the Fourth of July, 1946, into a Jewish family (Morgan was Episcopalian), he excelled in high school and graduated summa cum laude, Phi Beta Kappa from the University of California, Berkeley, in 1968. While in college he read *Corporate Bond Quality and Investor Experience* by economist and president of the Federal Reserve Bank of Cleveland W. Braddock Hickman.[4] This 530-page "abstruse" tome written in a dry, scholarly fashion was unknown outside the academy. It sold 934 copies when it was published by the Princeton University Press in 1958, and most of those were to college libraries.[5]

If you studied Hickman's findings and believed they were accurate, the information his book contained was of great importance to investors. He found that "issues in the high-quality classes [of corporate bonds]... have the lowest default rates, promised yields, and loss rates; but the returns obtained by those who held them over long periods were generally below those on low-grade issues."[6] That is to say, the investor did better with a portfolio of low-grade corporate bonds than with a portfolio of high-grade corporate bonds, if the investor held the investment "over long periods." What should have been front page in the *Wall Street Journal* was overlooked by almost everyone except Michael Milken.

Upon graduating in 1968, Milken married his high school sweetheart, Lori Anne Hackel, and they had three children. In 1969, he enrolled at the Wharton School at the University of Pennsylvania. Commenting on Wharton, another alumnus, Donald Trump, said, "I took a lot of finance courses at Wharton, and they first taught you all the rules and regulations. They then taught you that all those rules and regulations are really meant to be broken..."[7] Milken must have fit right in.

One of Milken's professors got him a summer internship in the Philadelphia office of an old-time (it traced its roots back to 1838) investment banking firm called Drexel Harriman Ripley. He worked there part-time while in school and moved to the firm's New York office to take a full-time position in 1970. (He left Wharton without graduating. He owed one paper, which he eventually handed in, and was awarded his degree in 1974.)

Milken spent his entire financial career with Drexel, through all its incarnations—from Drexel Harriman Ripley to Drexel Firestone to Drexel Burnham to Drexel Burnham Lambert. It is an intriguing choice. He could have gone to a first-class (known as major bracket in the trade) investment bank like Goldman Sachs or Morgan Stanley. I have not seen a discussion of why he stayed with what at that time was a second-class firm in the financial world, so one is left to guess. There are dozens of very smart, hardworking, and greedy young people at the top Wall Street firms. At a backwater like Drexel, Milken could write his own ticket, which he proceeded to do.

Despite the ancient pedigree of Drexel, the Burnham part of the firm was new and in the driver's seat. Founded by Isaac Wolf Burnham in 1935, the firm managed to survive some pretty tough times. When Burnham was contemplating buying Drexel, he spoke to Milken, who was thinking of leaving the firm in order to teach at Wharton. Burnham urged him to stay. "Mike worked away trading securities no one was interested in. I offered him $28,000 a year and increased the position he could handle from $500,000 to $2 million. I allowed him to keep a dollar for every three he made. He doubled the position's value in a year. Our deal never changed."[8]

This happened in 1974, a tough year for Wall Street firms but not for Drexel because of the money Milken was making "trading securities no one was interested in." In 1976, Milken made $5 million on this arrangement. In 1983, he made $46 million. In 1984, $124 million. In 1985, $135 million. In 1986, $295 million. And in 1987, $550 million. This figure was higher than the profits of most of the nation's largest companies. According to one calculation, Milken was paid $1,046 a minute assuming a fourteen-hour day. This was not counting the other income Milken received from his innumerable partnerships.[9] John D. Rockefeller once said, "I have ways of making money you know nothing of."[10] This was also true of Milken.

In 1978, Milken, who disliked New York and longed for his native Southern California, decided to move Drexel's junk bond operation to Los Angeles. "It was already obvious that Milken's success had little to do with Drexel, and that Drexel's success had everything to do with Milken... Why not simply move, using Drexel as an umbrella but effectively setting up an autonomous operation... under his total control?"[11] That is what he did. He made the decisions about junk bonds. He did well for Drexel, for many of his clients, extremely well for those Drexel traders he selected to come out to Los Angeles with him, and spectacularly well for himself.

It was in his Beverly Hills lair that the legend of Milken took root, grew, and fully blossomed. He showed up for work at four thirty in the morning, well before the markets opened in New York. He sat at the intersection of an X-shaped workplace so that he could see everything his chosen people were doing. The group he assembled was "not unlike a cult: intensely secretive, insular, led by a charismatic and messianic leader whom many of his followers came to see as larger than life." One of his people remarked, "We owe it all to one man, and we are all extraneous. Michael has denuded us of ego." Another said, "Michael is the most important individual who has lived in this century." Yet another opined, "Someone like Mike comes along once every five hundred years."[12]

In the years from 1978 to Milken's indictment on ninety-eight counts of racketeering and fraud by a federal grand jury in the Southern District of New York in 1989, the junk bond business exploded. During these years one could make the case that Michael Milken was the most important individual in American finance. There is a seemingly endless debate about whether he was a force for good or ill. His defenders credit him with providing liquidity for a new class of securities, junk bonds, which had formally been relegated to an insignificant place in finance. They also point to a number of companies the financing of which he made possible.

Milken's detractors question whether he was a value creator or a value taker. They charge him with pressuring companies to think short term. Most effectively, they point to his lack of ethics. In the end, he did plead guilty to six felonies, and this plea was entered not because of any lack of funds to mount an effective legal and public relations defense. He paid over a billion dollars in fines and was sentenced to ten years in prison, of which he served twenty months. He has spent the time since then in an effort to rehabilitate himself. A giant step in that direction was taken on February 19, 2020, when President Donald Trump granted him a pardon.

The securities Milken, the outsider, flogged would not at first be touched by major-bracket investment houses. There is no better illustration of his being an outsider than the fact that he exercised his greatest impact on the financial world when he left New York in favor of Southern California.

The most useful way to view Milken is as a symptom rather than a cause. He was a symptom of a basic trend, which he may have expedited but which would have asserted itself even if he had left Drexel Burnham back in the early 1970s and chosen to teach at Wharton. That trend was toward the increased power of financial considerations in determining the policies of American businesses. Shareholders were flexing their muscle as never before in the post–World War II era. Debt was weaponized to assemble large pools of capital with remarkable speed, enabling raiders to terrorize traditional managers. New technologies were threatening the business models that for decades had been the basis of stable oligopolies. New business strategies were overtaking somnolent incumbents. Suddenly the traditional general manager was under siege. Harlow Curtice never lost a night's sleep worrying about shareholder value. In the 1980s, that phrase was top of mind for the CEOs of even the best-run companies in the United States. From 1970 to 1979, the term *shareholder value* appeared in only one article in the *Wall Street Journal*. In the next ten years, the term appeared in 443 *Wall Street Journal* articles.[13]

The idea of shareholder value was nothing new. However, during the non-charismatic era after World War II, the goals of professional managers and shareholders were better aligned than they were to become. The value of well-run American corporations was increasing, so professional managers, even if they personally owned only a small number of shares of the corporations they managed, and shareholders had similar interests.

Even in the 1950s, however, poorly performing firms were subject to shareholder action. The classic example is the attempt by financier and self-made millionaire Louis E. Wolfson to take over the once great but ailing retailer Montgomery Ward in 1955. Montgomery Ward and Sears, Roebuck were the two leading general merchandise retailers, which competed with one another from the 1880s to World War II. Following the war, the CEOs of these firms, Robert Wood of Sears and Sewell L. Avery (known as SLAvery to his many detractors) of Montgomery Ward embarked on opposite strategies.

The two CEOs met for lunch at the Chicago Club soon after VJ Day. "This country's going into a tailspin within two years," Avery told Wood. "Every great war has been followed by a great depression..." Wood's view was diametrically opposite, and the two men managed their companies in accord with their outlooks. Sears built stores. Ward closed them. Sears invested in inventory. Ward sold it off. In 1954, Ward's sales had declined to $887.3 million from a peak of $1.2 billion and its profits from $74.2 million to $35.2 million. The company's net worth was $639 million. Its balance sheet showed $327 million in cash and securities. It became known as the bank with the store attached.[14]

By September 1954, Wolfson was planning the first high-profile hostile takeover of an American business since

World War II. He accumulated two hundred thousand shares of Ward stock in preparation for a proxy fight at the annual meeting on April 22, 1955. His strategy was "to show up Avery as weak, confused and nearly senile [he was almost eighty] by asking pointed questions and letting him hang himself..." When Avery rose to speak, he was incoherent. Wolfson failed his takeover attempt, but Avery was finished.[15]

Wolfson bears some intriguing similarities to Milken. Both were outsiders attacking the establishment. Both used novel techniques to do so. Both became very rich. Both served time in prison. And both were extravagantly praised by those who supported what they did. Henry G. Manne, dean of the George Mason University School of Law, said of Wolfson that his "contribution to human welfare far exceeded the total value of all private philanthropy in history. He invented the modern hostile tender offer. This invention, which activated and energized the market for corporate control, was the primary cause of the revolutionary restructuring of American industry in the 1970s and '80s, and the ensuing economic boom."[16]

The new world into which American business was entering is epitomized by the travail of the tire industry during the 1980s. Here we can see the conflict between the traditional approach of the professional manager (in this case Robert Mercer of Goodyear) and the charismatic capitalism made possible by Milken, which approached the corporation as a financial football to be kicked around. In this case, the charismatic capitalist is Sir James Goldsmith.

There was high drama generated by the conflict between these approaches in Akron, Ohio. This new world was characterized by the forces Milken played such an important role in setting in motion. The new reality included the demand for shareholder value, raids on all five of the major domestic tire manufacturers, and the transformation of equity into debt through the availability of junk bond financing.

Following World War II, the tire industry presented a classic oligopoly. It was dominated by five firms: Goodyear, founded in 1898; Firestone, founded in 1900; Uniroyal, founded as the United States Rubber Company in 1892; BF Goodrich, founded in 1870; and GenCorp, founded as the General Tire and Rubber Company in 1915. Four of these five companies were headquartered in Akron (Uniroyal was the exception), and the city became known as "the rubber capital of the world."[17]

Goodyear, nicknamed the gorilla, was the industry leader in 1970 with a domestic market share of 33 percent. Next came Firestone with a quarter. Of the remaining 42 percent of the market, about 22 percent was divided among the three firms mentioned above. A variety of smaller players accounted for the remainder. This oligopoly was remarkably stable. In 1919, the four biggest firms (those just mentioned but not counting General, which had only entered the industry four years earlier) accounted for 65 percent of tire shipments. In 1970, the top five firms (now counting General) accounted for 80 percent of shipments. Imports held under 4 percent of the market.[18]

The years from VJ Day to 1970 were good to the tire industry. New car sales increased dramatically, but that was not the key. Although about 30 percent of domestic tire production went to the Big Three automobile manufacturers in Detroit, it was next to impossible to make any money from that segment. Detroit could play one tire manufacturer off against another and get rock-bottom prices. The original equipment manufacturers could also credibly threaten to produce their own tires, as Ford did in the late 1930s. In the words of the founder of General Tire, "Detroit wants tires that are round, black, and cheap—and it don't care whether they are round and black."[19]

The tire manufacturers made their money in the replacement business. Original equipment tires sold for half the price of replacements. Even in the replacement business, profits were not assured. Some of the retailers to which the tire manufacturer sold—these were the great days of Sears—bargained hard on price and often demanded private-label merchandise.

These are the reasons why industry profitability was not as high as the concentration of the participants would suggest that it should have been. Nevertheless, between the war and about 1970, the tire manufacturers made money because of their sales through company-owned stores and through independent outlets such as gas stations.

By 1970, the replacement business was threatened by a new technological development. The domestic industry produced bias-ply and later bias-belted tires. In Europe, radial tires, manufactured in quantity by Michelin, swept the field. Radials lasted three to four times longer than bias-ply tires. Obviously, purchasers would be buying fewer replacements. The radial revolution did not go unnoticed on Wall Street. Fund managers saw little future in tires and began to sell shares in the early 1970s. Tire companies started underperforming the S&P 500 Index for the first time.

The tire companies were forced to invest in radials if they wanted to keep selling to Detroit because the automobile manufacturers demanded them. Investment in radial capacity was expensive. The tire companies thus had little choice but to spend money digging their own graves. Another option was to diversify into businesses with some profit potential. Yet a third option was to exit the industry altogether. Not an easy thing to do, but not impossible depending on the percentage of sales from tires.

Between 1982 and 1987, each of the big five tire companies was the target of at least one hostile takeover attempt. Three were raided twice. The most interesting effort and a useful lens through which to view the world Milken made possible is the case of Goodyear. The brief but action-packed "Goodyear War" illustrated the battle between the traditional corporate general manager and the corporate raider.

Michelin had been producing radials in Europe since the end of World War II, and they dominated the market. Charles J. Pilliod Jr. became Goodyear's CEO in 1974 and served until 1983. He joined the company in 1941 and spent his whole career with it, as was customary. He was not a provincial man. He spent a large part of his career abroad and saw how quickly radials captured the European market. Indeed, as early as the 1950s, Goodyear was manufacturing radials in Europe.

Through domestic American eyes, radials were a nightmare—a technological development that was good for your customers but bad for you. In addition to lasting longer than the standard American bias-ply or bias-belted tires, they generated less rolling resistance and therefore delivered better gas mileage. They held the road better, especially in wet conditions. No wonder Goodyear was in denial about their impact. As late as 1974, a Goodyear vice president said that the radial was "a sophisticated tire. If the American car owner doesn't learn to take better care of his tires, he's going to be badly disappointed with his radials. There is definitely the possibility of a disappointment with radials a few years down the road."[20]

Pilliod knew better than to believe this kind of nonsense. Michelin and the Japanese tire giant Bridgestone began exporting radials to the United States in 1971. *Consumer Reports* rated them a superior tire. Under Pilliod's leadership and in the face of internal resistance, Goodyear initiated radial investment in the United States, which eventually cost between $2.5 billion and $3 billion.

The company also determined that it needed to diversify out of the cyclical, highly competitive tire business. The goal was to become more than a manufacturing company in a mature industry. Early in 1982, a diversification task force was established to evaluate acquisition candidates.[21]

Pilliod reached the mandatory retirement age of sixty-five in 1983 and was succeeded by Robert E. Mercer on January 1 of that year. Mercer joined Goodyear in 1947 after military service and graduation from Yale. As usual, he spent his whole career at the company and had been chief operating officer since 1981. In December of 1982, Mercer said his goal was to "get into things that relate to our skills. We aren't going to be a conglomerate; we aren't going to buy oil wells."[22] However, on the recommendation of its diversification task force, Goodyear acquired the Celeron Corporation for $825 million in stock. Celeron operated natural gas transmission systems and explored for oil and gas. It was to be managed as a wholly owned subsidiary, but its CEO got a seat on Goodyear's board. The acquisition diminished Goodyear's sales to the automobile industry from 82 percent to 75 percent of total, but it did not make Wall Street happy. Goodyear's shares fell $3.50 to $30 when the deal was announced. This represented a loss of $260 million in market value. Goodyear had seventy-four million premerger shares outstanding. By the end of 1986, as a result primarily of this transaction as well as other developments, Goodyear had 109,435 shares outstanding.

Mercer's goal was to reduce Goodyear's sales exposure to the automobile industry to 50 percent. Celeron began an ambitious expansion program to help achieve this goal. It bought the All-American Pipeline Company, which was planning to build a heated oil pipeline from new oil fields opening up in California 1,250 miles to refineries in Texas at a cost of between $800 million and $900 million. In 1985, due to poor performance, Celeron was sold to Tenneco for $443.5 million. Proceeds from the sale were used to acquire oil and gas reserves.

By the end of 1985, the All-American Pipeline (still owned by Goodyear) had cost $1 billion. A revised plan called for it to be extended another five hundred miles at a cost of over $700 million. Meanwhile, crude oil prices dropped by half, calling into question whether the pipeline would ever be used. In addition to this initiative, Goodyear was expanding its aerospace business. Overall, the diversification program was costing a lot of money and not going well. The stage was now set for a classic confrontation between two men and profoundly different ideas of what private enterprise was all about.

Mercer was returning from Japan in October of 1986. He landed in Chicago on a commercial flight and was being picked up by the company plane to take him to Akron. Before the company plane took off, he was told he had an urgent phone call that he should take right away. The phone call was urgent indeed. It was his CFO informing him that movements in Goodyear stock led him to believe that the company was being raided. Mercer said, "I'll be home in an hour. Get the SWAT team together."[23]

The first rumors about a raid on Goodyear hit Wall Street on Monday, October 8, after the company's stock closed at $36.875, a five-year high. The price of Goodyear stock moved up sharply during October, from $32.75 in late September to $48.25 by Monday, October 27, after a one-day rise of $4.125. The stock had been trading heavily and repeatedly appeared on the most active lists. More than 12.7 million shares traded on October 27.[24]

Mercer and his team had been through a drill concerning the possibility of a raid six months previously. Mercer had consulted his financial advisers in New York City—Goodyear retained both Goldman Sachs and Drexel—about the chances of a raid. They estimated about 15 percent, so "it wasn't high on my radar screen." It turned out that the chances were 100 percent.

When Mercer arrived at the office, he asked, "What do we know?"

Answer: "There has been a big move in Goodyear stock."

Mercer: "Who's doing it?"

Answer: "They won't tell us."

Mercer: "I thought you guys had friends on the Street."

Answer: "Yeah, but those friends have all clammed up."

Mercer: "That tells me we're being raided."[25] Suddenly, a raid was the only item on his radar screen.

On Friday, October 24, Goodyear announced "a program for maximizing shareholder value over the near term," which might "include a restructuring of the assets and/or the capital structure of the corporation."[26] With this announcement came a sharp increase in the price of the stock on October 27.

The following day, it became known that the raider was Sir James Goldsmith. On Thursday, October 30, Goldsmith reported to the SEC that he and his backers—including Merrill Lynch, which had identified Goodyear for Goldsmith as an inviting target, and Britain's Hanson Trust—had accumulated 11.5 percent of Goodyear's 109 million shares.

Two men more different than Mercer and Goldsmith would be difficult to imagine. Mercer was as American as classic apple pie. He devoted his professional life to Goodyear. He was intelligent and hardworking. His father was a Ford dealer in a small town in New Jersey. When he became police commissioner, he could not sell cars to the municipality, which was his biggest customer. The family of six got along fine even with belts somewhat tightened.

Mercer enjoyed baseball. He played in high school and at Yale, which he attended courtesy of the GI Bill of Rights. He married his high school sweetheart, Mae, on July 5, 1947. He often joked to her that July 4 was his last day of independence. Their marriage was a lifelong, loving union.[27]

Goldsmith was an international bon vivant. He traced his ancestry to Moses von Schaffhausen, a goldsmith who was expelled from Nuremberg in 1499 because he was Jewish. He settled in Frankfort, changed his name to Goldschmidt and, like their more famous Rothschild cousins, he and his family provided financing for European governments.

Goldsmith was born in Paris on February 26, 1933, to a German Jewish father and French Catholic mother. His youth was characterized by wild gambling. At the age of twenty, he eloped with Isabel Patino, whose father was immensely wealthy. She died young and was followed by two more wives and numerous mistresses. The difference between Goldsmith and Mercer is perfectly captured by Goldsmith's observation that "if you marry your mistress, you create a job vacancy."[28]

At his death on July 18, 1997, Goldsmith possessed a fortune of about $2 billion. He had five residences: a hacienda in Mexico, a château in France, a mansion in southwest London, and a townhouse in central London. (He had sold the sumptuous townhouse on the Upper East Side of Manhattan where he had met with Robert Mercer.) He had his own Boeing 757, fitted out with two bedrooms, a kitchen, and an office.[29] He had a lot, but it was never enough.

Goldsmith launched a successful raid on Crown Zellerbach, a pulp and paper company, in 1984 and 1985. The result was that he wound up owning very large tracts of timber in the United States at next to no cost. He broke up Crown Zellerbach, which ceased to exist, and the raid yielded him a fortune of $400 million. He also acquired Diamond International and Continental Group for their timber holdings. He broke up Diamond International and made $500 million in the process. After these raids, he owned 3.5 million acres of American timberland.[30] Goldsmith posed an existential threat to Goodyear.

At Goodyear, Mercer and his colleagues engaged in "[m]ind-numbing strategy sessions [that] consumed the days and nights." The team shuttled between Akron and New York City. At one point, Mercer decided—to the horror of his advisers both inside and outside the company—to meet personally with Goldsmith. "Why not?" he asked. Goldsmith is "our largest shareholder. I ought to get to know him."[31]

Mercer went up to Goldsmith's townhouse on East Eightieth Street and knocked on the door.[32] He was informed that he was knocking on the wrong door. "But," remembered Mercer, "it looked grand enough to be the door. It was actually the door to the kitchen. So I went down a quarter of a block and knocked on the next big door. The same guy opened it and welcomed me in.

"And as I walked in, there are these two huge statues of naked women standing there. I looked around, and [the guy] said, 'Sir James will meet you on the second floor.'" Mercer walked up a winding staircase, and "Here's this huge guy [Goldsmith was six foot four], and it was all set up so that he could lean down and shake hands with me. We went into this dining room, and it was huge. It looked like something out of Hollywood. He sat in front of the fireplace. The table must have been twenty feet long. My place was on his right. He was at the head... Over the fireplace was this huge picture of this absolutely gorgeous, totally naked woman. And I said to myself, I'm not going to let him catch me looking at that, although I wanted to say, 'Your mother was certainly a nice-looking woman.'" Mercer refrained.

The two got down to business. Mercer said, "You apparently have an interest in Goodyear Tire and Rubber Company, and we're delighted." Goldsmith, according to Mercer, responded that his interest in Goodyear was to protect its shareholders. To which Mercer said, "That's a noble interest, and I applaud you for it." Goldsmith said the company had been very poorly managed, which was why the shareholders needed an advocate.

Mercer responded, "If what you're saying is you'd like me to step down, I don't have any trouble doing that, but I don't think the company's badly managed at all... The problem you have—can I call you Jimmy [to which Goldsmith responded affirmatively]—is that you don't understand the company." Mercer later recalled that Goldsmith "didn't even know about Celeron. He went through it with me, all these phrases—'unlock the value of the company'—and he never once mentioned Celeron... His whole line was a bunch of baloney."[33]

That was accurate. Goldsmith didn't know anything about Goodyear. Mercer was probably the only one of the company's 132,000 employees he had ever met. But Goldsmith did know about financial statements, and he agreed with his bankers at Merrill Lynch that there was a good chance to make a quick buck here.

Mercer said to Goldsmith, "Jimmy, our stock used to be twelve... Where were you then?" Goldsmith's reply tells the story of the impact of Milken's weaponization of junk bonds. "Money wasn't available then. Now, I can get all the money I want through junk bonds. That's the difference, Bob. Today, I can get the money. Then, I couldn't."[34]

This struggle received a great deal of publicity. Goodyear was a major corporation. However, according to Mercer, "amazingly enough, the Department of Commerce didn't feel that way." At one of the hearings in Washington, Malcolm Baldrige, secretary of commerce, said it didn't matter to him whether Goodyear was raided or not. "And you know," commented Mercer, "this was an old Yale guy." Baldrige died in a rodeo accident not long after this remark, and his successor was a little more sympathetic to Mercer's situation.[35]

Closer to home, Goodyear put on a full-court press, which was very effective. The mayor of Akron, providentially named Tom Sawyer, fought Goldsmith shoulder to shoulder with Goodyear. He was quoted as referring to Goldsmith as the "limey bastard," but later said he did not mean that. He meant "slimy bastard."[36] The unions and Goodyear's suppliers backed the company as well, in at least two instances by closing Merrill Lynch accounts.

In Washington, DC, a hearing on the raid was held by the Subcommittee on Mergers and Competitiveness of the House

Judiciary Committee. John Seiberling, who represented Akron in the House and whose grandfather cofounded Goodyear, said to Goldsmith, who was testifying, "My question is: Who the hell are you?" Goldsmith responded that he was an "active investor" endeavoring to save America from the "European disease" of "big business, big unions, and big government absolutely throttling out entrepreneurialism."[37]

When Goldsmith reviewed a tape of his testimony that evening, he didn't like what he saw. "I can't believe how nasty I look on this thing. I look like a monster. It's incredible!"[38] In any event, Seiberling's question made much more of an impact than Goldsmith's response.

The coup de grâce was legislation rushed through the Ohio legislature and signed by Governor Richard Celeste, making hostile takeovers more difficult and more expensive. Goldsmith couldn't live with this. It was all only a game for him, and he was not having any fun. He told Mercer it was time to wrap this episode up.

The two met in Washington. In brief, Goodyear agreed to pay Goldsmith $49.50 per share for his 12.5 million shares and to reimburse him for certain expenses he had incurred. Goldsmith's profit was estimated at $93 million. As Mercer told Lee Iacocca, "This particular raider earned over twelve times more from Goodyear in two months than I have in forty years of work with the same company." For his part, Goldsmith agreed not to buy Goodyear stock for five years.[39]

Goodyear remained in management's hands, but the company had been wounded. Once again, Mercer to Iacocca: the "one-year service on that debt [the $2.6 billion debt Goodyear took on to fend off Goldsmith] is enough to buy a brand-new state-of-the-art radial tire facility in Cumberland, Maryland.

Instead, we're closing down a plant in Cumberland and laying off 1,111 people."[40] Goldsmith did not repeat the success he had with Crown Zellerbach, but he made a fortune for rather little effort.

When the dust settled, we are left with two conflicting views of what business is. In an interview in 2001, Mercer said, "We have several constituencies we have to take care of. The number one constituency is the customer. We have to satisfy the customer. The second constituency are the employees. If we don't treat them like human beings and help them with all their hopes and aspirations, we don't have a team that can satisfy the customer, so then we don't have a business. The third group we have to satisfy are the suppliers... They [have] to understand we want the best quality they can give us at very competitive prices [and] delivered on time. The fourth constituency... are the government entities that we are responsible to... Even within those entities, we have a responsibility to the people of Akron and the other communities in which we reside. We want to be good neighbors. We feel that as a debt we owe society. It's the price of being in business. The fifth guy on the list is the shareholder. If you handle the first four properly, the shareholder is going to make out like a bandit."[41]

Mercer said that analysts never liked his placing shareholders fifth in line, but that is how he felt. This formulation is virtually identical to the credo that Robert Wood Johnson wrote for Johnson & Johnson in 1943, the year before that company went public.[42]

Mercer was not perfectly consistent in his views. At one point, he is quoted as saying, "I've never bought the idea that the shareholder is the owner of the company." Shareholders "own a piece of paper with the company's name on it, and they'll get rid of that paper at the drop of an eighth of a point in the stock price."[43] And yet elsewhere, this time before the House subcommittee at which Goldsmith also testified, Mercer said on November 18, 1986, "While I heartily agree that the shareholder is the major constituency of any public company, I regret the concept that such secondary constituencies as the company's customers, employees, and suppliers, and the communities host to the company's facilities have no rights."[44]

Despite these contradictions, the evidence from his business career points to the first set of constituencies (those enumerated on the previous page) as being closest to what Mercer really believed. Insofar as that may be true, he was fighting a noble battle, but it was a battle in defense of a past that would not be recaptured.

If Mercer had been a contemporary of Curtice, his career would have been very different. But because of a host of factors including Milken, you couldn't be Curtice in the 1980s. Not only Mercer but also Roger Smith at GM proved that. Milken helped kill the Detroit–Pittsburgh economy, the axis around which the nation's business had turned since World War II.

Goodyear survived. In 2021, it is the third-biggest tire manufacturer by sales in the world, behind Bridgestone, which bought Firestone, and Michelin, which bought Uniroyal and Goodrich. Continental, the German entrant in what is now the global tire oligopoly, bought General. Goodyear has sixty-two thousand employees, fewer than half the number it had when Mercer was CEO. Its market capitalization in 2021 was $4.63 billion. The next chapter in American innovation would be centered on the Pacific coast, not in the Midwest. Apple's market capitalization is hovering around $2 trillion.

Goldsmith was the charismatic figure in this drama. According to the *Wall Street Journal*, Goldsmith's "intellect and the ability he has to articulate his vision have no peers among corporate raiders... Force of personality and physical presence have often made Sir James's message difficult to resist... He is supranational... He is the center of a vast network of business, intellectual, and political enterprises." One man he fired said, "If I rang him up from darkest Africa saying I was deathly ill, he'd send a plane for me, I'm sure. My friends say I'm crazy to believe this, but I do." An English casino owner said, "Even at the age of seventeen, [Goldsmith's] life force, the power of his personality, captivated me. I admire lions and tigers, animals to fight back when attacked... He hates to feel safe."[45]

Charismatic figures have followers. These were some of Goldsmith's. The financial markets also followed Goldsmith. Almost single-handedly, he pushed the price of Goodyear stock up from $34.50 on October 1, 1986, to $48 on November 7. When Goodyear used greenmail to get him to go away, Smith Barney, whose arbitrageurs had accumulated 1.8 million shares of Goodyear, sued both Goldsmith and the company for breaking their word that there would be no greenmail.[46]

Goldsmith founded a political party in Britain, which polled eight hundred thousand votes in 1997. This turnout led to the defeat of some candidates. Margaret Thatcher said of him, "Jimmy Goldsmith was one of the most powerful and dynamic personalities that this generation has seen." The real truth about Goldsmith was that he was all about himself. The same can be said of Boesky, Perelman, Pickens, and the rest of the takeover kings in the aptly characterized "decade of greed."[47]

Michael Milken was the person most responsible for the transformation of corporate finance in the 1980s. If you saw him at Drexel Burnham's annual get-together known as the Predators' Ball—at which Sir James Goldsmith was a prominent guest and participant—or at his desk in the middle of his Beverly Hills headquarters, you would have had no trouble singling him out as a charismatic figure. Look at what his acolytes said of him. He "denuded us of [our] ego." In other words, we are mere extensions of Milken's will. Someone like Milken comes along once in half a millennium, we are told. Joan of Arc to Michael Milken.

Milken is one illustration of the danger of charisma. To abandon the responsibility for your own point of view in favor of the judgment of a more forceful, magnetic person is to run a risk not worth taking.

The sad truth is there are no heroes in this story. Milken, Goldsmith, and their ilk were value takers, not value creators. Mercer and the traditional managers like him were wedded to the past. One feels more sympathy for Mercer than for Goldsmith because Mercer had a sense of responsibility, and Goldsmith stood for nothing but self-enrichment. Nevertheless, the old-time companies like Goodyear have either died off or become irrelevant because the world was changing in ways with which they could not cope.

The masters of change who have created trillions of dollars of market value and hundreds of thousands of jobs in the United States and abroad had nothing to do with Milken or Goldsmith or Mercer. A new breed of charismatic business leader was needed. Some daring people arose to meet that need.

PART III

THE RISE
OF THE
SUPERSTAR CEO

From the mid-1990s to the present, the charismatic chief executive officer came into his or her own. CEO compensation increased dramatically. The search for that individual who could create a company or transform one from mediocre to magnificent became more intense than ever.[1]

In the political realm, the president of the United States from 1977 to 1981 was Jimmy Carter. Though an admirable man, his presidency is not remembered as a successful one. Stagflation—a combination of economic stagnation and rising prices—stalked the land. During the Carter years, inflation was at times in double digits, a terrible situation for those in the middle class trying to save money. On July 15, 1979, Carter gave a speech entitled "Crisis of Confidence: Energy and National Goals."[2] This will always be remembered as his "malaise" speech, although he did not actually use that word. Despite Carter's intelligence and sincerity, the crisis of confidence seemed only to deepen during his tenure in office.

Carter was defeated in his bid for reelection in 1980. Thus ended a tumultuous and unproductive decade for the nation's presidents, our CEOs. The decade saw Nixon forced from office in 1974, Gerald Ford, the only man in American history to serve as president who was elected neither to the presidency nor the vice presidency, failing in his election bid in 1976, and a one-term president in Carter.

Elected in 1980, Ronald Reagan became the first president to serve two full terms since Dwight D. Eisenhower (1953–1961). When asked during the campaign how an actor could be president, Reagan responded, "How can a president not be an actor?"[3] As actor/president, Reagan had his share of success.

On June 12, 1987, at the Brandenburg Gate in what was then West Berlin, Reagan delivered an address in which he said, "General Secretary Gorbachev, if you seek peace, tear down this wall."[4] Anyone who saw that wall could not help being impressed by its menacing size. When Reagan gave that speech, no one thought it would be torn down. Yet two and a half years later, on November 9, 1989, the unthinkable happened. The wall came down. Two years after that, in 1991, the Soviet Union fell apart. The West had won the Cold War.

George H. W. Bush followed Reagan into the White House in 1989. In 1992, Bush was defeated for reelection by Bill Clinton, a "dark horse" from Arkansas. During the Clinton years (1993–2001), America really did seem to be born again. He was a charismatic CEO of a country that was in the hunt for charismatic CEOs for its businesses.

In August of 1995, two landmark events took place in the business world. Microsoft launched Windows 95, and Netscape had its IPO, proving that the internet was going to be a force to be reckoned with. The following month, Pixar had its IPO, making its owner, Steve Jobs, a billionaire. *Time* chose Andy Grove, CEO of Intel, as its Man of the Year in 1997.[5] By then, everyone knew the names Gates, Jobs, and Grove.

Charismatic businesspeople were found not only in technology, nor were they only White men. Oprah Winfrey became the first African American woman to become a self-made multibillionaire. Indeed, the word *first* appears twenty-six times in her *Wikipedia* entry.[6] The Nobel Prize–winning African American novelist Toni Morrison called Bill Clinton "our first black president." He "displays almost every trope of blackness: single-parent household, born poor, working-class, saxophone-playing, McDonald-and-junk-food-loving boy from Arkansas."[7] Perhaps it is appropriate that the first self-made African American female multibillionaire should come fully into her own as the "Queen of All Media" during his years in the White House.

CHAPTER 10

THE ACCIDENTAL BILLIONAIRE

How many CEOs can you name who were fired by the company they cofounded, spent twelve years engaged in a variety of complicated ventures, and then returned to the company they cofounded and not only saved it from bankruptcy but transformed it into one of the most important enterprises in the world? There is only one. Steve Jobs defined charisma in business between 1997 and his death in 2011. The issue we will deal with in this chapter is the transformation that took place in Jobs between his firing from Apple in 1985 and his return to the company in 1997.

The English historian Frederic W. Maitland has cautioned us that when studying history, we must be mindful that what is now in the past was once in the future.[1] Ed Catmull, recently retired president and cofounder of Pixar, said, "Hindsight is not 20-20... Our view of the past is... hardly clearer than our view of the future. While we know more about a past event then a future one, our understanding of the factors that shaped it is severely limited. Not only that, because we think we see what happens clearly... we often aren't open to knowing more."[2]

When we look at history, everything seems inevitable. But imagine asking any technology-savvy person or any Wall Street analyst in, say, 1987, when Apple's market capitalization was over $7 billion, its sales were over $2.6 billion, and its profits were about $218 million and when John Sculley published his book about himself and Apple, what the chances were that Steve Jobs would triumphantly return to the company. This was the year that Intel introduced its 387 microprocessor, which signaled the beginning of the Windows/Intel bilateral duopoly that dominated personal computing during the 1990s. Bill Gates became the center of the industry's attention. He had been a mere footnote when Jobs was riding high at Apple in 1980. By 1987, their positions were reversed.

It is not unique for a business leader to return to a company he has left. David Packard, cofounder of Hewlett-Packard, left the company of which he was CEO to become secretary of defense in 1969. After serving in that position for two years, he returned to HP as chairman of the board. Charles Schwab left the company that bears his name in May of 2003 but returned fourteen months later after the board fired his successor. It is no accident that both these men were founders. Both returned after brief absences. Neither had been fired.

In order for this unprecedented turn of events to transpire, a number of developments were necessary. One set deals with Jobs himself. In a word, he matured. In 1985, he was thirty years old, wealthy, and world famous. Any call from him would be returned.

Although touched by genius, Jobs was his own worst enemy. It is difficult to write of him as one person. That is especially true of him in 1985 and the twelve years following. He was subject to extreme mood swings. Euphoria could be followed by hysteria. All his life, there had been an element of the child in him. Part of his appeal as co-founder of Apple in 1976 at the age of twenty-one and of his leadership of the company when he returned was that he never completely abandoned his childhood. His life story proved that growing up did not have to mean giving up.

However, there is all the difference in the world between being childish and childlike. Jobs gyrated between one and the other during these twelve years.

Three developments in Jobs's life during this period deserve our attention. The first is the computer company he launched upon leaving Apple. The second is what has been called his "side bet,"[3] the funding of Pixar and his relationship with its president, Ed Catmull. The third is the transformation of his private life made possible by his marriage to Laurene Powell.

Steve Jobs's next computer company, unimaginatively named NeXT, was launched as he left Apple, taking with him five executives so talented that Apple sued him for breach of fiduciary responsibility (a suit Apple soon dropped). Apple stock jumped a point when the news of Jobs's departure was announced. According to one technology analyst, "East Coast stockholders always worried about California flakes running the company. Now with both Wozniak and Jobs out, those shareholders are relieved."[4] There is no record of Jobs's reaction, if any, to this vote of no confidence. He owned 6.5 million shares of Apple, 11 percent of the shares outstanding, worth more than $100 million. His departure made him $6.5 million richer, at least on paper.

Of the five people Jobs took with him, two are particularly noteworthy. One is Dan'l Lewin, a 1976 graduate of Princeton who was deeply knowledgeable about the education market. His senior thesis in college was on Bob Dylan and charismatic leadership.[5] He did not return to Apple after NeXT but engaged in a variety of activities, the most important of which was the almost seventeen years that he spent at Microsoft, where he became a corporate vice president.

The other noteworthy defector from Apple is Bud Tribble. Tribble was in charge of software at NeXT until leaving for Sun Microsystems in 1993. As a hardware company, NeXT was a complete failure. It was saved by its software.

NeXT was a commercial failure that brought out all the worst in Jobs or, perhaps better put, in which Jobs acted out like a spoiled child. Despite the Wall Street reaction to his departure from Apple, he had no trouble attracting investors and followers, at least for a time. However, in the unsparing words of the biography coauthored by journalists Brent Schlender and Rick Tetzeli, NeXT became "the full, unfortunate blooming of Steve Jobs's worst tendencies at Apple. Yes, Steve had been a product visionary and a great spokesman for the company and the industry he had helped create. But he was hardly poised to be a great chief executive. In many ways, he wasn't even a grown-up yet. At the very moment when Steve had convinced himself that he had won a richly deserved freedom from an oppressive, dull overseer [i.e., Sculley], he was in fact slave to so much else: to his celebrity, to his unbalanced and obsessive desire for perfection in the most [unimportant] of details, to his managerial flightiness and imperiousness, to his shortcomings as an analyst of his own industry, to his burning need for revenge, and to his own blindness to these faults. He was immature and adolescent in so many ways—egocentric, unrealistically idealistic, and unable to manage the ups and downs of real relationships."[6]

Historian Randall E. Stross wrote a book about NeXT in 1993, and his portrait of Jobs and the company is equally unforgiving. The company's journey was "from blunder to blunder, disaster to disaster."[7]

"At NeXT's birth, one sees a strange paradox: the company that aspired to serve as the model for the twenty-first century resembled nothing as much as a throwback to the past, the mid-nineteenth-century American utopian community that was centered on a charismatic leader. Charisma... usually refers to some form of indefinable magnetism. The charisma that Jobs had, however, was more than this—it was the power that a leader... possesses that derives from a perceived connection to the overarching questions of human existence. Jobs was not engaged in the business of selling breakfast cereal or bathroom faucets; he was not even focused on the pursuit of profits, per se. Others could pursue the mundane. He was after the much larger quarry of *changing the world*, rescuing computer users from the existing prison of mediocrity, making a dent in the universe, carrying out revolution, claiming an enduring place in history; it was the extraordinary scope of his ambition that was the ultimate source of his appeal."[8]

Jobs's treatment of his team was the opposite of Mary Kay's or Sam Walton's. Most notable was "the frequent use of public mortification at [his] hands... This would be a critical component of NeXT culture—blistering, humiliating criticism by Jobs of designated individuals that could reduce the employee to tears…" "[H]umiliating public lashing, carrying out what some observers described as a 'gang rape,'" was the order of the day.[9]

The "extraordinary scope of his ambition" contributed mightily to the failure of NeXT. A reporter for *Fortune* wrote in 1993 that "it's hard to tell whether Steve Jobs is a snake-oil salesman or a bona fide visionary." This is a false dichotomy. At NeXT, he was both.[10] And when he encountered the consummate businessman in technology at the time, he was quite incapable of casting his spell.

Jobs pleaded with Bill Gates to write software for his beautifully designed, black NeXT computer. However, there was no question in Gates's mind that NeXT was a computer without a future despite its spectacular introduction in 1988. "Gates said with derision about his rival, 'He put a microprocessor in a box. So what?'" He was equally unimpressed with the new disk drive. The all-black design did not impress him, either. "Gates: 'If you want black, I'll get you a can of paint.'"[11] His view was, "In the grand scope of things, most of these features are truly trivial." When asked whether he would develop for NeXT, Gates left little doubt. "Develop for it? I'll piss on it." Not a ringing endorsement. When Gates at length made it crystal clear that Microsoft was not going to develop anything for NeXT, Jobs "wasn't livid…. He was deflated. He was at a loss for words, which wasn't typical. He knew what I was saying might be right. And it wasn't a particularly pretty picture in terms of what it meant for big black cubes changing the world."[12]

Jobs's infantile behavior was indeed on full display at NeXT. It was as if his experience at Apple had taught him nothing. His screaming, ranting, and micromanaging could be endured only by those who learned to ignore it. "And yet hardware and software engineers still could not resist working for Steve Jobs... [N]o one else seemed to care so much about their work."[13]

Executives at other companies did not have to put up with Jobs. The result was that possible deals that might have provided a niche for NeXT in the booming but highly competitive computer marketplace evaporated. In 1992, Jobs finally had to face unforgiving facts. He closed the hardware division of the company. This was the end of the vision of NeXT as a great computer. "There was no hiding the fact that NeXT's failure was primarily Steve's doing. This," in the words of Schlender and Tetzeli, "was the low point of Steve's career."[14]

In November of 1994, Steve contacted an attorney named Lawrence Levy, whom he wanted to be the chief financial officer of Pixar, which Jobs had purchased in 1986. Levy had read Stross's "scathing critique of Steve's behavior and business practices at NeXT." "...Steve Jobs might have been Silicon Valley's most visible celebrity, but that made it all the more glaring that he had not had a hit in a long time—a very long time... More and more, Jobs was looking like yesterday's news." When Levy told acquaintances that he was going to meet with Steve about Pixar, the response was usually "Why bother?"[15] These were the days in which Jobs was being compared to Orson Welles, whose career peaked at the age of twenty-five with the premiere of *Citizen Kane*.[16]

The vision of NeXT may have died, but the company did not. It lived on as a software company until it was acquired by Apple. Key to its viability was the development of NeXTSTEP, an operating system created by Avadis "Avie" Tevanian and his team. Tevanian had a PhD in computer science from Carnegie Mellon University, where he had also created an operating system. Six years younger than Jobs, Tevanian knew how to benefit from Steve's strengths without being intimidated by his weaknesses.

In addition to NeXTSTEP, Tevanian and his team also developed WebObjects, prebuilt code that could be used for building websites. The World Wide Web, which Sir Timothy Berners-Lee created in 1991 using a NeXT computer with the NeXTSTEP operating system, was taking off in the internet era in the latter half of the 1990s. WebObjects went on sale in 1996, and between that product and NeXTSTEP, NeXT showed an operating profit in 1996.[17] Tevanian is among the handful of people to whom Jobs owes the fame and glory he achieved when he returned to Apple.

What are we to make of NeXT?

The first lesson is that charisma alone does not an executive make. NeXT failed to achieve the goal for which it was created. That goal was to be the great computer a leap ahead from what Apple did in the heady days of the late 1970s. It was to be the computer of the future. The company was saved by NeXTSTEP and WebObjects and, critically, by the explosion of the internet, in the development of which Jobs played no part. The fact that Jobs extricated himself from the near catastrophe of NeXT used up more than one of his nine lives.

Sociologist Bryan R. Wilson has written the following about charisma: "If a man runs naked down the street proclaiming that he alone can save others from impending doom, and if he immediately wins a following, then he is a charismatic leader: A social relationship has come into being. If he does not win a following, he is simply a lunatic."[18] In 1997,

Jobs still fell into the first category. Avie Tevanian and other surpassingly talented people followed him from NeXT to Apple. But the misadventures of NeXT pushed Jobs perilously close to the second category.

The second lesson is that Jobs was going to have to grow up if he expected to save Apple. Charisma is, as the quotation above suggests, a social construction. Maniacal perfectionism and micromanagement are the road to oblivion. To become a true exemplar of charisma, Steve Jobs would have to change from who he was at NeXT, not to mention during his first years at Apple. But how? Who would teach him?

The person who best understood Steve Jobs was Edwin Earl Catmull, a computer scientist and the president of Pixar. Ten years older than Jobs, Catmull was born in Parkersburg, West Virginia, and raised as a member of the Church of Jesus Christ of Latter-day Saints. He went to college and graduate school at the University of Utah, majoring in physics and computer science as an undergraduate and earning his doctorate in the latter. With Catmull, as with Avie Tevanian and dozens of other people through the course of his life, Steve dealt with subject-matter experts with deep technical knowledge of a staggeringly complex emerging industry, knowledge that Steve did not have. This never seems to have bothered him.

Catmull and Jobs were similar in some intriguing ways. Both were tenaciously passionate about their work. Both were able to focus on their goals with an intensity that is possessed by very few other people in this world. Both understood that, as Jobs put it—and as we noted in the chapter on Edwin Land—technology alone is not enough. It must be married to the humanities.[19] Writing about *Toy Story*, Pixar's spectacularly successful first feature-length production, Catmull observed, "While there was much innovation that enabled our work, we had not let the technology overwhelm our real purpose: making a great film."[20]

As a boy, Catmull had two idols, Walt Disney and Albert Einstein. "Disney was all about inventing the new. He brought things into being—both artistically and technologically—that did not exist before. Einstein, by contrast, was the master of explaining that which already was."[21] *The Wonderful World of Disney* was an hour-long weekly television program that premiered in 1954 and affected all of us growing up in those days. The land Disney created was where dreams came true. "When you wish upon a star, makes no difference who you are."[22]

Nobody was more affected by the avuncular Walt Disney than Catmull. He wanted to be a Disney animator but believed he didn't have the talent. However, the dream never died. "At the age of twenty-six, I set a new goal: to develop a way to animate, not with a pencil but with a computer, and to make the images compelling and beautiful enough to use in the movies. Perhaps, I thought, I could become an animator after all."[23] Behind these placid words was powerful ambition. Catmull was going to make this dream come true or die trying.

In 1985, Catmull found himself leading a team working for George Lucas in Marin County just north of San Francisco. His team was creating special effects for Lucas's *Star Wars* franchise, among other films. Jobs got wind of their work when he was still at Apple. Catmull and Jobs first met in February of 1985.

After he was fired from Apple, Jobs's interest in the work of Catmull and his team increased. George Lucas, in the midst of a divorce, needed money. Steve had it. He paid Lucas

$5 million for Pixar, which became an independent company, and invested another $5 million in it. The deal closed on February 3, 1986.

"To be honest," recalls Catmull, "I was uneasy about Steve. He had a forceful personality, whereas I do not, and I felt threatened by him."[24] In these two brief sentences, Catmull showed more self-awareness than Jobs did in his whole life. Jobs was not an introspective man. Catmull is.

Jobs could detect when people felt threatened in his presence. He made a practice of leveraging that threat to gain an advantage in a relationship. He was superb at exploiting people's vulnerabilities. Yet he did not do that to Catmull. He seems to have respected him too much to subject him to the standard Steve treatment. Or perhaps he sensed that behind that benign exterior was an iron will.

In Catmull's words, the standard Steve treatment was "often impatient and curt. When he attended meetings with potential customers, he wouldn't hesitate to call them out if he sniffed mediocrity or lack of preparation—hardly a helpful tactic when trying to make a deal or develop a loyal client base. He was young and driven and not yet attuned to his impact on others. In our first years together, he didn't 'get' normal people—meaning people who did not run companies or who lacked personal confidence. His method for taking the measure of a room was saying something definitive and outrageous—'These charts are bullshit!' or 'This deal is crap!'—and watching people react. If you were brave enough to come back at him, he often respected it—poking at you, then registering your response, was his way of deducing what you thought and whether you had the guts to champion it."[25]

In the late 1980s and early 1990s, Pixar turned out some promising short animations. Unfortunately, the headline was that it was losing money. Lots of money. "At Pixar's lowest point," writes Catmull, "as we floundered and failed to make a profit, Steve had sunk $54 million of his own money into the company—a significant chunk of his net worth, and more money than any venture capital firm would have considered investing, given the sorry state of our balance sheet."[26] At length, Pixar had to get out of the hardware business, where it had never belonged anyway. Only three hundred Pixar Image computers were sold.

How "sorry" was the state of Pixar's balance sheet? When Lawrence Levy signed on as CFO in February of 1995, he described the situation as "dire." Pixar "had no cash, no reserves, and it depended for its funds on a person whose reputation for volatility was legendary." Fired from Apple. Failure at NeXT. "It felt like [Steve] had two strikes against him. One more and he might be out for good." "...Pixar was fraught with business risk... But Steve brought another layer of uncertainty." The more Levy learned, the worse things looked. "If I had known what I know now," he remarked to his wife, "I can't imagine I would have taken this job. Taking this company public seems like a crazy notion. No investor I know would come near this. Fifty million in losses, no profits, no growth, Disney holding all the cards." Levy wondered whether Pixar needed a CFO at all.[27]

After he bought Pixar, Steve was so wrapped up with NeXT that he didn't have much time for it. He came to Pixar's headquarters in San Rafael, more than fifty traffic-clogged miles north of Palo Alto, only once a year. He had to ask directions each time. Catmull came down to Silicon Valley to see him every couple of weeks. The news was always bad. Pixar needed more money. Three times between 1987 and 1991, Steve shopped Pixar around. He wanted $120 million for it. Microsoft offered him $90 million. The truth seems to be that "he could never quite bring himself to part with us."[28]

Catmull knew all too well that Pixar—and with it his lifelong dream—could not survive without Steve. More than once, though, he wondered whether the company could survive with him. "Steve could be brilliant and inspirational, capable of diving deeply and intelligently into any problem we faced. But he could also be impossible: dismissive, condescending, threatening, even bullying. Perhaps of most concern, from a management standpoint, was the fact that he exhibited so little empathy... [H]e was simply unable to put himself in other people's shoes, and his sense of humor was nonexistent. At Pixar, we have always had a pretty deep bench of jokesters and a core belief in having fun, but everything we tried with Steve fell painfully flat."[29]

Catmull's observation about Steve's inability "to put himself in other people's shoes" made the marriage between him and Pixar particularly problematic at first. "Seeing," "point of view," and "empathy" are what made Pixar's early movies great. This ability not just to look but to see in a profound way was not bought cheaply. Here is one example. In the making of A Bug's Life, the team felt it was essential to get a "bug's-eye view" of reality. How does one do that? The team put arthroscopic lenses on video cameras and went to a variety of landscapes, pushing the lenses along the ground to see an ant's point of view.[30]

Catmull and Jobs worked together for twenty-six years, probably the longest professional relationship of Jobs's life.

As they collaborated, the partnership became richer, and it was among the most fulfilling alliances in both men's lives. Catmull figured out how to manage Steve, and he did so by using his own strengths, which were considerable, and matching them with Steve's.

Catmull understood that one could not grasp Steve by asking him about himself. "We didn't get philosophical all that often. When we started to edge into personality and so forth, he'd just say, 'I am who I am.'" Steve did not say, as did Don Quixote, "I know who I am." He never really did. Catmull knew him better than he knew himself. Jobs "wasn't insensitive at his core—the problem was that he had not yet figured out how to behave in a way that let everyone see that."[31]

The great storyteller at Pixar was John Lasseter. *Toy Story*, the movie that transformed Pixar from a money sink to a billion-dollar company, was his idea. "John once described Steve's story as the classic Hero's Journey. Banished for his hubris from the company he founded, he wandered through the wilderness having a series of adventures that, in the end, changed him for the better."[32]

Shortly before Jobs bought Pixar, Catmull asked him how they would resolve conflicts. He responded without irony that he would continue "to explain why he was right until I understood. This," Catmull observed, turned out to be "the technique I used with Steve. I would state my case, but since Steve could think much faster than I could, he would often shoot down my arguments. So I'd wait a week, marshal my thoughts, and then come back and explain it again. He might dismiss my points again, but I would keep coming back until one of three things happened: (1) He would say 'Oh, okay, I get it' and give me what I needed; (2) I'd see that he was right and stop lobbying; or (3) our debate would be inconclusive [and I would] do what I had proposed in the first place... [W]hen this third option occurred, Steve never questioned me. For all his insistence, he respected passion."[33]

In 1993, with the release of *Jurassic Park*, it became clear that computerized special effects were going to be a major factor in the motion picture industry. Pixar made a deal with Disney that ceded to the giant of the industry a lot of the potential income from Pixar products. Pixar essentially became a contractor for Disney but also secured the financial and market muscle it needed to soldier on.

Two years later, *Toy Story* was released. Prior to its premiere, Steve told Catmull and Lasseter that he wanted to take Pixar public immediately after the film hit the movie theaters. They were reluctant. They wanted Pixar to establish a track record first, but Steve said, "This is our moment."[34]

IPOs are risky. In this case, the meaning of the IPO to Steve increased the pressure in what was already a pressure-packed situation. The IPO "carried with it the full weight of his return from the wilderness into which Apple had banished him ten years earlier. If there was one event that would unquestionably signify Steve's redemption, it would be Pixar's IPO. This would seal his comeback like nothing else could. It was no wonder," Lawrence Levy explained, "that whenever we talked about it, his tone took on a weight and importance of almost biblical proportion."[35]

This was a game Steve knew how to play. He was right when he said that this was "our moment"—more right than even he could have dreamed.

The IPO was all set for the week following the premiere of *Toy Story*. If the movie flopped, the IPO would, too. All would be lost. The stakes could not have been higher. Catmull, Lasseter, and Steve all believed in the movie. But the motion picture industry is the most fickle and unpredictable in the business world. No one could know how the movie would do. It was a shot in the dark.

When *Toy Story* premiered in 1995, it was a spectacular hit, breaking box office records. This was one movie the like of which no one had ever seen before. It was a remarkable story, exquisitely realized.

The IPO took place November 29, 1995, and it was a tremendous success. Suddenly, Pixar had a market capitalization of $1.4 billion. Steve owned 80 percent of the company. He had bought it for $5 million. A few years before the IPO, he had been willing to sell it for $120 million. Now, it had made him a billionaire. He phoned Larry Ellison, CEO of Oracle and Silicon Valley royalty, and said, "I made it."[36] The "side bet" delivered what NeXT never did—ecstasy. To call him an "accidental billionaire" may be a bit unfair. He played an essential role in Pixar's success. Nevertheless, one doubts he dreamed when he bought the company that this would be the outcome.

The headline in the *Wall Street Journal* the day after the IPO was: "STEVE JOBS IS BACK IN THE SADDLE AGAIN, BECOMING A BILLIONAIRE IN PIXAR IPO." "Any way you looked at it," according to Levy, "Pixar's fate had hung on the slenderest of threads."[37] The thread had not snapped.

When Pixar was finally purchased by Disney, as one feels was its destiny, the deal was consummated at the close of a frantic day. The deal was announced on January 24, 2006. The price: $7.4 billion. Just over half, almost $4 billion, went to Steve. At length, Catmull, Lasseter, and Jobs "had a chance to take a breath... The minute the door [to Catmull's office] shut behind us," Catmull has written, "Steve put his arms around us and began to cry, tears of pride and relief—and, frankly, love."[38] He had succeeded in transforming Pixar from a struggling hardware supplier into an animation powerhouse. In the process, he became one of the richest people in the world.

In his concluding discussion about Steve, Catmull observed that his "wife and children, of course, were paramount, and Apple was his first and most heralded achievement; Pixar was a place he could relax a little and play. While he never lost his intensity, we watched him develop the ability to listen. More and more, he could express empathy and caring and patience. The change in him was real, and it was deep."[39] And without it, his future accomplishments would not have taken place. Ed Catmull was the teacher he needed.

Steve Jobs's personality was a set of unsynthesized opposites. This shattered self was most apparent in his personal life, of which we know a good deal. Growing up, he was not like the other kids. In grade school, he was picked on because he was adopted. "What happened?" kids taunted. "Didn't your mother love you?" We can only speculate whether his adoption was the cause of this bullying or an excuse for it. Steve grew up "in remarkable nonconformity to the rest of the world, because he was so ahead intellectually and intuitively, but so behind emotionally."[40]

Steve told his parents he would not stand for the treatment he was getting and would not return to the school he was attending. His parents, remarkably obliging, moved from Mountain View to Los Altos so he could attend a different school.

It was at Homestead High School in nearby Cupertino where Steve and Chrisann Brennan fell in love. With his fractured personality, Steve was desperate for intimacy and terrified of finding it. He embraced and rejected it with Chrisann. They were seventeen, and even average children have a lot to learn about the opposite sex at that age. Chrisann wrote many years later that "Steve was a man with attachment disorder. His withholding was a form of intimacy through control..."[41]

Chrisann was (and is) an artist and an idealist. Her great-uncle was Branch Rickey, co-owner of the Brooklyn Dodgers, who recruited Jackie Robinson, and together the two of them broke the color barrier in Major League Baseball. She was proud of what Rickey and Robinson achieved. "These men embodied the kind of aspiration I had for myself: to be a leader and do something for others, to make a difference." "I knew he was a genius when I first saw him..." Brennan said of Jobs. She also noted that "There was a profound sadness about him that drew me in..."[42]

In her outstanding book, Brennan deepens our understanding of Jobs's relationship to his origins. "[N]ot knowing where he came from mattered so much to him... I think it must've been Steve's greatest hope to recover what was lost due to the adoption... Not only did Steve have a big hole in him from the adoption, he... fed on nearly everything to fill it up. Looking for the love he missed, he made sure all eyes were on him so he could get what he needed. He'd wipe people out in the process."[43]

Clara Jobs told Chrisann that "I was too frightened to love him for the first six months of his life. I was scared they were going to take him away from me. Even after we won the case [that involved Steve's biological mother trying to take him away from Clara and Paul] Steve was so difficult a child that I felt we had made a mistake. I wanted to return him."[44]

A strange way indeed to begin life's journey. One theme is constant—from the outset, nothing involving Steve was easy.

Chrisann did believe that Steve "had a huge capacity for empathy when it came to men's stories." *Empathy* is not a word often associated with Steve. His "huge capacity" for it was one of the tools that made him magnetic, powerful, and dangerous. In addition to his empathy, if that is the right word, Chrisann also commented that Steve "always had a profound sense of self-adoration."[45]

The most important minute in Chrisann Brennan's life was 10:38 p.m. on May 17, 1978. That is when she gave birth to her daughter, Lisa. Chrisann devoted herself to that child's welfare from that moment on. The same cannot be said of Steve. Years earlier, Steve had told Chrisann that "he was terrified he would 'lose his humanity in the business world.'"[46] In 1978, it looked as if something close to that had happened.

When Chrisann told him she was pregnant, "Steve's face turned ugly. He gave me a fiery look. Then he rushed out of the house without a word." "Steve was fully aware of the big picture, but I had no way of knowing that Apple would go public... and that my pregnancy would have been perceived as a threat to Steve's public image and therefore, the Apple brand." "Steve wanted to control what people thought of him. That's likely why he started to seed people with the notion that I slept around and he was infertile, which meant that this could not be his child. People believed him, I think, because people wanted a hero. Apple was succeeding, and Steve was brilliant, but mine was an old story, and no one really cared about a single mother."[47]

Steve was not present at his daughter's birth, but he did show up three days later to participate in choosing a name for the baby. He and Chrisann settled on Lisa Nicole Brennan. She was not to be called Jobs. He then disappeared from their lives. According to Chrisann, "He didn't want to have anything to do with her [Lisa] or with me."[48]

Brennan and her baby took up residence in Menlo Park, which borders Palo Alto. They lived on welfare. The county sued Jobs to prove paternity. He fought the case, promoting the story that Brennan had been sleeping around. In a sworn deposition, Jobs denied paternity, claiming that he was sterile and named another man who he said was Lisa's father. Brennan was a true product of the counterculture and was disarmed in the face of this assault. "At one point," she said, "I yelled at Steve on the phone, 'You know that is not true.' He was going to drag me through court and try to prove I was a whore and that anyone could have been the father of that baby."[49]

The next year, Jobs agreed to take a paternity test. DNA tests were new at the time and not as accurate as they are today. The report on Jobs read, "Probability of paternity... 94.41 percent." Jobs was forced to pay $385 a month in child support. For some reason, he decided to pay $500 a month. He was also required to reimburse San Mateo County $5,856 for back welfare payments and to submit a signed admission of paternity.

Nevertheless, Jobs periodically would deny that he was Lisa's father. He told Michael Moritz (then a reporter for *Time* and today one of the most successful venture capitalists in Silicon Valley) that statistics proved that "28 percent of the male population of the United States could be the father." Jobs's authorized biographer, Walter Isaacson, labels this claim not only "false" but "odd." Jobs's speculation struck Chrisann with the force of a physical blow. "After I read the

Time article," she said, "I was hit so hard that three days went by where I was hardly able to speak or focus."[50]

Fast forward to March 18, 1991. On that day, Steve married Laurene Powell. She was born in the town of West Milford, New Jersey (about forty-five miles northwest of New York City), on November 6, 1963. Her father was a Marine Corps pilot who died in a plane crash when she was three. Her mother remarried and stayed married even though, according to Isaacson, "it turned out to be a horrible situation..." For ten years Laurene and her three brothers "had to suffer in a tense household, keeping a good demeanor while compartmentalizing problems." From this experience, she learned that "I always wanted to be self-sufficient... My relationship with money is that it's a tool to be self-sufficient, but it's not... part of who I am." With an estimated net worth of about $19 billion in 2021, she can be said to have achieved self-sufficiency.[51]

Laurene double majored in political science and economics at the University of Pennsylvania. After a couple of unfulfilling years on Wall Street, she enrolled in Stanford's business school. It was there that she met Steve, who was delivering a lecture in October of 1989.

Steve was thirty-six on their wedding day and she was twenty-seven. She was pregnant with their first child, who was born in September. Both he and she were experienced with members of the opposite sex. Steve had numerous liaisons, most notably with Chrisann Brennan and Tina Redse. Laurene had turned down two marriage proposals. Smart, good-looking, shrewd, tough, and, in the words of Andy Hertzfeld, an original member of the Mac team, "armor-plated," Laurene knew what she was getting into, and she knew that she could handle it.[52] She had a strong sense of self and could have succeeded on her own.

Critically important, Laurene understood the difference between persona and person, between image and reality. The image she enabled Steve to project was one of a loving and caring husband and father of three—and, when Lisa was admitted to the family circle, four—children. Laurene welcomed Lisa into the family, and her last name was legally changed to Brennan-Jobs in 1992. The family photos are picture-perfect. In the midst of one of the most difficult periods of Steve's professional life, Laurene was exactly what he needed. The man who was known for his temper tantrums, hissy fits, and sadism found himself wrapped in a cloak of sanity and stability.

Nine years is not that large a gap between a husband and wife, especially in recent times; but these particular nine years, from 1955, when Steve was born, to 1963, when Laurene was born, mattered a lot. Steve grew up during the 1960s and in their shadow. The drug culture was new. Journeys to the East, literally and metaphorically, were the rage among those who prided themselves on being misfits. Laurene did not fully partake of this mystical, drug-induced, infantile behavior. She apparently learned growing up in a dysfunctional family that life could be tough and that you had to be tougher. There is no record of her dropping acid or even smoking marijuana.

Marriage and parenthood could be fun and funny and joyful. Steve's professional achievements were peerless in their glamour. But at the end of the day, living a sane life was serious business. Laurene wanted to build a family that worked. She welcomed Mona Simpson, Steve's biological sister, as well as Lisa Brennan-Jobs, into the family. She was appropriate with Chrisann and with others who had been a part of Steve's life.

Steve's vicious behavior came in two flavors. One was when he deployed it for effect, in order to get something he wanted. The second was when something within him that he could not control and of which he might not have even been aware snapped, and he would go off in a spasm of craziness.

Laurene knew how to discipline him. Chrisann recounts the following episode. She, Lisa, Steve, Laurene, and their infant son, Reed, were at Steve's home in Palo Alto "and about to go for a walk when, without warning, Steve blurted out the meanest, most ridiculous, terrible comments at me, like a machine gun spraying bullets across me. It was so unexpected and awful, something about why I was such a total failure of a human being that I gasped. You can't prepare for this sort of behavior, no matter how many times it happens. I fell silent, but… Laurene yelled at him to stop. Even she was indignant on my behalf."[53]

On September 4, 2018, Lisa Brennan-Jobs published a brilliant memoir of her impossibly difficult youth, entitled *Small Fry*. In her review of the book in *The New Yorker*, Katy Waldman writes, "Brennan-Jobs admires her father's brilliance and charisma, but her memoir elicits little sympathy for him, and *Small Fry*, a book of no small literary skill, is confused and conflicted, angry and desperate to forgive. It's central, compelling puzzle is Brennan-Jobs's continuing need to justify not just her father's behavior but her longing for his love. It is… mesmerizing, discomfiting reading."

Small Fry is a devastating account of an unworthy father. Lisa Brennan-Jobs was with her father as he was dying. He apologized profusely for the way he treated her, saying "I owe you one."[54] He did indeed.

Here is how Laurene responded to the book's publication: "Lisa is part of our family, so it is with sadness that we read her book, which differs dramatically from our memories of those times. The portrayal of Steve is not the husband and father we knew. Steve loved Lisa, and he regretted that he was not the father he should have been during her early childhood. It was a great comfort to Steve to have Lisa home with all of us during the last days of his life, and we are all grateful for the years we spent together as a family."[55]

A more perfectly crafted response to a memoir to which there can be no response cannot be imagined. One wonders how long it took for Laurene to write these words. Eight years after Steve's death, her response speaks volumes about what she brought to their marriage. She grounded and civilized Steve. She made this illegitimate man legitimate at last. Ed Catmull was right. Steve did change over the years. But he would not have been able to make the change he did—from childish to childlike—without a marriage that really was made in heaven.

So at last—with the NeXTSTEP operating system, with Pixar's spectacular success, and with the right woman at his side, Steve was prepared to play his historic role—to return to Apple, which was dying, and to endow it with the greatness that only he could.

CHAPTER 11

OPRAH WINFREY:
THE MAGNETISM OF MISERY

Charisma is necessary not only to do new things but for members of historically excluded groups to "break through" and succeed in realms already established. The first host of *The Tonight Show* was Steve Allen. A Caucasian male, his appearance in that role on that program at its premiere in 1954 was not particularly startling to viewers. Allen was an entertaining and appealing man.

The same year that Allen premiered on *The Tonight Show*, Oprah Gail Winfrey was born in Kosciusko, Mississippi. As the world knows, she is an African American woman. If she had been of age and had hosted *The Tonight Show* at its premiere, there would have been riots in the streets, at least in some parts of the country. The two senators from Mississippi in the year of Winfrey's birth were John Stennis and James Eastland, segregationist racists. According to his obituary in the *New York Times*, Eastland described Black people as belonging to an "inferior race," and he was "best known nationally as a symbol of Southern resistance to racial desegregation."[1] Eastland died in 1986.

Oprah Gail Winfrey was born on January 29, 1954. As she put it, "I came into the world in 1954 in Mississippi—a state with more lynchings than any other in the union—at a time when being a black man walking down the street minding your business could make you subject to any white person's accusation or whimsy. A time when having a good job meant working for a 'nice' white family that at least didn't call you *nigger* to your face. A time when Jim Crow reigned, segregation prevailed, and black teachers, themselves scarcely educated, were forced to use ragged textbooks discarded from white schools."[2]

But it is not Winfrey's way to dwell on such dreadful circumstances. "Yet the same year I was born, a season of change began." *Brown v. Board of Education* was handed down on May 17 of that year.[3] Kosciusko is a tiny town located in the middle of the state. Its most famous native other than Winfrey is James Meredith, who was born there in 1933. In 1962, Meredith became the first African American to attend the University of Mississippi. His matriculation was greeted by a race riot.

Winfrey spent the first six years of her life in Kosciusko, and against all odds—in his immortal "I have a dream" speech in 1963, Martin Luther King Jr. said "I have a dream that one day even the state of Mississippi, a state sweltering with the heat of injustice, sweltering with the heat of oppression, will be transformed into an oasis of freedom and justice"[4]—Winfrey actually thrived during those formative years. There were two reasons. One was Hattie Mae Lee's guardianship. "I came to live with my grandmother," Winfrey said, "because

I was a child born out of wedlock, and my mother moved to the North... like so many other black youngsters who are left to be taken care of by their grandmothers and grandfathers, aunts and uncles... I was one of those children. It actually probably saved my life... because my grandmother gave me the foundation for success that I was allowed to continue to build upon. My grandmother taught me to read, and that opened the door to all kinds of possibilities for me."[5] When it came to reading, Winfrey was a prodigy. She could read by the time she was three.

The second reason Winfrey thrived in racist Mississippi was that bulwark of African American life in the age of oppression, the Black church. "I was reciting speeches in the church. Then they put me up on the program, and they would say, 'And Little Mistress Winfrey will render a recitation,' and I would do 'Jesus rose on Easter day, hallelujah, hallelujah, all the angels did proclaim.' And all the sisters sitting in the front row would fan themselves and turn to my grandmother and say, 'Hattie Mae, this child is gifted.' And I heard that enough that I started to believe it... I didn't even know what 'gifted' meant, but I just thought it meant I was special. So anytime people came over, I'd recite... Bible verses and poetry... I did all of James Weldon Johnson's sermons."[6] When still very young, Winfrey got a reputation as a child who knew how to talk.

Winfrey's mother was Vernita Lee. Eighteen years old when Winfrey was born, Lee was unmarried, and Winfrey's conception was for a time thought to be the product of a one-night stand with her father, Vernon Winfrey. However, it has turned out that Vernon Winfrey could not be Oprah's father, although he has treated her as if she were his daughter. The identity of her father is unknown. Lee started a new life in Milwaukee after Oprah's birth. At the age of six, Oprah went up North to live with her mother. This inaugurated a time of troubles.

Lee was overmatched by the situation in which she lived in Milwaukee. She worked as a domestic all day, every day. She failed completely to protect her daughter from this new environment. The idyllic days of "Little Mistress Winfrey" were over.

At the age of nine, Winfrey was raped. This was the beginning of sexual violation by several different men including a cousin, an uncle, a family friend, and her mother's boyfriend. This continued between the ages of nine and fourteen. "It was just an ongoing continuous thing. So much so, that I started to think, 'This is the way life is.'"[7]

The result of these repeated traumatic experiences was confusion and guilt, because, in her own words (and among other reasons), "it does feel good." "She says she allowed [the abuse] to continue because she liked the attention and didn't want to get anyone in trouble." Even if she did speak up, she feared she would not be believed, a fear that proved justified.[8]

These harrowing experiences shattered Oprah's conception of herself. Winfrey became a belligerent delinquent. Her mother could not cope with her. In Winfrey's own words, "I became a sexually promiscuous teenager, promiscuous and rebellious, and did everything I could get away with, including faking a robbery in my house one time. I remember, you know, stomping the [eye] glasses in the floor and putting myself in the hospital and acting out the whole scene, and I used to pull all kinds of pranks—ran away from home—and as a result of that got myself into a lot of trouble and believed that I was responsible for it.[9]

"It wasn't until I was thirty-six years old—*thirty-six*—that I connected the fact, oh, that's why I was that way. I always blamed myself, even though, intellectually, I would say to other kids... 'Oh, the child is never to blame. You're never responsible for molestation in your life.' I still believed I was responsible somehow, that I was a bad girl..."

When she was fourteen, Winfrey became pregnant and gave birth to a son. The infant was born prematurely, and his brief life was snuffed out after a couple of weeks.[10] At one point, her mother tried to have her institutionalized; but the detention center did not have enough beds to accommodate her.

If you had met Oprah Winfrey when she was fourteen years old, what future would you have predicted for her? Oprah's mother had three more children after Oprah. Her son, Jeffrey, Oprah's half brother, died of AIDS in 1989. Her daughter Patricia, Oprah's half sister, died of cocaine addiction in 2003. Another daughter, also named Patricia and also Oprah's half sister, is still alive. Oprah only learned of Patricia's existence in 2010, and she had her as a guest on her show.

When she was fourteen, Oprah "ran away from home. I got to my father's house." The man who has played the role of her father, Vernon Winfrey, was in the army when he encountered Vernita Lee. He was born in Mississippi in 1933. By the time of Oprah's return to the South, he was married to Zelma (Meyers) Winfrey and living in Nashville, Tennessee. He worked as a janitor at Vanderbilt University (in 1963 he graduated from Hasla Barber College, and the following year he was able to open his own barbershop) when Oprah went to live with him and her stepmother.

Vernon Winfrey was a strict, demanding man. He was not happy with her first report card. "Troubled teen or not, I wasn't having any of that," he said. "My expectations of her were a mountain most high. I told her, 'If you were a C student, you could bring me C's. You are not a C student! Hear me?... If you bring me any more C's I'm going to place heavy burdens on you... Heavy burdens.'"[11]

Winfrey said she needed structure and attention. Her father provided the former. She was about to get the latter. Her arrival in Nashville marked the beginning of her upward climb.

In the fall of 1968, Winfrey enrolled in East Nashville High School, which her class integrated. She was elected vice president of her class, and she was also a speaker at all the Black churches in Nashville. She was making a name for herself. In 1971, she was selected as one of two students from Tennessee (two students were picked from each state) to attend the White House Conference on Youth. She was interviewed by a local radio station about it. By chance, there was a contest soon afterward in Nashville for "Miss Fire Prevention." The man who had interviewed her for the radio station about the White House Conference on Youth remembered that "I had given a nice interview and I was a kid, and they needed a teenager." She was seventeen. "So he said, 'What about that girl that [we interviewed] last year?' Suddenly I was representing this radio station in the 'Miss Fire Prevention' contest. Well, all you had to do was walk, parade around in an evening gown, [and] answer some questions about your life... [I]t was one of those little teeny, tiny beauty pageants. Well, nobody expected me to win the pageant because we were still Negroes at the time—I've been colored, Negro, black, now I'm African American. I was the only Negro in a pageant of all red-haired girls and it's the 'Miss Fire Prevention' contest. So... Lord knows, I'm not going to win."[12]

She recalled two of the questions that she was asked. One was, what would you do if you had a million dollars? "And I said, because I'm not going to win anyway, 'If I had a million dollars, I would be a spendin' fool. I'm not quite sure what I would spend it on, but I would spend, spend, spend. Spendin' fool.'" The other question the contestants were asked was what they wanted to do with their lives. She had seen Barbara Walters on *The Today Show*. Walters must have impressed her, because she said she wanted "to be a broadcast journalist because I believed in the truth. I was interested in proclaiming the truth to the world and all. And I won the contest. Well, what a shocked Negro, me."[13]

Winfrey had a gift for self-expression. Just as the congregations in the churches of her childhood in Mississippi and in Nashville had appreciated her ability to speak, the radio station that sponsored her beauty contest victory recognized her perfect broadcasting-style voice, free of dialect or even accent and hence suitable for all audiences. They put her on the air in January of 1974. Her ascent had begun.

"No way did I deserve the job," Winfrey said. "I was a classic token, but I was one happy token."[14] The man who hired her was the news director of her television station, Chris Clark. He believed in diversity and was willing to take risks to achieve it. "You have to remember it was a very racially tense time in Nashville, and she was the first black woman on television," he said. If she had failed, he would have been held responsible.[15]

Here are Oprah's own reflections on what it was like to get started in the media. She began on radio and immediately encountered the green-eyed monster. "All my friends just hated me," she remembered, "because they're cuttin' grass."

At nineteen, she made the leap to television. "It was because of the riots of the '70s that I think they were looking for minorities." When she had her interview, "I decided to pretend to be Barbara Walters because that's how I'd gotten into this... So I sat there, pretending with Barbara in my head, did everything I thought she would do, and I was hired.

"As a 'token,' [I] had to take the heat from my college classmates—I went to an all-black college—with them calling me a token, and I used to say, 'Yeah, but I'm a paid token.'"

"I was very defensive about it because I've always had to live with the notion of other black people saying, 'Oh, for any amount of success that you achieve... you're trying to be white, you're trying to talk white... which is such a ridiculous notion to me, since you look in the mirror every morning and you're black. There's a black face in your reflection... It was very uncomfortable for me at first... pretending to be Barbara Walters, looking nothing like her..."

"My [college] classmates were so jealous of me." Oprah tried to appease them by buying them pizza and lending them money. "That whole 'disease to please,' that's where it was the worst for me," she recalled. "I wanted to be accepted by them and could not be... It was very difficult for me socially, really one of the worst times in my life, because I was trying to fit in in school and trying to build a career in television."[16]

The great African American scholar and crusader for racial justice, W. E. B. Du Bois, wrote, "One ever feels his twoness—an American, a Negro; two souls, two thoughts, two unreconciled strivings, two warring ideals in one dark body, whose dogged strength alone keeps it from being torn asunder... He simply wishes to make it possible for a man to be both a Negro and an American, without being cursed and spit upon by his fellows, without having the doors of opportunity closed roughly in his face."[17]

This age-old dilemma was precisely what the young Winfrey was encountering. The situation for her was even more complex than that described by Du Bois. She was not only a Black person trying to make it in a White person's world. She was a woman trying to make it in a man's world, and she ran the risk of being rejected by everybody.

Winfrey showed the combination of toughness and empathy that would serve her well in the years ahead. An early assignment brought her to a segregated area of Nashville. She approached a shopkeeper and extended her hand. He said, "We don't shake hands with niggers down here." She responded without missing a beat, "I bet the niggers are glad."[18]

Her empathy became clear in her reporting. "She was wonderful with people," Clark said. "And that was her downfall as a journalist, because she could not be detached. She'd be sent to cover a fire, come back to the station, and work the phones trying to get help for the burnt-out family instead of writing a story for the evening news."[19]

Winfrey was a natural talent and soon received an offer to co-anchor the news at the leading station in Baltimore. She felt she couldn't turn the offer down. Even at the age of twenty-one, she negotiated a contract that suited her plans for advancement. "I was lucky, lucky, lucky..." she said. "[I]t's the right place at the right time." Later, she would say the offer was part of God's plan for her.[20]

From early in her life, Oprah held a set of beliefs that were mutually contradictory. While she acknowledged her luck, she also believed and preached to the world that one has control over one's life. You can do what you want to do and be what you want to be. "It doesn't matter how victimized any of us have been—we are all responsible for our lives." But she also believed in a God that played an active role in human affairs and in her life in particular. "God is with me," she would say years later. "That's why I always succeed... I am God-centered."[21]

Winfrey visited Auschwitz with one of its most famous survivors, Elie Wiesel, in 2006. She remarked to him that his surviving the Holocaust was a miracle. He responded that "If a miracle to spare me, why? There were people much better than me... No, it was an accident." This was an explanation she apparently found impossible to accept.[22]

It took Winfrey decades to be able to interact with people of Wiesel's stature. The years following her move to Baltimore were filled with enough drama and melodrama to sustain a soap opera: her endless struggles with her weight due to binge eating; her chronic "bad man troubles" ("I was one of those sick women who believes that life was nothing without a man... The more he rejected me, the more I wanted him... There is nothing worse than rejection. It's worse than death");[23] the never-ending battle between her desire to unburden herself of so many secrets and her desperation for privacy; and the tension between her tendency toward the tawdry and a genuine desire to do good in this world. And behind all these unresolved conflicts was her ambition to be the biggest, to be the best, to be number one, to be the first, to make a difference, and to make a fortune—a monumental ambition that both liberated and enslaved her. Her ambition was a gigantic engine that knew no rest.

Behind her ambition was a willingness to work however hard was necessary to fulfill her destiny. And behind her work ethic was the fact that Oprah Winfrey is possessed of a very special spark. The only full biography of her is by Kitty Kelley, known for not pulling punches and for dishing dirt at every possible opportunity. Kelley concludes her biography of Winfrey (published in 2010) by labeling her "the most influential woman of her generation."[24] An exaggeration? Perhaps. But there is no question that she has been an impact player. As the sisters in her church back in Kosciusko told her grandmother (whose grandparents had been enslaved), "Hattie Mae, this child is gifted." The church, the setting in which two millennia ago Saint Paul wrote to the Corinthians about charisma, is where Winfrey's charisma first became evident.

In Baltimore in 1976, Winfrey was hired because the news director of WJZ saw her demo tape. "It was very impressive; she had a compelling delivery..." She was hired to co-anchor the six o'clock news with a man whom Baltimore "adored," an adoration of himself which he shared. After eight months, he couldn't stand having her on his show, and on April 1, 1977, she was demoted to daytime TV at WJZ. "It's like your life is over," she said years later.[25]

Winfrey was not meant to be a news anchor. Her luck had not abandoned her, and her life was far from over when she lost that position. On August 14, 1978, WJZ premiered a morning talk show called *People Are Talking*. Winfrey was co-anchor along with a White man named Richard Sher. After the first show, "I came off the air, and I knew that was what I was supposed to do... This is it. This is what I was born to do... It just felt like breathing. It was the most natural process for me."[26]

235

By 1982, Winfrey was on the air at WJZ three times a day. She began with the early-morning news. Next came *People Are Talking*. Then she did the news at noon. Very taxing, but that was something she never shied away from. She was becoming well-known and even respected in Baltimore despite the fact that *People Are Talking* often descended into "trash TV." To see her on that show, which became very popular, was to see a person seemingly completely at ease in a medium that is difficult to master. Because she was at ease, she put her studio audience and viewership at ease as well. If there was any tension between her and her teammate, Richard Sher, it was well hidden.

What does startle today's viewer is that Winfrey wore her hair in an Afro. She was so symmetrically coiffed that it looks like it might have been a wig.[27] When one sees that Afro, one is reminded of Winfrey's observation that she migrated from colored to Negro to Black to African American. This is a remarkable odyssey. How many other racial, ethnic, or religious groups have traveled a road like this? When Oprah was born in 1954, the original inhabitants of the United States were referred to as Indians. Today, they are referred to as Native Americans. That is one change. Reference to African Americans today has changed three times. I can think of no other group that has changed so often, and most have not changed at all. Italian Americans are still Italian Americans, Chinese Americans are still Chinese Americans, and the numberless others that make up the American kaleidoscope are referred to the same way today as they were in the 1950s. Oprah was young and gifted. Her skin is also black—what the nineteenth-century Black abolitionist Frederick Douglass called an "unpopular color."[28] Oprah modeled herself on a White woman, Barbara Walters. She succeeded in the White world of broadcasting in the 1970s and 1980s. Yet as she herself said, when she looked in the mirror, a Black face looked back. It is difficult enough to locate one's identity in the public sphere. How much more difficult when race is added to the formula.

In 1983, it was time for Oprah to renew her contract at WJZ. Fate knocked on the door yet again. The host of a talk show in Chicago, *AM Chicago*, was leaving the program. Suddenly, there was an opening in a very large market. But jumping into this market was a big risk. *AM Chicago* was a failing program. This city was owned by the nationally known Phil Donahue.

At her interview, Oprah showed none of the insecurity that was so abundantly evident in her love life and in the management of her weight. She watched *AM Chicago* before her interview. She then proceeded to march into the offices of WLS, which aired the program, and to tell her interviewers point-blank that their show was no good and then she told them why.

In describing her own talent, she said, "I'm best at combinations. A sexual surrogate one day, Donny and Marie Osmond the next day. Then the Klan." Her interviewers asked her to jump through a couple of hoops, but the job was hers the moment the general manager of the station met her. In the words of one journalist, "Her astute merger of prurience and uplift proved irresistible." *AM Chicago* premiered with Winfrey at the helm on January 2, 1984. A couple of weeks short of her thirtieth birthday, she took Chicago by storm. There was a great deal of prurience in Chicago's future. And in the nation's.[29]

On September 8, 1986, *AM Chicago*, which had rocketed from last place to first in its market, was renamed *The Oprah Winfrey Show*, expanded from thirty minutes to an hour, and syndicated by King World to make it available nationally. "I'm thrilled at the prospect of beating Phil [Donahue] throughout the country," she said.[30] She received a $1 million signing bonus. This was just the beginning of a fortune that was to grow into the billions. She was rich and soon to become much richer.

Timing matters. The first television talk show with an African American host was aired on WRCV in Philadelphia in 1960. *The Del Shields Show* featured a thirty-year-old man who had been on the radio for a number of years. His television show lasted only a few weeks. Racism killed it. As Shields said, "[I]t only took fifty letters saying 'Get that nigger off your show or we'll stop drinking your beer' to make the sponsor drop the program. I limped away from that one," Shields lamented.[31]

For Winfrey, the time was right. When television enchanted the nation in the early 1950s, it "was explicitly and glaringly white." The only series on the air then featuring African Americans was *Amos 'n' Andy*, the actors in which were trained by the White men who played the roles on the radio "in the nuances of the stereotype." Television in the 1950s "told the Negro continually that he did not exist—except in insults..."[32]

Breaches in the "lily-whiteness" of television began in the 1960s. A milestone was reached with the premiere of *I Spy* in the fall of 1965 on NBC. The protagonists were spies for the United States. They were a White man and a Black man, played by Robert Culp and Bill Cosby. Cosby only took the role when he was assured he would be fully the equal of Culp, not an afterthought. That is how the role was written, and the show was successful.[33]

When Oprah premiered in Chicago in 1984, Cosby had already established himself as an entertainer and specifically as a television personality with whom a White audience could feel comfortable. No African American woman had achieved the same goal. Oprah was to change that.

Chicago was the right place for her to begin her ascent. The city elected its first African American mayor in 1983. At the age of thirty, Oprah already had ten years of experience on the air. She was more at home and at ease as a public personage than in her private life. In 1987, she was described in *Time* magazine (unflatteringly, to put it mildly) as a "black female of ample bulk" whose show explored the "often bizarre nooks and crannies of human misfortune." A decade later, *Time* included her in its list of the one hundred most influential Americans.[34] Quite a transformation, and one most other talk show entrepreneurs never made. What was her secret?

Guests on Oprah's program told stories about the pain they had endured. Their suffering appeared dreadful in the extreme. They confessed to Oprah, a live studio audience, and a television audience that grew to many millions stories they probably would not have shared with their most intimate friends. Oprah was an invitation. For the first time in their lives, these people had an audience. Someone was really listening to them.

Oprah's own story was well-known. When it came to pain, her life history took a back seat to no one's. Indeed, her ongoing battle with her weight was there for all to see. On November 15, 1988, a trim Oprah rolled out a wagonload of sixty-seven pounds of fat.[35] That was the weight she had lost.

Unfortunately, not permanently. "In a diary excerpt from 1991, Winfrey recounts that on vacation she 'gained eight pounds, bringing me to an all-time whopping 226 pounds. So big, disproportionate, fat in the face. Unable to move freely... I don't know this self. My body has betrayed me, or has it just acquiesced? I don't know who this is waddling through the airport. I caught a glimpse of myself reflected in the store window. I didn't recognize the fat lady staring back at me.'"[36] The suffering was real. So also was the color of her skin and her gender. The fact that she was an African American woman bespoke a history of pain without having to say a word.

"I transcend race," Oprah said.[37] All human hearts are the same. "Race is not an issue," she said in 1987. "It has never been an issue with me... Truth is, I've never felt prevented from doing anything because I was either black or a woman." According to one account, she built "a comfortable and unthreatening bridge between the white and black cultures."[38] (The same could be said of Cosby prior to his calamitous fall from grace.) She had to build this bridge in order to appeal to a mass audience. But since her show did not shy away from racial issues, she found herself engaging in a "delicate balancing act... Winfrey must be exquisitely sensitive to the potential for alienating her majority white audience..."[39]

Winfrey's race mattered for the very reason that it did not matter. Welcoming Winfrey (or Cosby) into your home was a way for the middle-class White audience to achieve what has been called "virtual integration." This "enables whites to live in a world with blacks without having to do so in fact. It provides a form of intimacy without any of the risks. It offers a clean and easy way for whites to [lay claim to a] commitment to fairness, tolerance, and color blindness..."[40]

The United States of the 1980s wanted to think of itself as a "post-racial" society. Bill Cosby and Oprah Winfrey were proof. He was "America's dad," "a genial father figure" who not only epitomized middle-class values but chastised those African Americans who did not live by them.[41]

Oprah has been America's therapist. She has welcomed people with dreadful, horrifying problems onto her show. Guests were not paid to appear. Oprah knew how to keep costs down. Her ability to get people to open up demonstrates a charismatic connection with her guests as well as with her fans. There has always been a seductiveness—difficult to describe but not sexual—about her. With her beautiful voice and the self-assured fashion in which she moved around the studio audience, she had an almost magical ability to put people at their ease. This demands real talent. She never judged. She celebrated. A good example is her superb interview with Marcia Clark, lead prosecutor in the "trial of the century" of O. J. Simpson in May of 1997.[42]

Once you confessed to Oprah and her audience, you could begin to heal. Time and again, she preached that "the only thing that can free you is the belief that you can be free."[43] It was your responsibility to think your way out of your troubles.

This is a traditional American message. It dates back to Benjamin Franklin and runs through the classics by Dale Carnegie (*How to Win Friends and Influence People*), Napoleon Hill (*Think and Grow Rich*) and Norman Vincent Peale (*The Power of Positive Thinking*).

These books are similar to Oprah's message in that they look not to institutional arrangements or macroeconomic conditions but rather strictly at the individual. It is remarkable that Dale Carnegie's book was published in 1936 and Napoleon

Hill's the following year, in the midst of the worst economic depression of the twentieth century. Your fate was in your own hands. Economic forces and institutional barriers were no match for your willpower and did not absolve you from personal responsibility for the situation you faced in life.

Oprah did use phrases like the "slave mentality."[44] This mentality was to be avoided. However, she did not opine on the institution of slavery and its impact upon African Americans in the nation as a whole. "[F]rom an early age, I have always known I was responsible for myself,"[45] she has written. Her message has been: so are you.

How does one gain control of one's life so as to be able to exercise this responsibility in a meaningful way? There are endless prescriptions. For example, T. D. Jakes, bishop of a nondenominational megachurch and a member of Oprah's "SuperSoul100," (a group "with the power to inspire and uplift"),[46] appeared on *Oprah's Lifeclass* on September 15, 2013. Jakes spoke from a stage. Oprah worked the crowd.[47]

Jakes, a big man with a powerful voice and an impressive self-presentation, declared, "When you hold on to your history, you do it at the expense of your destiny." "Oh my God," Oprah exclaimed into the microphone she was holding while standing in an aisle of the studio audience. "Wooo! That hit me. That just hit me... Did that hit you all? When you hold on to your history, you do it at the expense of your destiny. That makes me want to cry. That hit me that hard. That's deep."[48]

This is not an original thought. "History," Stephen Dedalus said in Joyce's *Ulysses*, "is a nightmare from which I am trying to awake."[49] Branches of psychiatry and clinical psychology are devoted to freeing patients from past trauma.

The need to free oneself from the past, as Oprah might put it, transcends race. This is something that all of us have to achieve to an extent. The question is: How? And that is a question that self-help salespeople rarely answer. My advice to you as an investor is to buy low and sell high. How? I have no idea.

Oprah Winfrey is a staggeringly successful businesswoman. One journalist wrote that the secret of her success lay at least as much in what she did not do as in what she did. She did not take her company public. She did not create her own book imprint. She did not license her name to any merchandise. She did not act in public in a way that might call her authenticity into question. She did not fall prey to big deals promising the often-spoken-of but rarely found "synergy." She kept a tight lid on corporate politics. In a word, she stuck to her knitting. Nothing distracted her audience from her message.[50]

In 2002, Oprah said, "I don't think of myself as a businesswoman,"[51] a remarkable statement from a person who made billions in one of the toughest industries there is. A businesswoman might have made the mistakes just listed. Oprah "thought different." She is reported to have had but a casual relationship with the balance sheet and was not an active manager of her vast wealth. She kept a small fortune in cash. But she was not profligate. She did say in the Miss Fire Prevention contest that if she had a million dollars, she would be a "spendin' fool." When she had more than $2 billion, she spent freely on herself, her friends, and her numerous charities, but she was never a fool with her great wealth. There is no better illustration of her business skill than her landing and then handling the Prince Harry and Meghan Markle interview in March 2021. According to the *Washington Post*, "Oprah Winfrey's Prince Harry and Meghan interview netted her $7 million and 17 million viewers. It also validated her larger business strategy."[52]

"Few," according to *Time* magazine, "would have bet on Oprah Winfrey's swift rise to host... the most popular talk show on TV... Guests with sad stories to tell are apt to rouse a tear in Oprah's eye... They, in turn, often find themselves revealing things they would not imagine telling anyone, much less a national TV audience."[53] A sociological study of Winfrey has as its subtitle "the Glamour of Misery." The words are well chosen.[54]

Winfrey's show was known as tabloid TV, and not without reason. On May 1, 1989, for example, she interviewed a woman with multiple personality disorder who participated in devil worship and said she had witnessed the ritual sacrifice of children. Oprah asked, "[D]oes everyone else think [yours is] a nice Jewish family?" The interviewee said they did and that hers was not the only such Jewish family. She did later helpfully observe that "Not all Jewish people sacrifice babies... It is not a typical thing." "I think we all know that," Oprah responded. This was the woman who saw Auschwitz in 2006 with Elie Wiesel, yet this was the kind of trash Winfrey trafficked in. She caught some negative publicity for this particular show, but she got away with a lot over the years.[55]

By the mid-1990s, Winfrey was a force to be reckoned with throughout the media. She reigned supreme on television, in which her mix of serious issues with trash defied categorization. Ever since her performance in *The Color Purple* back in 1986, she mattered in Hollywood. She launched Oprah's Book Club in 1996 as part of a remarkably successful effort to elevate her program and her image above the standard fare on talk TV. On April 14, 2000, she launched *O, The*

Oprah Magazine, which became the most successful magazine launch in history.

Oprah Winfrey is a phenomenally successful self-taught businesswoman. She trusted her instincts. She could have simply stuck with her television show and amassed a fortune to match the dreams of Hattie Mae Lee's granddaughter in the 1950s. If she had, she might have gone the way of other television talk show hosts from Steve Allen to Phil Donahue. The temptation to stick with a winning formula in the business world is very strong. But it is a recipe for decline into irrelevance if not worse. The world changes too quickly to keep running in place. The problem is you can't be certain in advance of what you are getting into. You risk failure. Nevertheless, as talk shows became ever more salacious in the 1990s, Oprah, with considerable daring, took a different tack. "Banking her franchise on the durable virtues of decency, hard work, and self-improvement, she found a bigger audience, eight million a day, and turned herself from a multimillionaire into a billionaire."[56]

Winfrey has had a lengthy career in the media—dating from her debut in Nashville in 1974 down to the present day—because she possesses assets shared by no competitors. As the leading charismatic figure on the air, she has built and sustained a special relationship with her viewers. They believe in her authenticity. They trust her judgment. They feel that, in some unfathomable way, she is looking out for them. This powerful bond is also delicate, and she well understands its nature. If she betrays her fans, her well-earned title of Queen of All Media will be at risk.

In addition to and aligned with this special connection to her audience, Oprah was extraordinarily astute about how far she could stretch her brand. Her instincts told her—no market research was involved—that a book club would strengthen the relationship with her followers. The same was true with her magazine. She is an expert brand manager, understanding that to stretch that brand too far weakens it, especially since, working as she does eighteen hours a day, she is in no position personally to vouch for all the products people might pay her to lend her name to.

Book clubs, however, presented a congenial opportunity. They were nothing new. The Book of the Month Club was founded in 1926. The Literary Guild was created the following year. Dozens of other book clubs followed. In his youth, your faithful author wrote advertising and jacket copy for four book clubs in the business and professional books division at Prentice-Hall, which is now a division of Pearson. Prentice-Hall alone must have had at least twenty book clubs in 1970.

No other book club, however, had Oprah Winfrey. None had anything like her charisma. One reporter wrote that "Winfrey's rapport with the camera cuts across class and race."[57] This is a breathtaking claim, but the sales of the books she boosted lend it some credence.

Oprah's Book Club was launched on September 17, 1996, with a novel by Jacquelyn Mitchard entitled *The Deep End of the Ocean*.[58] Viking, the publisher, began by shipping sixty-eight thousand copies. When one of Winfrey's producers contacted the publisher to say that the book would be chosen for Oprah's Book Club, Viking shipped another hundred thousand copies. Eventually, the book sold millions of copies. There are many similar stories of the stratospheric increase in sales resulting from Oprah's imprimatur.

Winfrey had book club episodes on her television program to introduce the next selection. "Few people will watch a discussion of a novel they have not read, so making fiction work on TV requires considerable show-biz skill (which Winfrey has, of course)."

Book club episodes began with a short documentary about the author, followed by a discussion over a meal among Winfrey, the author, and a couple of viewers. "They talk about what they thought about the book and... its relevance to their lives. Could they be friends with the main character? What did the book teach them about themselves? This is the real innovation that allowed Oprah to turn novels into TV. She focuses the discussion on the response from viewers and herself. Winfrey's own reactions tend to be the most vivid. To eat while talking about spousal abuse in a studio made to look like a dining room is a learned skill."[59]

Declaring in 2002 that "It has become harder and harder to find books on a monthly basis that I feel absolutely compelled to share," Winfrey decided to terminate her book club. The publishing industry went into well-justified mourning. One estimate held that her recommendations had generated $700 million in publishing revenue.[60] Single-handedly, she had turned some authors into millionaires. We are describing a great deal of power wielded by one woman. (I am presently reading a book entitled *Caste* by Isabel Wilkerson on my iPad. On its cover is an O in the middle of which is "Oprah's Book Club 2020." "Oprah's Book Club" appears as a running head on every page.)

Winfrey brought the book club back in 2003. The reboot ran until 2012. According to one estimate, sales of "Oprah editions" came to fifty-five million units, a fantastic total.[61]

Her book club morphed into version 2.0, sponsored by the newly created Oprah Winfrey Network (OWN) and *O: The Oprah Magazine*. On March 25, 2019, Apple and Winfrey announced a revival of the video version of her book club to air on Apple TV+.

There is one episode in the book club's history that deserves our particular attention. James Frey published a book entitled *A Million Little Pieces*, which purported to be a memoir of his life as a drug addict and criminal. The book was made to order for Oprah. She selected it for her book club for September of 2005, and it became the book club's best seller up to that time. Unfortunately, the book was riddled with sensationalized fabrications. These fabrications were discovered by a website called The Smoking Gun, which published its lengthy story, "A Million Little Lies: Exposing James Frey's Fiction Addiction," on January 4, 2006. Frey turned out to be the mastermind of an elaborate literary hoax. The first line of the exposé is "Oprah Winfrey's been had."[62]

At first, Winfrey stood by Frey. However, his deceptions were so egregious that she had to make a power move to separate herself from him. Frey's lies threatened the loyalty of her followers and thus her charismatic connection to them. That could not be tolerated.

On January 26, 2006, Winfrey had Frey back on her show. She eviscerated him. She had not worked as hard as she had for all those years in order to be taken down by a huckster. As she said about that show, "I was defending my turf and defending every single viewer who had bought that book. I am... here on behalf of the reader who is pissed off that it wasn't what we thought it was." She could not allow the charismatic cord—as fragile as it was strong—to be severed.

By the time Winfrey was finished with Frey, there wasn't much left of him but "a hank o' hair and some fillin's." He was symbolically castrated on live television. The takedown was so utterly devastating that years later Winfrey criticized herself for not being compassionate.

Winfrey asked a lot of blunt questions—"Why did you lie?"—to which the answer was obvious but unlovely—to sell books. She was widely praised in the mainstream media for her demolition of the pretender with whom she was dealing.

What is most remarkable about this story is that a Black woman destroyed a White man before the eyes of the world. The history of race in the United States had been the opposite. It had always been White men who have assaulted Black women. As for Black men, they have been lynched by White men for imagined affronts to White women for many decades. In 1955, Emmett Louis Till, a fourteen-year-old Black youth, was murdered by two White men for supposedly whistling at a White woman (accounts vary concerning precisely what Till was supposed to have done). The two men were acquitted by an all-White jury. A year later, they admitted their guilt but were protected by double jeopardy. This murder took place in Mississippi, the state in which Winfrey was born the previous year and in which she lived at the time.

In dealing with Frey, Winfrey showed how icy-cold fearless she could be. She also demonstrated an instinctive knowledge of her relationship with her fans—who were also her consumers. This was a mutual relationship founded on trust that she is the real thing, trust that must be defended.

In defense of this trust, Winfrey developed a reputation as a very difficult person for whom to work. Employees were on call 24-7. The Queen of Talk did not want her employees talking about her. They signed strict nondisclosure agreements. She was always on guard—not completely without reason—against betrayal by those closest to her. The more she disclosed about herself, the more hidden she became.

In 2007, Oprah took a giant leap outside her comfort zone. She endorsed Barack Obama for the presidency when he was in the midst of a hard-fought campaign for the nomination against Hillary Clinton. She made this endorsement clear and gave her reasons for it on *Larry King Live* in May.[63]

It is a long way from marketing unarguable but not very useful nostrums such as "When you hold on to your history, you do it at the expense of your destiny" to endorsing a political candidate. Oprah had remained resolutely apolitical. Now she was jumping in with both feet. And the ground under her was not that firm.

Oprah's favorability ratings had always been very high. In 1996, 78 percent of those polled rated her favorably. That remained steady until a poll in August 2007 showed her with a favorability rating of only 61 percent, down 13 percent in just seven months from a comparable survey. A poll taken in December 2007 had her at 55 percent favorable with 33 percent unfavorable. By late March 2008, respondents were saying they preferred Ellen DeGeneres to Oprah. This was the first time in decades that Oprah was not on top of such a poll.[64]

Oprah supported Obama early, when it looked to everyone that Hillary Clinton would be the Democratic nominee. However, this remarkable gamble paid off. Part of the reason that she won her bet was her charismatic connection to her fans. According to one estimate, she was responsible for generating a million votes for Obama in the primary alone, a critically important contribution.[65] In 2013, President Obama awarded her the Presidential Medal of Freedom.

A charismatic African American woman from Kosciusko, Mississippi, played an important part in the ascent of an African American man from Hawaii to the White House. But his successor has demonstrated that the United States has a very long way to go before it can claim to be a post-racial society.

Oprah Gail Winfrey did not become the first self-made female African American billionaire by accident. Today, she is an icon. She has been urged to run for the presidency of the United States. The nation has proven it could do a lot worse. She has emerged from a life fraught with innumerable barriers to a position of respect bordering on reverence.

Oprah said she is God-centered. She certainly is special. When she visited the Harvard Business School unannounced a number of years ago, everyone wanted to see her. Everyone wanted a piece of her. Through decades of hard work, courage, and innate judgment, she has established herself as a charismatic figure transcending the deepest fissure in American society—race.[66]

CHAPTER 12

ELON MUSK:
CHARISMA AT THE EDGE OF REALITY

In 2012, Elon Musk was inspecting the yet-to-be-released Tesla Model S. He got into the car, looked around, and focused on the sun visor. He saw the seam around the edge. The fabric of the visor was pushed out. "It's fish-lipped," he said. The screws that attached the visor to the body of the car were visible. Each time he saw those screws, he experienced them as tiny daggers stabbing him in the eyes. That was his way of saying this was not good enough. "We have to decide what is the best sun visor in the world and then do better," he commanded. An old saying in Detroit is that "every car is a compromise." Musk was not prepared to accept that standard for Tesla. This incident, related by Musk's biographer Ashlee Vance, is a window into Musk's approach to his car company. Nothing less than perfection in every detail is called for.[1]

The demand for excellence places enormous pressure on any attempt to mass-produce automobiles. The industry is unforgiving. Cars are complicated machines. There are numberless mistakes that can be made every step of the way from concept to design to production to distribution. These mistakes range from visible screws on sun visors to failures that can cause accidents and cost lives. The stakes are high.

There has been no successful domestic start-up in the automobile industry since the Chrysler Corporation was founded in 1925. The domestic industry was beaten at its own game by foreign companies once the industry became global in the 1970s. For years, there has been overcapacity, and cyclical gyrations have not made life any easier for the incumbents.

The failures of the past, such as the DeLorean in the early 1980s, have been the result of attempting to do better what the incumbents were already doing or of doing the same thing with subsidies squeezed out of one government or another. True, Tesla also received government subsidies. The difference is that this was truly a mission-driven company. It was to produce only electric cars and by doing so to save the planet from choking on exhaust fumes and from global warming.

The idea of powering cars with electricity is nothing new. It dates back to the turn of the last century, when the industry was born. Steam-, electricity-, and gasoline-fueled internal combustion engines competed with one another. The internal combustion engine prevailed because it posed the fewest problems.

Tesla was founded in July of 2003 by three engineers, Martin Eberhard, Marc Tarpenning, and Ian Wright. Musk joined the company in the process of its first round of funding the following year, and he became chairman of the board. He never planned to play merely a ceremonial role. He also became the head of product design.

Wright left after a year. In his words, "Tesla was all about progress and doing everything they can to make sure that everybody's driving an electric car. And I'm not really a true believer..." He was more interested in the racetrack than the highway. In 2008, Musk became CEO, forcing out Eberhard. The parting was anything but amicable. In February of 2020, Musk said of Eberhard, "He is literally the worst person I've ever worked with."[2] Tarpenning left when Eberhard did. Musk is now often referred to as the company's founder, although he is not.[3]

Tesla became a key component of Musk's ambition to do nothing less than transform the way we live. If transportation does not make the transition from internal combustion to electricity, air will become unbreathable and climate change will make the world uninhabitable. Tesla thus fits with Musk's other commitments—to SpaceX and Solar City. The goal of SpaceX is to colonize Mars. Musk believes that unless the human race becomes interplanetary, it will perish. His grand—some might say grandiose—goal is to save humanity.

SpaceX is what we can call a backup plan. If Musk does not succeed in ending the era of carbon combustion, solving commuter congestion, and rewiring the brain, then he will give humanity a second chance to get things right on a different planet. That planet is incontestably far more hostile to human life than the ocean, the Gobi Desert, or Antarctica. No one imagines a city the size of, say, Cincinnati in any of these locales, but for Musk that's a trivial objection. If he gets us there, we will build it. For all this, a welcoming world is supposed to respond with admiration, gratitude, and government subsidies.

To Musk, the Tesla is not just another car. "It's the most fun thing you could possibly buy ever." "It's not exactly a car," Musk said in a 2018 interview. "It's actually a thing to maximize enjoyment... Maximize fun."[4]

What is genuine here and really does set Tesla apart from the numerous also-rans of the past is the desire to reinvent the automobile, not to copy others. Tesla almost went bankrupt in the 2008 economic crash. The government saved it, as it did with other car companies. The fact is that Teslas are on the road today and in increasing numbers. They are environmentally friendly. They are beautiful inside and out.

Nevertheless, the company has a lot of critics. One report published on July 4, 2020, pointed out that Tesla's "market cap [is] approximately 2.5x that of Ford, GM and Fiat-Chrysler combined, despite selling around 400,000 cars a year while Ford, GM and Fiat-Chrysler sell 5.4 million, 7.7 million and 4.4 million vehicles respectively."[5] The stock fluctuates wildly. As of this writing, Tesla is now not only the most valuable domestic automobile company, it is the most valuable automobile company in the world, surpassing even Toyota. In fact, it is more valuable than all these companies combined.

Tesla has always accumulated debt. Musk has consistently disappointed with regard to schedule. There are those who do not think the company can survive (although their numbers are dwindling). It has proven that it can produce sales but has not yet demonstrated that it can produce steady profits.

Without Musk, the company would probably not exist. If he left now, its stock would plummet, and it might have to be sold. With him, we can say only that the story will take many more twists and turns.

Who is he? How did he come to play such an important role in an industry at the center of the global economy? Why is it customary to compare him to Steve Jobs? Why is it also customary to describe him as charismatic? Where has all this come from?

Elon Reeve Musk was born on June 28, 1971, in Pretoria, South Africa. His mother's family started out in the upper midwestern United States, then moved to Canada, and then, because of Musk's maternal grandfather "enduring lust for adventure," relocated on a whim to South Africa, where no member of the family had ever been before.[6]

Maye Haldeman, Musk's mother, married his father, Errol Musk, in 1970. She was beautiful. According to her, he pursued her relentlessly, in love with her, she said, "because of my legs and my teeth."[7] Errol Musk was a mechanical and electrical engineer. His work as an engineer and real estate developer made him wealthy.

Maye and Errol were married from 1970 to 1979. In addition to Elon, they had two other children. Kimbal, born in 1972, started Zip2 with Elon and another entrepreneur in 1995. This software direction service company was bought by Compaq in 1999 for $307 million. The proceeds were invested in X.com, an online financial services company. This in turn was merged with Peter Thiel's Confinity to form PayPal, which became the foundation for Musk's wealth.

Musk's sister, Tosca, born in 1974, is still another technology entrepreneur. She has produced feature films and is the CEO and cofounder of the streaming media platform Passionflix. There are few, if any, other families in the world with three siblings each of whom has become a notable technology entrepreneur, and one of whom has become world famous in that role. Not only is Musk world famous, he is fabulously wealthy, surpassing Jeff Bezos as the richest person in the world on January 7, 2021. Musk's net worth was estimated at over $185 billion. (On January 11, he fell behind Bezos again. It is not improbable that there will be more such back and forth.)

Elon was odd from the beginning. "He seemed to understand things quicker than other kids," said his mother, perhaps not the best witness on such a question, but it does appear that she was right. He also, according to his biographer, "seemed to drift off into a trance at times. People spoke to him, but nothing got through when he had a certain, distant look in his eyes."[8]

"Sometimes," his mother said, "he just didn't hear you." There was some suspicion that he might have a hearing deficit. His adenoids were removed because that was supposed to improve hearing. "Well," said his mother, "it didn't change. He goes into his brain and... is in another world. I do think Elon was always a little different but in a nerdy way. It didn't endear him to his peers."[9] Mom expressed that mildly.

As a youth, Elon was a compulsive reader. Among other things, this is a way to avoid interacting with other human beings, which he was not very good at. Sometimes he read ten hours a day. His retention was remarkable. He often corrected other kids when they got a fact wrong. This doubtless did not endear him to his peers, either.

After his parents were divorced, Musk lived with his mother for a few years. He then decided to move in with his father. Musk said, "My father seemed sort of sad and lonely, and my mom had three kids, and he didn't have any. It seemed unfair." Musk's mother could not comprehend his decision. Why would he "want to leave this happy home I made for him—this really happy home. But Elon is his own person." Musk's first wife, Justine, observed that, "I don't think he was particularly close with either parent."[10]

Musk came to loathe his father. "[My father is] good at making life miserable—that's for sure. He can take any situation no matter how good it is and make it bad. He's not a happy man. I don't know... fuck... I don't know how someone becomes like he is."

"He was such a terrible human being," Musk told *Rolling Stone*. "You have no idea. My dad will have a carefully thought-out plan of evil... He will plan evil."[11] Errol killed three men who broke into his home. He was not criminally charged. At the age of seventy-one or seventy-two, he had a child with his 30-year-old stepdaughter. This was, he explained, "God's plan."[12] Errol Musk was not your average dad.

At school, Elon was not a leader and hardly seemed like he was on the road to making a mark in the world. His biographer interviewed those who knew him then, and the consensus was that Elon was "quiet" and "unspectacular," two words that would not be used to describe him today. One student said, "There were four or five boys that were considered the very brightest. Elon was not one of them." Another observed, "Honestly, there were just no signs that he was going to be a billionaire. He was never in a leadership position at school. I was rather surprised to see what has happened to him."[13]

Like Steve Jobs, Elon was bullied when he was young. Eighth and ninth grades were especially difficult. One day, he and his brother, Kimbal, were sitting at the top of a flight of concrete stairs at school having a bite to eat. Elon describes what transpired. "I was basically hiding from this gang that was fucking hunting me down for God knows fucking why. I think I accidentally bumped into this guy at assembly that morning, and he'd taken some huge offense at that." The guy in question kicked Elon in the head, pushed him down the stairs, and along with his friends beat him mercilessly. Elon lost consciousness. "They were a bunch of fucking psychos," he said. He was out of school for a week and eventually had to have surgery on his nose. "For some reason, they decided that I was it, and they were going to go after me nonstop... For a number of years, there was no respite. You get chased around by gangs at school who tried to beat the shit out of me, and then I come home, and it would be just awful there as well. It was just like nonstop horrible."[14]

According to Elon, his father took him on a trip to the United States "when I was about ten. And I remember it was really an awesome experience because the hotels all had arcades. So my number one thing when we went to a new hotel, was to go to the arcades."[15]

Musk loved video games and was particularly adept at *Dungeons and Dragons*. He found video games "incredibly engaging, and they made me want to learn how to program computers. I thought I could make my own games. I wanted to see how games work. I wanted to create a video game. That's what led me to learn how to program computers."[16]

Back in South Africa, Musk's family owned a Magnavox Odyssey, the first video game device. "And then it went from there to the Atari to Intellivision. And then one day... I saw a Commodore VC-20. And I was like 'Holy crow! You can actually have a computer and make your own games.' I thought this was just one of the most incredible things possible. It came with this manual about how to program BASIC. I spent all night several days in a row absorbing that... I was definitely obsessive. When you first do it, you realize it's incredible. You can type these commands and then something happens on the screen. That's pretty amazing."[17]

When Musk was twelve years old, he wrote the code for a space-based game he named *Blastar* and sold the code to a South African magazine called *PC and Office Technology* for $500. It is a simple game by today's standards. Even Musk, not a man to hide his light under a bushel, called it "a trivial game." It was not trivial, however, for a twelve-year-old to write 167 lines of code and sell the game he created to a computer magazine for $500 in 1984. A Google engineer rebuilt the game for HTML 5. You can play it today if you so desire.[18]

It is not surprising that Musk was captivated by the solipsistic activity of playing a game one-on-one with a computer. His childhood and adolescence were pretty awful. At home, no one understood him. At school, he was bullied and beaten. He lived inside himself. His constant reading stimulated his fantasies. He was attracted to computers because they made sense. In an unintelligible world, computers follow rules—"You can type these commands and then something happens on the screen." They don't throw you down stairs and beat you. They don't plan evil. They do as they are told. You can control them.

His attitude toward his schoolwork was to question authority. He had no interest in doing an assignment simply because it was assigned. "I just look at it as 'What grades do I need to get where I want to go?' There were compulsory subjects like Afrikaans, and I just didn't see the point of learning that. It seemed ridiculous. I'd get a passing grade and that was fine. Things like physics and computers—I got the highest grade you can get in those. There needs to be a reason for a grade. I'd rather play video games, write software, and read books than try and get an A if there's no point in getting an A."[19]

From the beginning, Musk was a nonconformist. He had no interest in doing things simply because others were and no interest in following rules that didn't fit in with what his goals were for himself. His early life brings to mind Edgar Allan Poe's poem "Alone": "From childhood's hour I have not been / As others were; I have not seen / As others saw..."[20]

Musk spent five uneventful months at the University of Pretoria before making his way to Canada at the age of seventeen. For a brief time, he worked at odd jobs before enrolling in Queens University in Kingston, Ontario. His brother and sister followed him there.

Musk studied as little as possible at Queens, spending his time fixing computers to make some money. His next stop after Queens was the University of Pennsylvania, where he studied business and physics and where he found people with whom he could relate. He knew his future was in technology. "I'm not an investor. I like to make technologies real that... are important for the future and useful..." The question he asked himself in college was "What will most affect the future of humanity?" He came up with the following list: "the internet; sustainable energy; space exploration, in particular the permanent extension of life beyond Earth; artificial intelligence; and reprogramming the human genetic code."[21] Whether or not that list was really made, he certainly has pursued those goals. They beg for ridicule and smack of juvenile fantasy. Yet he has raised and spent billions convincing others to enable him to pursue each of them.

The most important event in his life at Queens was that he met Justine Wilson in 1990. She was eighteen; he was nineteen. They began an on-again, off-again courtship that lasted a decade. "She looked pretty great," Musk recalled. "She was also smart and this intellectual with sort of an edge. She had a black belt in tae kwon do and was semi-bohemian and... the hot chick on campus."[22] Wilson was an aspiring (and now a published) novelist. She did not particularly need Elon. By this time, there was no trace of the shyness in him that could have resulted from his wretched childhood and adolescence. If ever a man was born to reject rejection, it was he.

"He would call very insistently," Justine remembered. "You always knew it was Elon because the phone would never stop ringing. The man does not take no for an answer. You can't blow him off. I do think of him as the Terminator. He locks his gaze on to something and says, 'It shall be mine.' Bit by bit he won me over."[23]

Elon continued his pursuit of Justine after leaving Queens. They were finally married in January of 2000. He showed a certain romantic flair in luring Wilson to the altar. On their wedding day, however, she began to learn the difference between being wooed and being won. "As we danced at our wedding reception, Elon told me, 'I am the alpha in this relationship.'"[24]

"I shrugged it off," she recalled in an article she wrote in 2010, "just as I would later shrug off signing the postnuptial agreement, but as time went on, I learned that he was serious. He had grown up in the male-dominated culture of South Africa, and the will to compete and dominate that made him so successful in business did not magically shut off when he came home."[25] When Wilson met Musk at Queens, he appeared to be your average geeky, next-to-penniless kid. By the time they were married, he was a millionaire many times over.

Justine and Elon had six children. The first, Nevada Alexander, was ten weeks old when he took his usual nap. This time, he stopped breathing. Sudden infant death syndrome. In Justine's words, "By the time the paramedics resuscitated him, he had been deprived of oxygen for so long that he was brain-dead. He spent three days on life support in a hospital... before we made the decision to take him off it. I held him in my arms when he died.

"Elon made it clear that he did not want to talk about Nevada's death. I didn't understand this, just as he didn't understand why I grieved openly, which he regarded as 'emotionally manipulative.' He was very much in the mode of stiff-upper-lip, the-show-must-go-on, let's-get-it-over-with. He doesn't do well in the dark places." In the words of a journalist, "[L]oss—the place he had to make in his life for its invisible enormity—baffled him."[26]

Six weeks after their son's death, Justine began in vitro fertilization. The couple had twins in 2004 and triplets in 2006, all boys. Two of the five were diagnosed as autistic. Justine says that one of the two boys is no longer on the spectrum. Justine repeatedly told Elon that "I am your wife, not your employee." He regularly responded, "If you were my employee, I would fire you."[27] Musk filed for divorce in 2008, and the two now share custody of the five boys.

Musk's personal life is as chaotic as his business life. His brand of charisma seems to thrive in chaotic situations. In this he is quite the opposite of Edwin Land, illustrating once again how difficult it is to generalize about charismatic personalities.

Musk has had a number of highly publicized liaisons since his divorce. The most recent is with a Canadian musician named Claire Elise Boucher, who goes by the stage name Grimes. She has stated that she is changing her name to c. On May 4, 2020, she gave birth to their child, a son. She thought up his name: X Æ A-12. "She's great at names," said the proud father. This particular name may be illegal in California, where the child was born, but no matter—Musk was created to break rules.[28] (My own suggestion for a nickname is Bud.)

After the University of Pennsylvania, Elon planned to study physics and materials science at Stanford. That plan lasted two days. When he hit Silicon Valley, he had an acute case of what today is known as FOMO—fear of missing out—on the internet boom. He and Kimbal founded Zip2, a software company that sold an internet city guide to newspapers and also sold web services to small businesses.

The funding of this venture is controversial. One school of thought is that Musk's despised father gave his sons $28,000 to get going. Always quick to deny his father credit for anything, Musk declared, "He was irrelevant. He paid nothing for college. My brother and I paid for college through scholarships, loans, and working two jobs simultaneously. The funding we raised for our first company came from a small group of random angel investors in Silicon Valley."[29]

The truth about his father's contribution will remain unknown. We do know that the venture capital firm Mohr Davidow put $3 million into his company in 1996 and that in February 1999, at the peak of the internet bubble, Compaq Computer bought Zip2 for the incredible price of $307 million. "It was like pennies from heaven," said a Zip2 executive.[30] Twenty-two million dollars of this went to Elon, and

Kimbal got a check for $15 million. At $60 million, Mohr Davidow made twenty times its original investment.

As usual, this seems inevitable because it happened. But there was nothing inevitable about it. Start-ups, especially first-time start-ups, fail far more often than they succeed. Two young men who know nothing about how to run a business and have limited, if any, personal resources drive three thousand miles to a part of the country they have never seen, and in four years, they are worth $22 million (over $35 million in 2021) and $15 million (over $24 million in 2021). Elon was twenty-eight. Kimbal was twenty-seven. If they had so chosen, they could have retired for the rest of their lives on the money they made prior to reaching the age of thirty.

There was never any thought of retirement. Musk founded X.com in November of 1999 with $10 million of his own money. This has been described as "one of the world's first online banks." Deposits were insured by the FDIC.[31] In less than half a year, in March of 2000, X.com merged with its competitor Confinity, owned by Silicon Valley big shot Peter Thiel. Thiel pushed Musk out of the executive suite, but Musk remained the company's largest shareholder with an 11.7 percent stake. This company, renamed PayPal, was acquired by eBay for $1.5 billion in 2002. Musk's take was $165 million. In his authoritative history of venture capital, Harvard Business School professor Tom Nicholas describes PayPal as "Perhaps the most important venture capital investment from the standpoint of its effects on serial entrepreneurship..."[32]

Now Musk was really rich by any standard. And he showed once again that he was a perpetual motion machine.

In May of 2002, Musk founded Space Exploration Technologies, known as SpaceX. Still privately held, this company has an estimated seven thousand employees. Musk established it with $100 million of his own money. Since its birth, he has expended a tremendous amount of time and effort on it. Why?

Here is what he says: "To figure out what is truly significant, we have to take the longest possible view. There have only been about a half dozen genuinely important events in the four-billion-year saga of life on earth: single-cell life, multicell life, differentiation into plants and animals, movement of animals from water to land, and the advent of mammals and consciousness." Becoming multiplanetary would "serve as a hedge against the myriad—and growing—threats to our survival. An asteroid or a supervolcano could certainly destroy us, but we also face risks the dinosaurs never saw: an engineered virus, nuclear war, inadvertent creation of a micro–black hole, or some as-yet-unknown technology could spell the end of us. Sooner or later we must expand life beyond our little blue ball—or go extinct."[33]

For the sake of discussion, let us grant that everything Musk says is true. Earth was almost struck by an asteroid recently. New diseases—Ebola, brain-eating amoebae, flesh-eating bacteria—appear regularly. Whether or not COVID-19 has been "engineered," its devastating impact lends force to this observation. Nuclear Armageddon has been a threat for decades. If you really believe that Job One is to colonize Mars so that the human race can survive, one would think that effort would consume your waking hours. The challenge of building a rocket that can get anyone to Mars cannot be overstated. Neither can the expense involved nor the lives that will inevitably be lost be ignored.[34]

Musk may believe every word he says, but his attention is so divided that it makes us question the chances of his bringing any of his initiatives to fruition. In addition to being the founder, CEO, and lead designer for SpaceX, Musk is the CEO and product architect of Tesla, co-founder and CEO of Neuralink, founder of the Boring Company, cofounder of Open AI, and chairman of SolarCity, a company founded by two of his cousins and which, like Tesla, had a load of debt and no profits and which was acquired by Tesla in November of 2016. Any one of these positions could be a career in itself. The Boring Company, for example, constructs tunnels under congested areas in cities. In April 2017, Musk said this initiative has taken only about 2 percent to 3 percent of his time.[35] Will that prove to be enough for an enterprise of this magnitude? A reporter noted in February 2021 that Musk himself thought he was "stretched too thin" and complained of what he described as an "insane" work schedule. Critics thought Tesla was being neglected. Could it run on "autopilot?"[36] Everything with which Musk has been engaged for the last decade is incomplete. Nothing is certain to be fully realized. But Tesla, as of this writing by far the most valuable automobile company in the world, looks like a very good bet at present.

Just as Musk declared himself to be the "alpha" in his marriage to Justine Wilson, he has to be the alpha in every endeavor in which he takes part. He was already a star in Silicon Valley by the time he began raising money for Tesla. People who invested their money with him since 1995 have done very well indeed. He has access to people of great wealth such as Larry Page and Sergei Brin, the founders of Google, and all the venture capitalists give his ideas serious consideration. He is a big shot in a way that Eberhard, Tarpenning, and Wright were not.

Musk was more than a moneyman. He was and is an out-standing technologist. His public presentation skills do not rise to those of Steve Jobs. He is not above speaking untruthfully or inaccurately. This is not a necessary attribute of being a salesman, but it sometimes comes with the package. And Musk is a great salesman.

Time and again during the more than a decade and a half that Musk has been the alpha—and some would say the omega as well—of Tesla, the company has disappointed in innumerable ways. Very late with product. Red ink even when the sales volume has increased. Mounting debt. You name it. Tesla has suffered it. But it is still on its feet, and if it can survive financially (which looks quite likely at this writing), Elon Musk will go down as equal in importance in the history of the automobile industry to Henry Ford. Here are some of the similarities and differences between Ford's approach to the industry and Musk's.

To begin with the similarities, Henry Ford, it has been said, was a man "of vision and of visions."[37] Vision is essential, and it points to an attainable future. "Visions" are dangerous. They are mirages. Musk, too, is a man of vision and visions. He is a visionary with regard to the electric vehicle. He is beset by visions when it comes to colonizing Mars.

When Henry Ford was developing the market for automobiles in the United States, there was a good deal of skepticism about them. In order to publicize the automobile as something that, although genuinely new, was also practical, Ford needed free publicity. Advertising would have been prohibitively expensive and unpersuasive. Therefore, Ford raced cars, sponsored races, and even won some, though his eye was always on the mass market.

Musk had to deal with the stereotype of electric cars as golf carts. Boring. Ugly. Slow. So he got involved in racing as well. "Racing provides a valuable environment for carmakers to test new technology..." It also provides publicity as well as sex appeal. "Race on Sunday, sell on Monday" has long been an industry saying. Tesla's Model S became "a presence in the world's racing subculture."[38] As far as "boring" and "ugly" are concerned, the first car Tesla sold—the Roadster—was based heavily on the Lotus, one of the flashiest cars ever built.

One final similarity deserves to be mentioned. The Ford Motor Company was founded on June 16, 1903. The Model T hit the market on October 1, 1908. It was manufactured for almost two decades and was named the Car of the Century by the Global Automotive Election Foundation in 1999.[39] One of the most remarkable aspects of Henry Ford and his Model T was that there was very little infrastructure to support a mass-marketed automobile powered by an internal combustion engine in the first decade of the twentieth century in the United States. The roads were terrible. There were few gas stations. Indeed, refining gasoline (as opposed to kerosene) had yet to become a big business. There were few repair shops. If you bought a Model T in the early years, you had to know a great deal about how it operated, and you had to be able to repair it yourself.

Infrastructure was also lacking for electric vehicles at the beginning of this century. There was no network of charging stations. The result is a new phrase in our lexicon: "range anxiety." Both Ford and Musk faced the chicken and egg problem—which comes first, the car or the infrastructure? They both made the big bet that the car would be so compelling that the infrastructure would arise to accommodate it.

Ford was proven right. It appears that Musk will be, too. Even if Tesla should fail to survive as an independent company, it is more likely than not that electricity will be the future not only of the automobile but also of buses and trucks.

The biggest difference between Ford and Musk is that Ford targeted the low end of the market first. This was always his plan: to put America on wheels. "I will build a car for the great multitude constructed of the best materials by the best men to be hired after the simplest designs that modern engineering can devise… so low in price that no man making a good salary will be unable to own one and enjoy with his family the blessing of hours of pleasure in God's great open spaces."[40] This quotation is worth reading twice. It is truly a vision of the future around which a corporation can rally.

Musk is also thinking big. He wants to change the dominant design of global mobility to electricity from gasoline. He is building cars "after the most beautiful designs that modern engineering can devise." He is eliminating independent dealers, a fundamental revolution in the automobile business model. He is making cars safer through progress in software that will eventually lead to fully autonomous driving. All told, Tesla represents a breathtaking reconceptualizing of mobility.

Musk's road map was to start at the top of the market, the opposite of Ford's approach. Tesla's first product, the Roadster, was priced very high and produced in small numbers. It was introduced in 2008 beginning at $109,000. In 2010, Tesla had its IPO. The Roadster was discontinued in 2012; 2,450 units were sold.

The Tesla Model S was introduced in 2012. This was the first automobile that was Tesla from the ground up. Lotus was not involved. This is a sedan. More than a quarter of a million have been sold. The price ranges from a low of $75,000 to a high of $133,000.

The Tesla Model X, described as a midsize luxury SUV, was introduced in September 2015. The price ranged from a low of $80,000 to a high of $144,000 for the "signature version." As of September 2018, 106,689 have been sold.

Tesla introduced the Model 3 on July 7, 2017.[41] As of March 2019, 198,700 units have been sold. The price is $35,000, but that only accounts for a basic version of the vehicle. There are plenty of options, which can easily drive the price up another $20,000.

The Model 3 is the most important car Tesla has introduced. This is the car that is supposed to do for electric vehicles what the Model T did for automobiles in general—bring them to a mass market. "Since we created the company, from the beginning, this has been the goal," Musk has said. Reaching that price point "has been a long journey through what Musk has called 'production hell'..."[42] The company had to learn how difficult it is to mass-produce an automobile.

Here is what Musk said on April 22, 2013, on a visit to the Khan Academy in Mountain View. He arrived late because he was working at the Tesla factory in Fremont, on the southeast corner of San Francisco Bay. "There's always something wrong because there's too many things going on," he said. There are "thousands of unique components in cars, and... if any one of those things is missing, you can't make cars." "Today's fiasco," he told Sal Khan, "was, I kid you not, we were missing a three-dollar USB cable... It's part of the wiring harness, so you can't put the interior in without this cable... It's literally three dollars, so I had to send people throughout the

Bay Area to buy three-dollar USB cables."[43] There is one story after another just like this. That is what it means to mass manufacture automobiles.

Many people have made expensive automobiles in small numbers. The problem has always been mass production. No matter how technologically advanced a factory is, it cannot operate without the required parts. That three-dollar USB cable proves the point. It is a small problem compared to the fact that automobile manufacture today entails a global supply chain. If imports are interrupted for any reason, sending people running around the Bay Area to buy the required missing part is not an option.

The clarity of Musk's vision—transportation without fossil fuels—is compelling. His commitment to it is powerful. His charisma is unquestionable. People from all over the world are drawn to him. What he wants to do is so much more exciting than measuring clicks for advertisers on the internet that his magnetism is increased by what is going on around him. Tesla would not have survived in a world populated by companies as well run as Toyota without Musk. The question is: Can Tesla survive with him?

Musk has a deserved reputation for attracting outstanding talent. He has an equally deserved reputation for not being able to hold on to that talent. The exodus from Tesla of first-class engineers, financial people, public relations executives, and experts in every other function vital to the company has been lovingly catalogued by the legion of short sellers who are betting that this company will fail. "Tesla's active short community has made a sport of tallying up executive departures: they count at least thirty gone since June [of 2018], including the chief information officer, a senior project manager for the supply chain, and the system leads for both architecture and design on Autopilot. If you look at the past year, the number rises to sixty-four." Perhaps most concerning was the departure of J. B. Straubel in July of 2019. Straubel, the chief technology officer, had been with the company since 2003. He has been looked upon as one of the founders. Obviously he knew how to handle Musk, and it must be said that his departure was reported as amicable. [44]

The first time Musk's biographer Ashlee Vance met his subject, Musk asked, "Do you think I'm insane?"[45] It is not a bad question. Vance did not answer. The answer is "no." Musk is not insane in a clinical sense. He is, however, a man who believes that the rules do not apply to him. Great things have been done by men and women who did not follow the rules. Musk's problem, which may eventually prove devastating, is that he is unable to tell the difference between rules that are worth following and those that are not.

The single most troubling event—of many—with regard to Musk's leadership of Tesla was his tweet on August 7, 2018: "Am considering taking Tesla private at $420. Funding secured."[46] This message was made immediately available to the 21.4 million people who followed Musk's Twitter feed at the time and quickly became known to every other interested party thereafter. The biggest problem is that the tweet was a lie. An undebatable lie. The funding was not secured. Tesla was not taken private. Now everyone associated with the company—employees, customers, suppliers, and everybody else—knows that its CEO is a liar.

This was no garden-variety lie. It is against SEC regulations for executives of public companies to disseminate incorrect information about material issues, and taking a company private is as material as one can get. Musk hates short sellers because of their "constant defamatory attacks… resulting in great harm to our valuable brand."[47] Their votes of no confidence in Tesla are votes of no confidence in him.

To arrive at a price of $420 a share, Musk added 20 percent to the price of the stock at the time. That brought him to $419. Then he added a dollar because "he had recently learned about 420's significance in marijuana culture and thought his girlfriend 'would find it funny… '"[48] This is a rather unscientific procedure for a man who boasts of his mastery of physics.

This tweet "set off a trading frenzy," according to the SEC and compelled the NASDAQ to suspend trading in Tesla's stock. Musk eventually got off easy. He and Tesla were both fined $10 million. He paid the company's fine. The amount was so trivial in the context of Musk's wealth that it will not deter future behavior such as this. He was required to relinquish the chairmanship of the company, although he was permitted to remain as CEO, which is all that matters. Musk's comment: "Worth it."[49] One wonders whether this escapade did more damage to the Tesla brand than all the short sellers on the market. Insane? Not quite. Astute? Judge for yourself. Since the tweet, Tesla stock has skyrocketed in value. On May 1, 2020, at 8:11 a.m., Musk took to his Twitter account yet again. "Tesla stock price is too high [in my opinion]." What prompted this inappropriate remark is unknown. What is known is that on May 1, 2020, the price of Tesla stock dropped over 10 percent.[50] Since then, the performance of Tesla's stock has been the stuff that dreams are made of. On January 6, 2021, it closed at 755.98, which is one reason Musk is so wealthy right now.

There are more such stories about Musk and Tesla, but in evaluating him as a charismatic figure, one must pay at least passing attention to his much-publicized ambition to colonize Mars.

People of great wealth routinely discover that they don't know what to do with their money. It is common to see people of great wealth building mansions or, as in the case of William Randolph Hearst, a castle, which he built near San Simeon on the California coast. The super-rich pursue a variety of quixotic ventures.

Elon Musk, Jeff Bezos, and Richard Branson are all interested in space travel. For Musk, this is more than just an interest. It is an obsession. For decades, he has wanted to colonize Mars because he is convinced the human race is in peril if it remains on Earth and on Earth alone. The tool for Musk's ambition to save the human race from extinction is the firm he founded in 2002, SpaceX. Privately held, SpaceX is headquartered in Hawthorne, California, in southwestern Los Angeles County. Musk has raised billions of dollars to fund its capital-intensive activities. At the beginning of 2021, SpaceX was valued at between $80 billion and $100 billion, making it one of the most valuable privately held companies in the world.[51] The Musk magic—pure charisma—has attracted not only capital but thousands of talented engineers to build and launch rockets that can land and be reused.

Musk has said he wants to die on Mars but not on impact. In 2019, he predicted that people would land on that planet in four years.[52] In the words of biographer Ashlee Vance, "While the 'putting man on Mars' talk can strike some people as loopy, it gave Musk a unique rallying cry for his companies. It's the sweeping goal that forms a unifying principle over everything he does... When Musk sets unrealistic goals, verbally abuses employees, and works them to the bone, it's understood to be... part of the Mars agenda. Some employees love him for this. Others loathe him but remain oddly loyal out of respect for his drive and mission. What Musk has developed that so many of the entrepreneurs in Silicon Valley lack is a meaningful worldview. He's the possessed genius on the grandest quest anyone has ever concocted. He is less a CEO chasing riches than a general marshaling troops to secure a victory. Where Mark Zuckerberg wants to help you share baby photos, Musk wants to... save the human race from self-imposed or accidental annihilation."[53]

There is a lot of enthusiasm for Mars among a cadre of true believers. When you take a step back and think about what this really means, you pause. Highly recommended is George Dvorsky's article "Humans Will Never Colonize Mars." Aeronautics engineer Louis Friedman says that unfounded Mars enthusiasm is like the futurology of the 1940s and 1950s. "Back then, cover stories of magazines like *Popular Mechanics* and *Popular Science* showed colonies under the oceans and in the Antarctic. But this just hasn't happened."[54]

According to astrophysicist Martin Rees, "By 2100 thrill seekers... may have established 'bases' independent from the Earth—on Mars, or maybe on asteroids... But don't ever expect mass emigration from Earth. And here I disagree strongly with Musk and with my late Cambridge colleague Stephen Hawking, who enthuse about rapid build-up of large-scale Martian communities. It's a dangerous delusion to think that space offers an escape from Earth's problems. We've got to solve these problems here. Coping with climate change may seem daunting, but it's a doddle compared to terraforming

Mars. No place in our solar system offers an environment even as clement as the Antarctic or the top of Everest. There's no 'Planet B' for ordinary risk-averse people."[55]

Insofar as the Mars fantasy distracts first-class talent and investment dollars from the problems here on Earth, it is a barrier to their solution. The truth is that there is no way around dealing with the problems the human race faces on this planet. This leaves one wondering what Musk is up to. Has he been blinded by his own charisma? Does he really believe what he says about colonizing Mars? Or is this a way to motivate the troops in his innumerable other business ventures?

If it is the former, he is delusional. If it is the latter, he is the most charismatic leader in the business world today.

CHAPTER 13

STEVE JOBS: TRIUMPH AT APPLE

Steve Jobs was the only man in the whole world who could have saved Apple in 1997. And Apple needed to be saved. Mismanaged successively by Sculley, who was kicked out in 1993, Michael Spindler, fired in 1996, and Gil Amelio, a member of the board who took over from Spindler and was fired five hundred days later, the company was failing. Without going into the gory details, Apple's products had deteriorated, its marketing was dreadful, and its finances would have collapsed had it not been for CFO Fred Anderson's work. The world of computers was dominated by Microsoft, especially after the introduction of its breakthrough product, Windows 95, in August of 1995.

Apple went shopping for a new operating system in a desperate attempt to remain relevant in the world of Windows 95. In a remarkable turn of events, Apple's then CEO, Amelio, engineered the purchase of NeXT in December of 1996 for the startlingly high price of $429 million in cash and stock.[1]

NeXTSTEP and WebObjects saved Steve and his investors in NeXT. Steve was at last free from that incubus. Apple not only acquired an operating system, it acquired Avie Tevanian, a gifted engineer, as chief of software. On the hardware side, the equally talented Jon Rubinstein, also from NeXT, became chief engineer.

But what about Steve? What role would he play? We are given to believe that Steve was very much of two minds about his next move. He was not a boy wonder anymore. He was forty-two, with a family and with more than a billion dollars in assets. His marriage was a success. He loved the children he had with his wife and fully acknowledged that he was the father of Lisa Brennan-Jobs, although the mixture of cruelty and kindness with which he treated her would have driven a less innately well-grounded person crazy. Pixar was a screaming success. Those who viewed *Toy Story* and the productions that followed found them deeply touching. They would not have existed without Steve, who knew a great story when he saw one.

NeXT was a failure. Steve had wanted to achieve at NeXT what he had wanted to achieve at Apple from its founding in 1976 to his firing in 1985. He still believed that the future was all about the computer. He agreed to act as an advisor to Amelio, promising to "help Gil in any way he asks me to," illustrating that when Steve offered to help, one was well advised to watch one's back.[2]

Amelio was an able technologist. He held a PhD in physics from Georgia Tech. He had extensive experience in the semiconductor industry and deeper knowledge of technology than Steve. He might have been a successful CEO in the era of Harlow Curtice. He was utterly without charisma. As he himself wrote, "Some reporters weighed me against Steve Jobs and rated me low on the charisma scale... I'm a good administrator... Steve captivates audiences."[3] Amelio was preparing for Apple's bankruptcy soon after he became CEO.

At a dinner party one evening at which Larry Ellison was present, it was reported that Amelio described Apple's situation as follows: "Apple is a boat. There is a hole in the boat, and it's taking on water. But there's also a treasure on board. And the problem is, everyone on board is rowing in different directions, so the boat is just standing still. My job is to get everyone rowing in the same direction." After Amelio left, Ellison is said to have asked another guest, "But what about the hole?" Amelio said the report of this remark was "meant to make me look foolish, and succeeded, but I found [the story] funny nonetheless."[4] Steve enjoyed telling this story.[5] Doubtless it is among the reasons he felt comfortable doing to Amelio what Sculley had done to him.

Apple was circling the drain when the computer industry was booming. It was obvious to any sentient being that Amelio was not the man to save it. Michael Dell said it should be liquidated. Did Steve really want to put himself through what was needed to fix this company? At one point, he phoned Intel's Andy Grove at two o'clock in the morning and walked him through the pros and cons. Grove's advice? "Steve, look. I don't give a shit about Apple. [He should have.] Just make up your mind."[6]

There are two reasons that only Steve Jobs could have saved Apple in 1997. First, Jobs persuaded Bill Gates to continue supporting Apple by announcing a five-year commitment to writing software, specifically Office for the Mac. Microsoft Office was and still is the standard, and without it, the hole in the Apple boat Amelio described in his comic-opera way would have only grown larger. Jobs also convinced Gates to invest $150 million in nonvoting shares of Apple. Amelio had attempted to negotiate a similar arrangement with Gates and had failed.

Second, Steve was able to endow the work of others with meaning as no one else at Apple could. Fred Anderson, who was hired as chief financial officer in 1996 and did yeoman work keeping Apple afloat financially despite its declining sales, said Steve "understood the soul of Apple. We needed a spiritual leader that could bring Apple back as a great product and marketing company. And nobody else great, who had those skills, was going to take on Apple... So we had to have Steve."[7]

So they had to have Steve. They got him. Amelio was summarily ousted on September 16, 1997. He wrote, "I had, along with many others... been trapped by the charisma and boldness of this unusual man."[8] Steve became "interim" CEO, a title he held for three years. This is where the *i* comes from in Apple's products. The "interim" was dropped in 2000.

In the years from 1997 to his death in 2011, Steve became an icon of the business world—the man who defined charisma in the context of enterprise. Four reasons stand out: the creation of Apple Retail, the iPod, the iPhone, and the iPad. We will take a look at each.

In order to transform Apple into the vehicle to fulfill his ambition, Jobs had to whip the company into shape. His goal was not only to make a dent in the universe but also perhaps, in the far-off and unimaginable future, to put himself on par with Bill Gates. In the words of a book published in 2005, "Like all the best fights, this one is personal. Steve Jobs is going to best Bill Gates. This fight is Shakespearean, elemental, and emotional..."[9] Jobs had complete, dictatorial control. He selected his own Board of Directors. He was the dog that had caught the freight train. Now he had to figure out what to do with it. The computer industry creates more has-beens more quickly than any other. Steve was determined not to be one of them.

This meant firing a lot of people to cut costs. Head count dropped by almost 40 percent, from 10,896 to 6,658.[10] Products were fired, too. Apple in the years preceding Steve's return had fallen into the hands of its distributors. Each wanted a customized computer that it could claim was made only for its stores. So Apple spent a lot of time and money producing different machines for different retail outlets. These represented no advance in technology. This is an approach a desperate company adopts when any sale on any terms that makes any contribution to the bottom line has to be jumped at. No more effective way to annihilate the magic that Apple had once been can be imagined.

Moreover, SKU creep—that is, product proliferation—increases the complexity of managing a company. Every computer needs engineers and marketers. Inventory management can become a nightmare. In 1998, unsold, unsellable inventory was ruthlessly reduced from $400 million to $78 million.[11]

When Steve returned to the company, there were numerous product platforms: the 1400, 2400, 3400, 4400, 5400, 5500, 6500, 7300, 7600, 8600, 9600, 20, e-Mate, and Pippin, with, as Jobs put it, "a zillion variants with each one." "How are we going to explain this to others," Jobs asked, "if we don't even know which products to recommend to our friends?"[12]

Jobs's solution became known throughout the company: the two-by-two matrix. On the horizontal axis, Consumer and

Pro[fessional]. On the vertical axis: Desktop and Portable. In the upper left cell, there is the iMac, Apple's first success after Jobs's return. In the lower left cell, iBook. In the upper right cell, Power Macintosh. And in the lower right cell, PowerBook G3.[13] These were bold moves. It is easier to start something than to stop it, but in one day Steve put a stop to a lot. These are products that the company had been selling to its customers as the best in class. Suddenly, they were no more.

A key to rebuilding Apple was engineering an efficient supply chain. There was no one at Apple with the necessary expertise. Tim Cook had made a name for himself first at IBM and then at Compaq, where he was happy with his position. Apple had tried to hire Cook a number of times, but he was not interested. When Jobs called, however, it was a different matter: "Steve created the whole industry that I'm in. I'd love to meet him."[14]

"Any purely rational consideration of cost and benefits lined up in Compaq's favor," Cook said, "and the people who know me best advised me to stay at Compaq. One CEO I consulted felt so strongly about it he told me I would be a fool to leave Compaq for Apple."[15]

Now we see Steve's charisma in action. "Five minutes into my initial interview with Steve, I wanted to throw caution and logic to the wind and join Apple. My intuition told me that joining Apple would be a once-in-a-lifetime opportunity to work with a creative genius."[16]

The first day that Cook arrived at Apple's headquarters at 1 Infinite Loop in Cupertino, he had to cross a picket line made up of customers angry that the company was no longer supporting the Newton.[17] This was a handheld personal digital assistant championed by Sculley that was supposed to be able to recognize handwriting. It never worked well and had limited sales, but nevertheless it did attract some devoted customers. Steve directed that the picketers be offered free coffee and doughnuts. Legend has it that the refreshments were offered at the far end of the parking lot so that when reporters interviewed the picketers, the company's headquarters did not appear in the background.

Two phrases circulated through the company soon after Steve's return: "Focus and Simplify" and "Think Different." The former is an enactment of the latter.

When these phrases were making the rounds at Apple, I was teaching cases at the Harvard Business School, celebrating executives such as Alfred P. Sloan Jr. as masters of complex organization. I do not remember teaching a case in the thirty-one years I spent on the HBS faculty on an executive celebrated for simplifying complex organizations and managing simplicity. That is what Jobs did with the two-by-two matrix. His presentation of the new approach was exceptionally daring.

A great deal happened at Apple with Steve's leadership from 1997 to 2000. Old products were killed. New products and services developed. Most important, a team equal or superior to any other in the industry was assembled. They were a "mature, experienced, and disciplined" group willing to push back "fiercely" when they thought Steve was misguided.[18]

Unfortunately, the numbers did not indicate much progress. Eddy Cue, a key member of the new team, said early in 2001, "We can't make things better than we're making them. Yet we're in the same place we were in 1997." Steve told him to be patient. "People will come around."[19] Steve's counseling patience showed how much he had grown.

The numbers were, in fact, problematic. In fiscal year 1997, sales and profits were $7.1 billion and $1.5 billion respectively. Market capitalization at the end of the year was $2.8 billion. Those numbers in 2000 were $8 billion, $2.3 billion, and $8.4 billion. In 2001, the year of the great technology bust, the numbers were $5.4 billion, $1.2 billion, and $7.71 billion. On the last day of 1999, Apple's market capitalization was $10.2 billion. Microsoft's was $619.3 billion. On Wednesday, May 26, 2010, Apple's market capitalization exceeded Microsoft's.[20] Waiting did pay off.

APPLE RETAIL

There are a lot of reasons why forward integrating into retail was a bad idea for Apple. Retail is difficult. It demands a lot of employees, and in the case of Apple products, it demands employees who understand and can explain complex devices. Store site location is a science unto itself and one with which Steve had no familiarity. More threatening in a business where products become outdated quickly and therefore inventory becomes worthless, there is always the danger that the retail outlet will stock not what the consumer wants but what the factory has made too much of. Other computer companies, most notably Gateway, had opened their own stores and failed to execute successfully. Gateway closed a hundred stores.[21]

Steve, however, felt that Apple products were special. Stores that retailed them did not understand how they should be displayed, and their salespeople did not know the difference between one computer and another. So Steve made the decision to take the plunge into retail. And he decided to locate Apple's stores in high-traffic areas in upscale shopping malls. This is yet another "Think Different" decision. A computer at the turn of the century was hardly an impulse purchase item. It was an expensive consumer durable that most people would keep for more than three years. What was the point of paying the leasing costs for a store across from a high-traffic apparel retailer in the heart of a shopping mall?

Steve Jobs was a man at the edge of history, the quintessential charismatic business leader. He translated the future to the present.

Apple redefined retail. Apple's stores are the sites at which Steve and his company forged a distinctive charismatic connection with the customer. Consider the remarkable Apple flagship store at Fifth Avenue and Fifty-Ninth Street in Manhattan, opened in 2006. That store is actually in the basement. But above it is suspended the Apple logo within a translucent cube. Apple transformed the skyline of Manhattan with a thirty-two-foot-high cube. It is no accident that when Steve died, so many people placed flowers in front of and wrote notes posted on the windows of the retail stores.

In the late 1990s, Steve was not quite the know-it-all he had been as a youth. He was aware that he was no retailer. So he recruited Millard "Mickey" Drexler to the board in 1999. At the time, Drexler was CEO of The Gap, a power chain of clothing retail stores at the peak of its success.[22] The fact that Jobs could persuade Drexler to join the board is testimony to his charisma. Drexler was a retail maven running what at the time was a company that was hot as a pistol. Apple still looked to the world like an also-ran.

Equally if not more important, Jobs hired Ron Johnson to serve as senior vice president for retail in 2000. Johnson, a graduate of the Harvard Business School in 1984—interestingly enough, the only HBS graduate to play a key role in the rebirth of Apple—had turned down the standard Wall Street career path for HBS graduates in favor of retailing. He had made a name for himself by bringing class to the masses at Target, where he was vice president of merchandising.

Target seems an out-of-the-way place for Steve to look in order to find an executive who could reinvent retail. By this time, however, Steve's ability to spot talent was unequaled. Johnson is a charismatic man himself, not afraid to work on loading docks or clean floors in stores that needed it. In 2021, Apple had about 147,000 employees, probably half of whom worked in retail. Ron Johnson is a people person. He had a lot in common with Steve, especially in his willingness to depart from the conventional wisdom. As one journalist put it, "Necessity and inspiration led Apple to toss out the conventional textbook on computer stores and to ignore the rules of location, design, staffing, and services provided."[23] Four years younger than Steve, Johnson saw Apple as an opportunity to build retail stores from scratch with a man he regarded as the most creative executive in business.

Steve's obsession with secrecy was everywhere apparent in the retail project. When Johnson arrived in Cupertino, he was—it is said—given an alias to use at Apple—John Bruce. Johnson was well known in the retail world—he had climbed the ladder at Target for sixteen years—and Steve did not want questions asked about why Apple hired him.

This is odd. First, Apple wasn't followed that closely in 2000. Second, Ron Johnson is not an uncommon name. Third, the assumption that people would make the leap from hiring a very successful executive to the conclusion that Apple was going to jump into retail with both feet is at least questionable. Fourth, it was public knowledge that Drexler had joined the board the previous year. But such was life at Apple when Jobs was running the company. Since there was no record of anyone named John Bruce being hired, it took a bit longer than usual for Johnson to get his identification badge.

In keeping with the secrecy surrounding the birth of Apple retail, a prototype was set up well away from Infinite Loop. An incident in the development of retail is a good illustration of what it was like to work with Steve in his forties rather than his twenties. After months of working on the prototype, Johnson suddenly believed that they had it all wrong. As he and Steve drove to see the prototype, he proposed a fundamentally different idea.

Steve's reaction? "Do you know how big a change this is? I don't have time for this. I don't want you to say a word to anyone about this. I don't know what I think of this." Not another word was said on the drive. When two men got to the prototype, Steve said to the team, "Ron thinks we've designed our stores all wrong. And he's right, so I'm going to leave now and you should just do what he's going to tell you to do."[24]

This was the impact of Ed Catmull on Steve. Later that day, Steve said to Johnson, "[Y]ou reminded me of something I learned at Pixar. On almost every film they make, something turns out to be not quite right. And they have an amazing willingness to turn around and do it again till they do get it right. They have always had a willingness to not be governed by the release date. It's not about how fast you do something, it's about doing your level best."[25]

Apple opened its first two stores on May 19, 2001, at Tysons Corner Center Mall in McLean, Virginia, near Washington, DC, and in the Glendale Galleria in Glendale, California, not far from downtown Los Angeles. In 2021, Apple had 511 stores around the world. Scads of statistics could be marshalled to illustrate the success of Apple's retail strategy. But let's take a step back.

Think of your own first visit to an Apple Store. If it was on a usual business day, you probably would have encountered the busiest store in the mall. Plenty of customers and plenty of help. Nevertheless, the store did not seem crowded. The tables at the center were clean and simple and appealing. The graphics on the walls were beautiful. Attention had been paid to every detail.

The salespeople were not actually selling. They were not on commission. If you did not know which computer to purchase, they were as likely to advise a less expensive as a more expensive one. If you wanted to use your computer more efficiently, there was a Genius Bar where experts on Apple's products could, usually by appointment, show you how to do what you wanted done. If by chance none of the geniuses could solve a problem, there was a red phone, a hotline, on which they could directly contact an engineer in Cupertino. They would take as much time as was necessary. You were receiving expert help. Apple, as high a high-technology company as exists, had undertaken a foray into the oldest form of business, retail. Steve succeeded because he redefined the retail experience. The staff was there not to sell but to serve.

Steve was criticized for all the obvious reasons for opening retail stores. Today, there is not one city in the world without an Apple Store that would not welcome one. Nor is there one city that has one that would not welcome another. For two decades, retailing has been in a secular decline. Store closings and bankruptcies regularly headline the news. But

Apple Retail has been on a tear. This is what happens when a charismatic leader invents the new.

THE IPOD

Apple announced the iPod on October 23, 2001, and shipped it on November 10. No one in the company, the industry, or the whole world dreamed at that time that Apple would sell four hundred million units of the product.[26]

The idea of combining music with mobility was nothing new. Radios in cars began to appear in the late 1920s, but they only became popular after the Galvin Manufacturing Company introduced the Motorola 5T71 Radio in 1930.[27] Indeed, Motorola is a combination of "motor" and "Victrola," and that became the company's name in 1947.[28] The transistor was invented late in 1947, and transistor radios were introduced in 1954. A great many were sold, and young people carrying them around and listening to music on the go became a common sight by the end of the decade. This was followed by the boom-box craze in the latter half of the 1970s.

Sony developed the Walkman in 1979. Domestic demand was so great that exports could not begin until the following year. The original Walkman consisted of a cassette deck and headphones. Two hundred million of these were sold. Sony developed eighty different models of the Walkman as "Walkman became a household word around the world..." By 2009, Sony had sold 309 million Walkman and Discman devices.[29]

Not only did Sony have an outstanding experience with mobility, it owned a great deal of music. Sony purchased CBS Records in 1988 and has been an important player in the industry ever since. If any company was going to dominate the industry in the twenty-first century, it should have been Sony. It had everything... except Steve Jobs.

On January 9, 2001, Jobs introduced Apple's "Digital Hub" strategy. Digital was the future; analog the past. At a time when many were saying that the glory days of the PC were drawing to a close, Jobs doubled down on the Mac.[30] He saw it as the center of the "digital lifestyle" that would characterize life in the twenty-first century. There was a veritable "explosion of new digital devices." These included cell phones, portable music players such as "CDs and their cousins the new solid-state MP3 players," digital camcorders, DVD players, digital cameras, which "now constitute 15 percent of all cameras sold in the US. It'll be 50 percent in a few years" (he was more prescient than he knew), and handheld organizers.[31]

Why did you need a PC when the digital world was fragmenting all around you? Jobs offered four reasons. The PC could run complex applications. The devices he mentioned could not do so. "They don't have enough horsepower." Second, the PC had a big screen, which permitted a much better user interface. User interface (or UI, as it is known in the trade) had always been critical to Jobs. That is why he understood the value of the mouse way back in 1979.[32] Third, PCs could burn discs, which digital devices could not do. Fourth, computers had large, inexpensive storage. In addition, the PC offered faster internet access than any of the digital devices just mentioned. The PC could not only add value to these devices, it could interconnect them.

The focus of this presentation was the relationship between the camcorder and Apple's new iMovie2 application. What was not mentioned was the iPod. It had not yet been created. And it was music rather than video that would transform Apple. "I felt like a dope," Jobs said. "I thought we had missed it. We had to work hard to catch up."[33]

Apple did more than catch up. The company transformed both the technology industry and the music industry with the iPod. The product was put together with remarkable speed. The idea of a digital music player had been around for a long time. The first such device was invented in Britain in 1979 and patented there in 1985 and in the United States two years later.[34] Here we see again the important lesson that technology casts a long shadow.

Jobs started talking about a digital music player in the fall of 2000, but hardware chief Jon Rubinstein told him the necessary components did not exist. However, in February 2001 during the Macworld show in Tokyo, Rubinstein made one of his regular visits to Toshiba, which supplied Apple's hard drives. Executives there showed him a tiny hard drive newly developed. Its diameter was 1.8 inches. The hard drive Fujitsu supplied to the MP3 players on the market was 2.5 inches in diameter.

This tiny hard drive posed a problem for Toshiba. "They said they didn't know what to do with it. Maybe put it in a small notebook."[35] Rubinstein said nothing in the moment, but he knew exactly what to do with it. He met with Jobs that evening at the Hotel Okura in Tokyo. "I went back to Steve and I said, 'I know how to do this. I've got all the parts.' [Steve] said, 'Go for it.'" For $10 million, Apple obtained exclusive rights for all the 1.8-inch disk drives Toshiba could supply.[36]

There were a lot of hurdles yet to be jumped. "No one had any idea what the end product would look like, or how users would control it..." No one knew a myriad of things. All they knew was that the device had to look great, ease of use was essential, and Steve wanted it right away.[37]

As a leader of the team, Rubinstein recruited Tony Fadell, who at the age of thirty-one had already made a name for himself as an entrepreneur and technologist. Fadell put together an outstanding group and got help from around the company. It was the iPod that vividly illustrated the advantages of having hardware, software (iTunes), design (run by Jony—soon to be Sir Jonathan—Ive), audio engineers, microprocessor experts, battery experts, and more all working in the same firm. By this point in Apple's history, Steve's charisma had recruited the top people in each of these fields to Apple.

There were other MP3 players and portable music players of various description on the market. Apple was not the first mover. But the competition was hamstrung by being difficult to use, by being able to play only a limited amount of music, or by some other serious shortcomings. In the words of Greg Joswiak (known universally as Joz), an Apple marketing vice president, "The products stank."[38] Apple was going to create a device the like of which had never been seen.

There are innumerable features that made the iPod special. One of these was the click wheel, also referred to as the scroll wheel. If you were going to have a device the size of a deck of cards that could hold a thousand songs, how were you going to navigate it? How were you going to find the track to which you wanted to listen?

The click wheel was the brainchild of Phil Schiller, senior vice president of marketing. "One day I went into Steve's office and said, 'Hey, all these other competitive devices make you click on the buttons and go next song, next song, next song. If you've got a thousand songs, you don't want to press it a thousand times. We had been talking about how great the device should be if you go running, which meant you had to be able to do it one-handed. And the idea came to me that we can apply the idea of a wheel to a music player. If you could rotate around continuously on a wheel, and you could have acceleration, that would really be great.'"[39] He was right. It was.

During the development process, Jobs had ideas every day. In Fadell's words, "We would have this swirling thing of Steve's latest idea, and we would all try to stay ahead of it. Every day there was something like that, whether it was a switch here, or a button color, or a pricing strategy issue. With his style, you needed to work with your peers, watch each other's back."[40]

When Steve introduced the iPod on October 23, 2001, he observed that the product put a thousand songs in your pocket. Your entire music library, or at least a large fraction of it, could be with you all the time. That was the first "major breakthrough" that Steve featured in his keynote. The iPod was "ultraportable." It was 2.4 inches wide, four inches tall, and 0.78 inches thick. It weighed 6.5 ounces, lighter than most cell phones.

The second breakthrough was made possible by Apple's "legendary ease of use." With all your music on an iPod, you had to be able to search by "playlist, artist, album, and song." The "unique scroll wheel" made that possible. The third major breakthrough was "auto-sync," which meant that it was seamless to transfer music from the Mac to the iPod. Only a firm that owned the hardware and software could create this experience.[41]

When Bill Gates saw the iPod, he said, "It looks like a great product." This is a far cry from his reaction to NeXT. He then asked, with a note of incredulity, "It's only for the Macintosh?"[42] Macs had only 5 percent of the market. The question Gates asked was vital.

The iPod was priced at $399 at a time when you could buy an MP3 player for a lot less than that. The Sony Discman (mobility but not an MP3 player) retailed for under $100.[43] This high price—in this instance a bit too high—was classic Apple. The company disrupted markets from above, by bringing out a product that was much better than what was available on the market. Apple has always been a premium products company that sold products at premium prices.

Neither Steve nor his executives knew how big the iPod was going to be. The keynote introducing it was held in Town Hall, a rather unattractive auditorium on the Infinite Loop campus, which accommodates about two hundred people. All the reporters attending received a free iPod. The reviews of the product were excellent. Nevertheless, the iPod did not fly off the shelves immediately. The first quarter the product was available, Apple sold 150,000 units.[44]

Given the excellence of the product, why were sales not greater? There are a lot of reasons. First, Apple was known as a computer company. In the words of Schlender and Tetzeli, computers were its "focus and raison d'être."[45] It was not known as a digital device company. Second, the price was high, even by Apple's standards. When Apple introduced a new and improved version, Steve cut the price of the original by $100.[46] Third, the iPod was available only to Mac owners. This ruled out the great bulk of the potential market.

Sales kept climbing, helped by outstanding advertising and publicity. The iPod was the star of a special edition of Oprah's "Favorite Things" on *The Oprah Winfrey Show* in May of 2003. (The iTunes Music Store had launched on April 27.) "This music player is truly genius," Oprah told her studio audience as well as the millions watching the program on television. The latest edition of the iPod held thirty-seven hundred songs. "This fifteen-gigabyte Apple iPod cost $399, but," she told her ecstatic studio audience of 350, "I got some music for your ears because you're going home with your own iPod for free." (It is believed that Apple provided these iPods to Winfrey free of charge.) "Enthusiastic" fails to convey the way the Queen of All Media pitched this product. When the fifth generation iPod hit the market in 2005, she called it one of her favorite things for that year. Only she could endow a product with the American equivalent of a royal imprimatur.[47]

A vital decision about the iPod's future was made in 2003. Should it be made available to Windows users?—the very question Bill Gates raised when he first saw the iPod in 2001. Steve was opposed. He insisted the iPod was driving sales of the Mac. To him, that was the point. But every other executive on the iPod team disagreed. "It was really a big argument for months, me against everyone else." Steve was adamant. Windows would get the iPod "over my dead body."[48]

The iPod team kept pushing. At one point, Jobs said, "Until you can prove to me that it will make business sense, I am not going to do it." The team wanted Steve to think in terms of "iPod, Inc." If it were a standalone company, what was the right decision for this remarkable product? A spreadsheet was developed, which, said Phil Schiller, demonstrated beyond peradventure that there was no amount of cannibalization of Mac sales that would outweigh the sales of iPods. Steve's reaction on hearing his challenge met? "Screw it. I'm sick of listening to you assholes. Go do whatever the hell you want."[49] Hard to imagine Harlow Curtice talking this way.

The story has one more chapter. If the iPod were to be made available to Windows users, was iTunes software to be made available to them as well? This time Schiller and Jobs switched sides. Jobs said yes. If the consumer was to have an Apple experience, it had to be outstanding. But Schiller "thought that was crazy, since we didn't make Windows software."[50]

A middle way was decided upon. Software was provided by a company called MusicMatch. Opinion was unanimous that the result was really bad. "That was the worst of all worlds," observed Jobs, "because [MusicMatch] was controlling a big piece of the user experience. So we lived with this crappy outside jukebox for about six months and then we finally got iTunes written for Windows."

Jobs announced iTunes for Windows at a Macworld special event in October of 2003. He talked about the new features of the second generation of iTunes. Then he paused briefly and said, "But there is one more feature. This feature a lot of people thought we would never add until this happened." When he said "this happened," he pointed to a large screen behind him on which were written the words, "Hell froze over." After pointing to the screen, the letters in "Hell froze over" fell to the bottom and dissolved. Then he brought the house down: "iTunes for Windows is probably the best Windows app ever written."[51] Steve bet that the combination of iTunes software and the iPod would introduce a whole new market to Apple quality. He was right. The iPod is still very much alive in 2021. In fact, it is still being used to introduce consumers to Apple.[52]

With phenomenal speed, the iPod became an iconic product. Journalist Steven Levy, author of *The Perfect Thing: How the iPod Shuffles Commerce, Culture, and Coolness*, noted that people were swapping iPods to learn about one another. "Simply handing over your iPod to a friend, your blind date, or the total stranger sitting next to you on the plane opened you up like a book. All somebody needs to do is scroll through your library on that click wheel, and musically speaking, you're naked. It's not just what you like—it's *who you are*."[53] Schlender and Tetzeli are right in saying that "The iPod had changed everything for Apple."[54] Consumer electronics is a much faster-moving business than computers. The world expected and received a new and improved model of the iPod every year.

The iPod was supported by the iTunes Store, which "opened its virtual doors" on April 28, 2003. In less than a decade, it became the largest music vendor in the world. "How did [Apple] get the music companies to go along?" asked a senior executive at Microsoft when he first saw the iTunes Store.[55] The answer is that by the early 2000s, Steve had become perhaps the most skillful negotiator in business.

Sales and profits at Apple were outstanding, growing from $5.4 billion and $1.2 billion respectively in FY 2001 to $8.3 billion and $2.9 billion in FY 2004. Market capitalization during these years almost tripled to $15 billion. This happened despite the fact that Mac sales were declining. Observers who had predicted back in 2000 that the growth era of the PC was over were correct.

The iPod combined with the iTunes Store did more than arrive in the nick of time to save Apple from the secular decline in the computer industry. They made possible the gathering together of a group of technologist executives second to none in the world. Creating a product that consumers can't get enough of, and are willing to pay a high price for, is a powerful drug. All the key players at Apple became addicted.

The first Apple product I bought was an iPod. It was a twenty-gigabyte model, oddly enough cobranded with Hewlett-Packard. When Oprah Winfrey featured the iPod among her favorite things, she said, "I'm such a techno-illiterate, I was saying [to a man with her on the stage], how does the music get in there [pointing at the iPod]?"[56] I had the same question when I bought mine. My solution was not to rip, mix, and burn scores of CDs into a computer and then transfer them to an iPod. I simply brought the iPod and my CDs to a teenager and asked him to make it happen.

THE IPHONE

The iPhone was born in 2007. The world was already awash in mobile phones. Billions had been sold. The first handheld mobile phone was produced by Motorola in 1973. It weighed two and a half pounds and measured nine inches in height. You could talk for thirty-five minutes. Recharging took ten hours.[57] The iPhone story is yet another example of technology casting a long shadow.

By 2007, mobile phones were ubiquitous. Some brands were well-known. Nokia, a company in Finland established on May 12, 1865, to make paper, found its way into the telecommunications business and by the early twenty-first century was a major player in mobile phones. So was BlackBerry, manufactured by the Canadian company Research in Motion. When he was a candidate for the presidency in 2008, Barack Obama used a BlackBerry, and that made news. These devices were so addictive that they were nicknamed "CrackBerry." Motorola also had a hit with its Razr.

Once again, Apple was late to the party. Once again, it disrupted the industry from above by producing an expensive smartphone that was worth the money. Steve Jobs was the driving force behind this initiative. He was the decider in chief on all the most important issues in the creation of the device.

It all seems so obvious now. We are used to the iPhone. Two billion two hundred million have been sold.[58] This accounts for 20 percent to 40 percent of the market, depending upon the country in which market share is being measured. In terms of profit, Apple's performance has been commanding. In 2016, for example, Apple captured almost four out of every five dollars of smartphone profits worldwide. Most other smartphone makers must have lost money on each phone they sold. The iPhone is the most successful consumer product of this century so far. It is the standard against which all other smartphones are measured. Samsung, the Korean giant, copied it pixel by pixel.[59]

In fact, nothing was obvious. It was not even clear in 2003 and 2004 that Apple would enter the already crowded phone industry. Perhaps it should break some new ground in the computer space by coming out with a tablet, which Apple eventually did in 2010 when it brought out the iPad. Schlender and Tetzeli report that "five cell phone– and tablet-related products" were "percolating" in 2004.[60]

In addition to all this uncertainty, the matter of life and death reared its ugly head. In October of 2003, Jobs was diagnosed with a pancreatic neuroendocrine tumor. This shocking, startling news was orthogonal to all the major business decisions on which he had to focus.[61] Immediate surgery was called for. Not until July 31 of the following year did he consent to have the tumor surgically removed.

Steve postponed his surgery because he was simply not ready to have his body cut open and because he wanted to allow time to regress to the magical thinking that characterized the mystical musings of his youth. What these nine months were like for his wife is unimaginable. Equally hard to figure out is how he himself was affected during this period.

When you have potentially terminal cancer, each morning you die a little. You wake up, and it doesn't hit you at first. Then it does. You have to have lived through this experience to know how horrifying it is and what willpower is required to think about anything else.

Jobs was a very public person by this time. Apple's stock price would move on news of a health crisis. He had to keep his condition strictly under wraps until the time was right.

The day after his surgery, Jobs wrote a blast email to Apple employees informing the "team" of what had transpired. He wrote that he had "a very rare form of pancreatic cancer," which was true. He continued that his disease "can be cured by surgical removal if diagnosed in time (mine was)," which was not quite true.[62] It is not known when Steve was told that the surgeons spotted metastases to the liver. He had always believed he would die young. This belief was to be proven correct. It is against this backdrop that the future of Apple was being decided.

The decision that was taken was to put the tablet on hold and go for the phone. "Everybody carried two devices. A cell phone and an iPod," according to Eddy Cue. "We knew you could add iTunes to a phone and it would be almost like an iPod. It was mostly a software problem."[63] Therefore, both for defensive reasons (a competitor who made a phone could add an iPod to it, and it is better to cannibalize yourself than to be cannibalized by someone else) and for offensive reasons (the market for mobile phones was competitive but very large), the phone was to be the next big thing for Apple.

What was the iPhone to look like? What materials would it be made of? What carrier would be chosen to transmit its signal? What was the optimal user interface? These questions and a host of others needed answers.

Stories about the iPhone are endless. There was plenty of argument. You could fight Jobs, but it took a lot of courage. You really had to know what you were talking about. No question about it, he was smart. By this time, his words were law at the company.

For the UI, one thought was the scroll wheel because it was working so well with the iPod. It turned out to work very well for looking up phone numbers but could not be adapted to dialing them.

Another possibility was a physical keyboard like the Black-Berry. But the physical keyboard was clunky. There was nothing clever about it, and aesthetically it left much to be desired. Perhaps worst of all, it left very little room for the screen. The phone was a small device. Steve wanted the screen to have as much space as possible. To make matters more problematic, the buttons and controls of a physical keyboard can't change. They were fixed in plastic, thus limiting what the phone itself could do. The ideal would be a software keyboard that was there when you wanted it but disappeared when you did not. No one knew in 2004 whether it was possible to build such a feature. A normal company would have market tested various approaches. However, that was never the Apple way. Jobs believed, as did Edwin Land, that consumers did not know what they wanted. It was up to Apple to tell them.

Eventually, what was decided upon was the screen we have today. A touch-screen keyboard appears when you want it and disappears when you want something else. It was the perfect solution to a critically important problem. Jobs cracked the whip on every aspect of the phone. At one meeting with the UI team, for example, he said their work was unacceptable. They had to "start showing me something good soon, or I'll give the project to another team." Greg Christie, the vice president managing this project, rented rooms in the Cupertino Inn, a short walk from the Infinite Loop campus, and had his team sleep there for two weeks. They literally worked 24-7 to come up with something that pleased Steve. And they succeeded. In the words of Tony Fadell, the whole iPhone project was "a roller coaster ride, and if it ain't scary, it ain't fun."[64]

One of the best illustrations of the challenge and response involved in the development of the phone was gorilla glass. Originally, the plan was to make the phone's screen of plastic. Legend—and it's nothing more or less than that—has it that Jobs was walking around Palo Alto with a prototype of the phone in his pocket. His keys scratched the screen. This would never do. The answer was glass.[65] The question was where to find it.

A mutual friend suggested that Jobs get in touch with Wendell P. Weeks, CEO of Corning. Founded in 1851, Corning had been in the glass business for a long time. Jobs phoned Weeks, and the switchboard put him through to an assistant who offered to give Weeks the message that Jobs wanted to speak to him. "No," said Jobs, who by now expected defer-ence, "I am Steve Jobs. Put me through." He did not get his way and called the person who told him to contact Weeks to complain about the "typical East Coast bullshit"[66] to which he was being subjected. Weeks heard about this and called the Apple switchboard asking to speak to Jobs. The switchboard operator told him to write his request and fax it, thus demon-strating what might be called "typical West Coast bullshit." Such is life among big shots.

The two men finally managed to arrange a meeting in Cu-pertino. Weeks told Jobs that years ago, Corning developed a very strong product, which it called gorilla glass. Unfortu-nately, the product could not find a market, so Corning did not manufacture it. Jobs told Weeks that it probably was not what Apple wanted anyway and proceeded to explain to him how glass was made.

Weeks, who graduated from Lehigh, which is famous for its engineering, as well as from the Harvard Business School, was infinitely more knowledgeable about glass than Jobs. Rather than sitting through Jobs's tutorial, he interrupted: "Can you shut up and let me teach you some science?" The re-sult was that Jobs said he wanted as much gorilla glass as Corning could make, and he wanted it within six months.[67] What we see repeatedly is that when people push back against Jobs's arrogance, the best results ensue. Not when they kowtow. This seems to be the important message about his charisma—his ability to be pushed against and the magic that can happen with that friction.

Weeks told him he couldn't have gorilla glass. "We don't have the capacity. None of our plants makes the glass now." Weeks then discovered that Jobs did not take no for an answer. "Don't be afraid," he said. "Yes, you can do it. Don't be afraid. Get your mind around it. You can do it."[68] We should pause at this exchange. Jobs echoed Mary Kay's mother—"You can do it!" Charismatic people are persuasive.

Corning did it "in under six months. We produced a glass that had never been made. We put our best scientists and engineers on it, and we just made it work." In an unusually graceful gesture, Jobs sent Weeks a note on the day the iPhone was announced. "We couldn't have done it without you."[69] This episode is reminiscent of Jon Rubinstein finding the tiny disk drive at Toshiba. A product was created that a company did not know what to do with, but Apple did.

The iPhone was announced on Tuesday, January 9, 2007. This keynote was held not in Town Hall but in San Francisco's gigantic Moscone Center. Naturally, Jobs took center stage, speaking for just under eighty minutes. "Every once in a while, a revolutionary product comes along that changes everything." The packed auditorium, shouting and applauding, was introduced to one such product on this occasion. Jobs began by saying that Apple was introducing three new products: a wide-screen iPod with touch controls, a revolutionary new mobile phone, and a breakthrough internet communications device. "Are you getting it? These are not three separate devices. This is one device. And we are calling it iPhone. Today Apple is going to reinvent the phone." Multitouch was the UI for the new era. Jobs said it "works like magic," has no stylus (you use your fingers), was unfailingly accurate, ignored unintended touches, and responded to multifinger gestures.

The keynote was a masterpiece of high-tech showmanship. The stage looked gigantic, perhaps forty feet wide by fifteen feet deep. The screen behind Jobs was also huge, about thirty feet long and ten feet high. The Apple executives in the audience held their breath. This was a live demo. They knew how unfinished the phone was. Any problem with it would be on display globally. They were naked before the world. With the exception of one small glitch advancing slides—which had nothing to do with the phone itself and was quickly remedied—the presentation was flawless. Steve was animated and enthusiastic, but he seemed relaxed.[70]

The phone had strained every neuron of the best engineers at Apple for two and a half years. It was looked upon by some as a "bet the company" project. According to one journalist, the iPhone effort was "so complex that it occasionally threatened to derail the entire corporation. Many of the top engineers in the company were being sucked into the project, forcing slowdowns in the timetables of other projects. Had the iPhone been a dud or not gotten off the ground at all, Apple would have had no other products ready to announce for a long time. Worse, its top engineers, frustrated by the failure, would have left Apple."[71]

Steve was on that stage alone for about seventy minutes. It was man and machine. One's thoughts are drawn to May 20, 1927, when Charles Lindbergh took off in *The Spirit of St. Louis* from Roosevelt Field on Long Island to land thirty-three hours and thirty minutes later at Le Bourget Aerodrome in Paris. One writer observed that Lindbergh "thought he had simply flown from New York to Paris. What he had really done was far greater. He had fired the imagination of mankind." Others had already flown across the Atlantic. But Lindbergh was the first man to do it alone. "He was the 'Lone Eagle,' and a full exploration of that fact takes one deep into the emotional meaning of his success." Lindbergh himself insisted that his flight was a team effort, as the name of his plane suggests. However, he was alone in that cockpit, and, as the *New York Times* observed, that fact "made the strongest impression."[72]

Steve was finally joined on stage by Eric Schmidt, CEO of Google. He spoke for about a minute. Schmidt was a board member of Apple. He and his company were soon to be cordially loathed in Cupertino for bringing out Android. As Jobs said at an employee meeting early in 2010, "Google wants to kill the iPhone. We won't let them. Their Don't Be Evil mantra? It's bullshit."[73]

After Schmidt, next up was Jerry Yang, CEO of Yahoo. He spoke for two minutes. Google was on its way up. Yahoo, once the hottest company in technology, was on its way down. Such is the way of Silicon Valley. The third guest speaker was Stan Sigman, CEO of Cingular (soon to be part of AT&T). He spoke for about five minutes, which were the only dull five minutes of the keynote.

With the exception of those nine minutes, it was all Steve all the time. He concluded by observing that 957 million mobile phones were sold worldwide in 2006, far more than game consoles, digital cameras, MP3 players, and PCs combined. One percent of that market meant ten million phones. That was Steve's goal for 2008, the first full year the iPhone would be on the market.

Steve himself did not fully understand what he had on his hands with the iPhone. Here are two examples. First, he did not want third-party software developers creating applications for the phone. He wanted complete control. He changed his mind quickly. Four months after shipping, Apple announced the availability of a software development kit for third parties that wanted to put their applications on the phone.[74]

The App Store has been a spectacular success. "Suddenly," according to an expert, "that was all anyone was talking about in the Valley and in the VC community. Hundreds of little guys signed up, and the race was on."[75] The App Store has delivered billions of dollars to developers and to Apple.

Second, Steve did not appreciate how important the camera was going to be. He mentioned very briefly that the iPhone would have a two-megapixel rear-facing camera. Today the camera is (my guess would be) one of the top five apps on the phone. Indeed, the phone has been described as a camera with a phone attached.

The best camera is the one you have with you, and people take their phones everywhere. As much as anything Apple produces, the integration of hardware and software is vital for creating a camera of outstanding quality. Equally important is the co-location of the hardware and software teams in Cupertino. The iPhone's camera leads the way in the smartphone industry. And smartphone cameras have gotten so good that they are making life increasingly difficult for digital single-lens reflex (DSLR) cameras.[76]

When Apple launched its phone, Steve Ballmer, who had succeeded Bill Gates as CEO of Microsoft in 2000, laughed at it. "Five hundred dollars fully subsidized with a plan! ...That is the most expensive phone in the world, and it doesn't appeal to business customers because it doesn't have a keyboard, which makes it not a very good email machine... You can get a Motorola Q phone today for $99. It's a very capable machine... I look at that, and I say I like our strategy. I like it a lot."[77]

In 2019, Bill Gates said that his "greatest mistake ever" was not developing Android at Microsoft. "Android is the standard non-Apple phone... platform. That was a natural thing for Microsoft to win. It really is winner take all. If you're there with half as many apps or 90 percent as many apps, you're on your way to complete doom. There's room for exactly one non-Apple operating system, and what's that worth?" Gates's answer to his own question was $400 billion, money that could have accrued to Microsoft rather than Google.[78] One of the reasons Windows phones failed was because of the failure of its app store. Its phones couldn't keep their apps after they were developed.[79]

The iPhone did experience some difficulties after launch. Especially notable were the dropped calls resulting from AT&T's inadequate network. Once it got traction, however, there was nothing to which to compare it. Apple brought out a new iPhone annually, and the excitement surrounding the announcements grew ever greater. Through the supply chain and even within Apple itself, industrial espionage became a serious problem. Everyone wanted to know what the next iPhone would look like and what new features it would support. Long lines formed early and stretched around blocks at Apple stores to purchase the iPhone on the day of release. People paid surrogates to hold a place in line. Nothing like this had been seen since the nylon riots following World War II, when the shortage of nylon "led to several riots by impatient women who had stood in line for hours waiting for the opportunity to buy stockings."[80]

Jobs concluded his keynote that January day in 2007 by saying that "Maybe our name should reflect [us] a little more than [Apple Computer Inc.] does. So we're announcing today we're dropping the 'Computer' from our name. From this day forward we're going to be known as Apple Incorporated to reflect the product mix we have today." Steve then quoted the hockey star Wayne Gretzky: "'I skate to where the puck is going to be, not where it has been.' [W]e've always tried to do that at Apple... and we always will."[81]

This was a remarkable moment. Companies die because they are not able to make this kind of change. The Mac was Steve's first love. He always overrated it. This repositioning demonstrated a flexibility that was to make the next decade and more golden years at Apple.

THE IPAD

Jobs knew his cancer was back as early as January of 2006.[82] The recurrence did not become apparent to the outside world until 2008. From January to the end of May 2009, he took a medical leave during which he had a liver transplant in late March. The surgery was successful, but doctors observed that the cancer had spread. In an unrelated procedure, Jobs refused to have his stomach pumped before surgery, aspirated some of its contents, developed pneumonia, and almost died. He was back at work that summer and had, according to Isaacson, "recovered most of his strength" by the beginning of 2010.[83]

As soon as his body permitted, Jobs was back at work, this time on the last of his great products, the iPad. The tablet that became known to the world as the iPad at the keynote on January 27, 2010, had been in the works for years. It was put on the back burner because the decision had been taken to bring out the phone first. The years from the introduction of the iPod in 2001 to the announcement of the iPad in 2010 were as successful a decade as a corporation can experience.

An idea of the intensity involved in bringing forth the new product can be grasped thanks to the outstanding book by software engineer Ken Kocienda, entitled *Creative Selection: Inside Apple's Design Process During the Golden Age of Steve Jobs.* Kocienda viewed Apple not through the business school eyes of an organization chart but as a series of concentric circles. "Steve was at the center of all the circles... He used... demo reviews as his chief means of deciding how Apple software should look and feel and function."[84]

Steve "was always easy to understand. He would either approve a demo or he would request to see something different... Nevertheless, some mystery remained. No matter how good your work was, or how smoothly it had sailed through the preliminary reviews leading up to him, you could never know how he would react. Sometimes he'd say he loved or hated something but then reverse himself in midsentence. Perhaps his change of heart might come a day or two later. Other times his opinions, once stated, held in place for years.

"Then there were his moods. On any given day, he might give you a tongue-lashing during a demo if he didn't like the work you brought him. Nobody was exempt, either—not top-level executives he worked with every day and not programmers like me whom he didn't know beyond a passing recognition. This was the price of admission to his demo room—either accept it, or don't demo to him."[85]

Kocienda delivered his demo to Steve in a meeting room in Infinite Loop 4 rather inappropriately named Diplomacy. The room was drab. There was nothing to distract Steve. Present at the demo were Henri Lamiraux, vice president of iOS software engineering, his boss Scott Forstall, senior vice president of iOS software engineering, Greg Christie, the leader of the human interface team, and Bas Ording, a designer on Greg's team. Of course Steve was there. He was on the phone when Ken entered the room.

After he finished his phone conversation, Steve's "eyes met mine. Over the years, many people have commented on Steve's special ability to tell you something, whatever it was, no matter how implausible, and make you believe it. This reality distortion field, the RDF, has become legendary. Yet, in the moment Steve fixed his eyes on me, I felt an opposite force, the RDF with the polarity reversed. Like flipping on a light switch, Steve had turned on a no-nonsense zone around himself, one that banished all flummery and neutralized all pretense. His look wasn't obviously unfriendly or threatening, but surely he knew his unblinking gaze could intimidate people in my position, and it certainly had that effect on me. I saw his look as a signal that he wasn't going to let me pull the wool over his eyes. He was now ready to see my demo."[86]

"Scott Forstall said, 'Okay, let's look at this demo. Steve, this is Ken. He worked on the iPhone keyboard. He has some keyboard designs to show you.' Scott introduced me as if it were the first time I had ever met Steve, even though I had demoed for him just a couple of weeks earlier...

"Steve was still looking at me. Continuing the demo introduction from where Scott left off, I said, 'Right, there are two designs. One has more keys, like a laptop keyboard, and the other has bigger keys, like a scaled-up iPhone. We're thinking of offering both. Try the zoom key to switch between them.'

"Steve then slowly swiveled his chair around to the demo table. He looked down. In front of him, the iPad was in landscape, with the home button to the right of the display... Steve moved his eyes all over the iPad screen, rotating his head slowly in small figure eights, in what I took to be an attempt to get a view of every corner of the display, both straight on and in peripheral vision.

"After several long moments of study, he reached out to tap the zoom key... to switch the keyboard to my bigger-keys design. No reaction, no hint of what he was thinking... Now that the screen looked different, Steve started his study all over again. He took his time... Once satisfied, he tapped the zoom button again, returning the iPad to the more-keys layout. It now looked exactly as it had at the start of the demo. Steve studied again, still betraying no sign of what he thought or felt. He tapped the zoom key one more time, changing to the bigger-keys layout again... He turned to look straight at me.

"'We only need one of these, right?'

"Not what I was expecting. I think I may have swallowed hard. Steve was still looking at me, and so, with a half shrug, I said, 'Yeah... uh... I guess so.'

"Steve sized me up a little and then asked, 'Which one do you think we should use?'

"A simple question, clearly directed at me and only me. Steve didn't shift in his chair or motion toward anyone else in the room. It was my demo, and he wanted me to answer. And then something happened. Standing there, with Steve Jobs staring at me, waiting for me to respond to this question, I realized that I knew what to say, that I had an opinion.

"'Well, I've been using these demos for the past few days, and I've started to like the keyboard layout with the bigger keys. I think I could learn to touch type on it, and I think other people could, too.'

"Steve continued looking at me as he thought about my answer. He never moved his eyes to anyone or anything else.

He was completely present. There he was, seriously considering my idea about the next big Apple product. It was thrilling. He thought for a few seconds about what I had just said and what he had seen on the iPad. Then he announced the demo verdict.

"'OK. We'll go with the bigger keys.'

"That was it." And this is as good an explanation of how the sausage was made that you can find. Demos, Kocienda observes, are "the primary means to turn ideas into software." Making great software was a core corporate goal, "and that came straight from Steve."

Forstall, senior vice president of software, was in the first of the concentric circles surrounding Steve. Vice presidents were in the second. "At the pre-Steve level, Scott was the executive editor. He was the 'decider.'" Scott had to edit carefully, because if he brought Steve something he deemed unworthy of his time, there would be hell to pay. Scott would have lost face.

In all of the concentric circles, there was a "push for simplicity." Everything about Kocienda's demo was stripped down to the bare essentials. Forstall used the minimum number of words to introduce Kocienda, who in turn used the minimum number of words in his demo. One vice president at Apple never sent Steve an email that could not fit on the screen of a small iPhone without scrolling.

Steve's decision on Kocienda's keyboard also bespoke simplicity. He was presented with two keyboards, both of which could have been included on the iPad. When he chose one rather than both, "it had a cascade effect toward greater simplicity." The zoom animation and zoom button, which got you from one keyboard to another, could be removed.

"We could also take away possible confusion about which keyboard to show in different situations. For example, should the software remember that you used the bigger-keys keyboard in the Notes app and the more-keys keyboard in Mail, and should these keyboard choices be restored in some situations but not in others? These questions became moot, and that's good, because they don't necessarily have easy answers. Steve figured that the best way to answer difficult questions like these was to avoid the need to ask them."

This demo was merely another episode in what was doubtless a busy day for Jobs. He probably did not remember Kocienda after this demo just as he had apparently not remembered him after the previous demo. Kocienda, however, marveled at "how much Steve taught me in one meeting where he spoke just four sentences."[87]

This is how Jobs's attitude permeated all of Apple. Kocienda is a very talented software engineer, and, judging from his videos on YouTube, he is quite articulate. From his book, it would appear that in addition to his technical abilities, he is liberally educated. Having joined Apple in 2001 and worked there for a decade and a half, he experienced the great years. Playing a central role in the creation of the keyboards for both the iPhone and the iPad meant that he was employable anywhere.

Look at how he describes the moment just before Jobs makes his decision at the demo: "It was thrilling." Later in his book, Kocienda describes Jobs as "the most famously charismatic person in Apple history."[88] The thrill he felt at that demo—that is charisma in action.

The keynote introducing the iPad took place before another packed house, this time at the Yerba Buena Center for the

Arts in San Francisco on January 27, 2010. It was quite different from the iPhone keynote three years earlier. Steve started things off on the big stage, wearing his signature outfit of blue jeans and a long-sleeve black turtleneck. He received a standing ovation when he walked on stage. His face, however, looked thin. So did his body, as far as one could tell. His voice was slightly raspy.

Jobs seemed relaxed as he prepared to introduce Apple's latest "truly magical and revolutionary product" to the world. The keynote lasted for about 130 minutes. Steve was only onstage about 40 percent of the time. There were a host of other presenters as well as a video of Apple executives. Steve's thin body was in stark contrast to the others who participated.[89]

When the iPad was announced, a number of reviewers were underwhelmed. Some mocked the name because of its supposed similarity to feminine hygiene products. But the complaining came to a screeching halt as soon as the iPad was released on April 3. The public gobbled them up far more quickly than the iPod or even the iPhone. Three hundred thousand were sold the first day they were available. Sales reached the one million mark in less than a month, twice as fast as the iPhone. In less than a year, fifteen million units were sold. It was a success beyond anyone's expectations.[90]

On March 2, 2011, Jobs hosted the launch of the iPad2. It was to be his last product keynote. On June 7, 2011, he delivered his last public presentation. This was to the Cupertino City Council concerning the new campus Apple planned to build, nicknamed iSpaceship, because it looked like a flying saucer. The word *cachectic* is defined as "physical wasting with loss of weight and muscle mass due to disease."[91] Steve appeared cachectic that June evening, although he was well spoken and certainly had his wits about him. He had four months to live.

As we know, when he died on October 5, there was an outpouring of grief over the world. "In China more than sixty-three million messages were posted on a popular microblogging site; world leaders from Barack Obama to Nicolas Sarkozy to Dmitry Medvedev issued condolences; and candles, mounds of flowers and notes such as 'iSad' and 'iThankYou' piled up outside Apple stores from New York to the Ginza shopping district in Tokyo." Rupert Murdoch, CEO of News Corp., noted Jobs's passing, saying, "Today, we lost one of the most influential thinkers, creators, and entrepreneurs of all time. Steve Jobs was simply the greatest CEO of his generation."[92]

What explains this reaction?

If you search the internet for "mourning Steve Jobs," you will get a lot of hits. Not only did millions mourn his death, a good deal was written about why there was such grief. Some of this writing was academic in nature, and not all of it was inviting to the reader. Here is one example from the abstract of an article entitled, "Vernacular mourning and corporate memorialization in framing the death of Steve Jobs": "Using the concept of heterotopia to explore the spatio-temporal power relations of contemporary organizational memorialization, we show how the construction of contemporary shrines and visual imagery rendered spaces and objects temporarily sacred and maintained Jobs as an ongoing presence in the lives of consumer-believers."[93]

My own thoughts are less involved.

First and foremost, Steve Jobs was a charismatic man. He had a magnetism that affected some people very powerfully.

This derived from who he innately was and was heightened by certain of his acquired characteristics. He had followers. Not only billions of consumers but scores of executives who respected him sometimes to the point of veneration for his instincts, which could make magic, for his forcefulness, decisiveness, and taste. There are people who believed he could help them do the best work of their lives.

These people believed he was a one-off. For all the anxiety and aggravation involved in dealing with him, the excitement of discovering how good you could be was worth it to many people. There were indeed some things that only Steve could do.

It must also be said that there is a dark side to charisma, and Jobs illustrates it. There is a story that he once got into an elevator on the Apple campus with an employee he did not know and asked him what was new. The response was "nothing much." To which Jobs said, "In that case, you're fired."

This probably never happened, but the fact that the story was told illustrates the fear Jobs inspired in unoffending people. Apocryphal though it may be, the story is not implausible. There were people at Apple afraid to ride in an elevator with him.[94] There are few individuals in leadership positions about whom such a story would be told, true or not.

The terror Jobs inspired did not necessarily help the day-to-day operation of his business. Ken Kocienda, who appears to be as sane as a software engineer can be, reports, "One exceptionally talented and experienced colleague told me flat out that he refused to demo his own work in Diplomacy... because of the way Steve treated people in these face-to-face meetings. My friend continued to respect Steve's taste, even though he deplored his temperament."[95]

It may be that it is because of this kind of behavior rather than in spite of it that people, especially those who did not interact with Steve and did not have to put up with this sort of thing firsthand, were drawn to him. Steve was a rule breaker. Some of the rules of decent human behavior exist for a reason. But he felt as free to break those—as the treatment of the daughter he had out of wedlock, Lisa Brennan-Jobs, illustrates—as he was to break the bars of the "iron cage," to use Max Weber's famous metaphor, that encases so many people in bureaucracies characterized by pointless, moronic rituals.

Steve's charisma extended far beyond those who knew him personally. Billions of people owned the products his company produced. Many millions had seen Pixar movies, but, even though Pixar's headquarters are located in what has been named the Steve Jobs Building and the company owes its existence to his financial backing, Jobs is associated in the public mind with Apple.

Jobs felt love-starved because of the circumstances of his birth and adoption. Apple's products were the vector through which he captured the love he had been denied because of the rejection of his biological mother and father. There is a picture of him with a broad smile on his face looking at a young girl hugging an iPad. This is how he wanted customers to feel about Apple's products, and this is why he was so vicious toward Apple employees who made mistakes on those products. They were stealing the love of the public from him.

Beauty was a key component of Apple products—the beauty of the software, of the hardware, and of the materials used in the hardware. Jobs meant it when he talked about the marriage of the humanities with technology. This was an important point of differentiation. Few other technology executives thought in these terms. (Edwin Land did, which helps explain why Jobs was attracted to him.) A key characteristic of the beauty of Apple products was simplicity. With simplicity came ease of use. There are many examples in which ease of use was privileged over more technologically sophisticated approaches to a product.

Yet another reason for the identification of so many people with Jobs is the story of his rebirth. He was fired in 1985, and he never forgot or forgave that event. He came back to the dying company he had cofounded and turned it into a force to be reckoned with by breaking the rules business schools teach about how to run a company.

Lastly, from a dramatic point of view, Steve Jobs died at the perfect moment. He left this world on top of his game. Having suffered defeats, he emerged victorious.

CHAPTER 14

CHARISMA AND CORRUPTION: TWO TALES FROM RECENT HISTORY

The New York Times, February 22, 2019: "Jeffrey K. Skilling, the former chief executive of Enron whose lies contributed to the sudden collapse of the energy company in one of the country's most high-profile cases of corporate fraud was released from federal custody on Thursday [February 21] after serving more than 12 years in prison, the federal authorities said."[1]

Two decades previously, no one imagined that such a sentence would ever appear in the nation's newspaper of record. Back then, in the late 1990s, Skilling was admired, emulated, and feared. He was never a celebrity on the scale of Oprah Winfrey or Steve Jobs, but to business school students and their professors, he was the gold standard. In 1997, Skilling became the chief operating officer of Enron. On February 12, 2001, he became the company's chief executive officer. The previous year he took home $132 million in compensation. Enron's sales had skyrocketed from $13.5 billion in 1991 to

$100.8 billion a decade later, making it the seventh largest company in the United States. At the beginning of 2001, its market capitalization was $62.5 billion, a figure made possible by a price/earnings ratio of 64. In the previous five years, Enron delivered a 507 percent return for its shareholders. For six straight years, *Fortune* named it "America's Most Innovative Company."[2]

Bethany McLean, one of the nation's leading business journalists, said, "From a distance, Jeff Skilling seems like the perfect CEO for the modern age. Hip, brilliant, captivating, brave, edgy—all these things that every executive wanted to be. He had a little bit of that wild man, macho flavor to him, even though he was also clearly an intellectual. People were fascinated by him..." Just as executives envied Skilling, other companies envied Enron. Their leaders "were aggressive. They were pioneers. They were changing markets. They were everything you were supposed to be."[3]

Jeffrey Keith Skilling was born on November 25, 1953, in Pittsburgh, the second of four children. His father was a sales manager for a company that made large valves for heavy machinery. The family moved from Pittsburgh to Westfield, New Jersey, a suburb of New York City, when Skilling was still a baby because his father had been transferred. When Skilling was twelve, the family moved to Aurora, Illinois, a suburb of Chicago, because his father had taken another job.[4]

Skilling's adolescence in Aurora was rather lonely and unhappy. He did well in school, graduating sixteenth in a class of six hundred, but he found it "sheer boredom." The family lived on the lower edge of the middle class. To earn some money, Skilling got himself a job at a local television station. When the position opened up, he became the station's production director. He was fourteen years old and, apparently, worked at that station for fifty hours a week while in high school. He saved $15,000, speculated in the stock market, and lost everything. By chance, he came into another $3,500. He played the market again.[5] He lost everything again. By the age of eighteen, Skilling had demonstrated a lifelong penchant. He was a gambler.

Skilling attended Southern Methodist University, where he took engineering courses he did not like and in which he did not do well. Then he switched to business, and there he found his métier. His grades were perfect. Upon graduation, he got a job at a bank in Houston and quickly became the bank's youngest officer.

The next step was business school. He applied to only one— Harvard. According to *The Smartest Guys in the Room*, the authoritative book by McLean and Peter Elkind, he was interviewed by the dean at the Hyatt in Houston. The dean asked, "Skilling, are you smart?" "I'm fucking smart," he replied.[6]

It is not clear whether the dean being referred to is the dean of admissions, which is a staff position and not an academic appointment, or the dean of the faculty, which is a highly prestigious tenured academic position. The dean of the faculty is the CEO of the school. It is hard to believe that he used this language in a discussion with Larry Fouraker, the dean of the faculty at the time. In any case, describing himself as "fucking smart," which he did do, is as big a gamble as an applicant to the Harvard Business School could take. He was either going to be summarily rejected or accepted because no other applicant described him or herself that way. The gamble worked. Whoever it was who took the chance on the Harvard Business School side must have been happy with the result. Skilling graduated as a Baker Scholar in 1979, which means he was in the top 5 percent of a very competitive group of nine hundred people.

Skilling's next stop was McKinsey, a well-known management consulting firm founded in 1926. The path from HBS to McKinsey was, and still is, well trodden. McKinsey is an "up or out" organization, and Skilling moved up, making partner in five years and director in ten. He started off in the Dallas office and soon moved to Houston, where he was the third employee of an office that has since grown very large.

The management consulting industry grew rapidly in the 1970s with aggressive competitors including McKinsey, the Boston Consulting Group, and Bain fighting to hire the leading students at the Harvard Business School and offering what at the time were astronomical starting salaries of around $60,000. These companies are in the business of giving advice. They are all about strategy. Implementation is up to the client. McKinsey was an excellent fit for Skilling, who enjoyed big ideas and ignored details.

The 1970s and 1980s were decades of deregulation of many industries. Natural gas was no exception. Traditionally, it was moved from producer to local utility through privately owned pipelines with the government setting the price. By the late 1980s, the unregulated market determined the price.

Skilling's philosophy was that people were motivated by money and fear. Unsurprisingly, he was a devotee of the free market. To him, deregulation meant nothing but opportunity. Working in the city that was the energy capital of the United States, there was a historic opportunity to do for natural gas what Michael Milken was doing for junk bonds—create a market where none had existed before.

The job of a small McKinsey office is to become a big one. The method is to pitch clients headquartered in the area. The technique is to present transformative strategies. Skilling sold a big idea to Enron. It became his principal client, and for a time perhaps the most celebrated McKinsey success story.

Enron was much in need of a new strategy. It was an old, boring company in a stable, low-margin, low-growth market. Enron's roots went back to 1925, but its modern history dates from 1985 with the merger of Houston Natural Gas and InterNorth, an Omaha-based energy holding company.

The CEO of the newly formed company was Kenneth Lee Lay. Born in Tyrone, Missouri, in 1942, Lay graduated from the University of Missouri, where he was a member of the Beta Theta Pi fraternity (by chance, the same fraternity that Skilling joined at SMU). Lay migrated from the public sector to the private sector, picking up a PhD in economics from the University of Houston in the process. In 1984, he became CEO of Houston Natural Gas.[7] With the InterNorth merger the following year, Lay found himself at the head of a large company that adopted the name Enron. He bought and sold numerous subsidiaries. His goal was to get big fast. But how?

The company was not making much headway. Lay was a mediocre businessman who liked to live well and who did understand that it was important to be close to political power. He was the Bush family's favorite businessman. George W. Bush referred to him as "Kenny boy." The more time he spent schmoozing with and raising money for politicians, the less he spent on Enron's business, in which he became progressively less interested and less knowledgeable.

Along came Skilling with what he regarded as a breakthrough way to connect buyer and seller in the new, unregulated world of natural gas and for Enron to grow rich as a market maker. The idea was the "Gas Bank," which Skilling pitched to twenty-five Enron executives in late 1987. The company eventually adopted the idea. As the name implied, Skilling proposed to change the firm into a financial product trading house. The company's natural gas assets, and reliable revenues, would be a springboard for launching intangible goods in markets that the firm created or expanded to unprecedented size.

Skilling "[freed] natural gas from its physical qualities, from the constraints of molecules and movement." Trading meant that Enron did not "[have] to own assets in the production and transportation of natural gas... [It] could simply own a portfolio of contracts that would allow it to control the resources it needed. Instead of seeing a commitment to delivering natural gas as [involving] a pipeline, Enron saw it as a financial commitment. It was a whole new way of conceptualizing the business..." This "whole new way" came to be called "asset light." Less capital was needed. The opportunity for a higher return on capital thus beckoned. Perhaps it is not surprising that when people described Skilling, they used phrases like "incandescently brilliant" and "the smartest person I ever met."[8] The larger-than-life image of Jeff Skilling was beginning to take hold.

At first the Gas Bank and associated trading activities did not fulfill their promise. Skilling thought he knew why—he was not running them. In June 1990, he left McKinsey to become CEO of a newly created division, Enron Finance. Before taking the job, Skilling made what McLean and Elkind have correctly called "a very strange demand." He insisted that his business use mark-to-market accounting rather than historical cost accounting, which was standard practice in the natural gas industry. "This was so important to him—'a lay my body across the tracks issue'"—that he told Lay he would not join Enron without this arrangement.[9] Why was this change a make-or-break issue for Skilling?

Accounting has rightly been called "the language of business." Its purpose is to provide an accurate picture of the economic reality of a business for the benefit of investors, management, suppliers, and all other parties with an interest in the company in question. This is not easy to do.

For some industries in some situations, mark-to-market accounting, which is quite legal, provides the most accurate picture of a business that it is possible to obtain. Indeed, it was standard bookkeeping practice in the United States in the nineteenth century. It is an "accounting method that values an asset to its current market level. It shows how much a company would receive if it sold the asset today," which is why it is also called "fair value accounting."[10] Under historical cost accounting, by contrast, an asset is valued at the original nominal monetary cost of a purchase. Neither method is inherently good or bad. At different times and with different assets, one or the other might generate a truer picture of reality.

Enron declared bankruptcy on December 2, 2001. The company's market capitalization on January 1, 2001, was $62.5 billion. All that wealth disappeared in eleven months in what was at the time the biggest bankruptcy in the history of American business.

Much attention has been focused on mark-to-market accounting for this calamity. In the conventional, historical method, if you enter into a twenty-year contract, you book the revenues that result as you acquire them year by year. With mark-to-market accounting—at least as it was employed by Enron in the Skilling era—you can book the estimated value of that contract for all twenty years on the day you enter into it. You are obliged to record changes in that contract's value in subsequent years.

Why did Skilling favor mark-to-market accounting with such religious zealotry? One reason that McLean and Elkind offer is that Skilling "never let go of the consultant's conceit that the idea was all and the idea, therefore, should be the thing that was rewarded... [A] business should be able to declare profits at the moment of the creative act that would earn those profits. Otherwise businessmen were mere coupon clippers, reaping the benefit of innovation that had been devised in the past by other, greater men."

"There's no way around it," Skilling said. "It reflects the true economic value."[11]

Skilling may very well have said such things. However, the distance between what he said and what he did was great indeed. He spent his eleven years at Enron doing everything possible to separate accounting statements from "true economic value." In this endeavor, he succeeded so well that he wound up in jail for more than twelve years.

Any accounting system can be abused by someone as fundamentally dishonest as Skilling. Mark-to-market accounting may have been especially ripe for such abuse in the natural gas industry in the late 1980s because deregulation had rendered the old rules irrelevant. No one knew what would replace them. Skilling had an answer to this question.

Another aspect of the Enron fiasco dealing with accounting is the way the company hid its debt. For this purpose, Enron set about constructing "special purpose entities," which through sleight of hand enabled it to keep its mountain of debt off its balance sheet.

The assertion that Enron was "asset light" was never true. It had major ownership interests in hard assets all around the world. A good example is the gigantic Dabhol power plant located a hundred miles south of Mumbai. This construction project soaked up cash and produced no income, like so many other Enron investments in hard assets. But the company's financial statements were so obscure that it took a lot of work to find this out. The people who should have been doing this work—from business journalists; to rating agencies; to equity analysts; to Arthur Andersen, the accounting firm serving as Enron's auditor; to corporate lawyers; to the audit committee of the board of directors on which sat, among others, Robert K. Jaedicke, the dean of Stanford's Graduate School of Business from 1983 to 1990 and a professor of accounting—did not. Either it was not in their own interests to do so—many of them were feeding off Enron's carcass—or they were just dazzled by the dot-com expansion of market capitalization of which (hard to believe but true) Enron seemed a comparatively modest example. In March of 2000, the NASDAQ p/e was 175.

Natural gas contracts could go ten or twenty years out. The price of natural gas two decades from when a contract was signed left a lot of room for optimism, for lack of a better word. Since mark-to-market accounting required that the value of that twenty-year contract be booked the day it was signed, whoever negotiated it just captured a luscious bonus, and the top line on Enron's income statement (i.e., sales) was appropriately beefed up. This merry-go-round demanded that another such contract be entered into next year, and then another, and on and on without regard to a prudent evaluation of the unpredictable volatility in gas pricing over a decade or two into the future.

Skilling multiplied these risks by wandering into steel, metals, advertising time and space, broadband, the weather(!), you name it. The idea was to make money trading on the prospects of other people's assets. "In the old days," according to Skilling, "people work for the assets. We've turned it around—what we've said is that assets work for the people."[12] Read those sentences again. They sound good, but they are meaningless.

Skilling hired Andrew Fastow in 1990 to work for him at Enron Finance. Fastow was twenty-nine years old. Married to a wealthy woman, his hunger for more money was the equal of anyone else's at Enron, which is saying a lot. Fastow saw Skilling as the rising star to which to hitch his wagon. No opportunity to ingratiate himself was passed up. He named his first son Jeffrey. Fastow's off-balance-sheet special purpose entities, in the operation of which he more than once sacrificed Enron's interest for his own, made him millions. When the music stopped, he was sentenced to six years in prison and two years of probation.

As the 1990s progressed, Skilling became ever more powerful in the company, beating out rivals in a snake pit of an environment. In 1997, he became Enron's president and chief operating officer, second only to Lay, who by this time had little idea of what was going on at the company. Lay touted the stock constantly while selling millions of dollars on his own account. Skilling, meanwhile, "offered the world a powerful, even charismatic, vision of the new Enron."[13] It was to become an impact player in the "new economy" the internet was creating. Its stock, he was certain, should be priced much higher than it was, given the valuations of dot-com companies in the late 1990s.

Charisma often has a dimension dealing with personal appearance, and Skilling's case was no exception. In the late 1980s, he "wasn't a physically striking man—he was smallish, a little pudgy, and balding." He wore glasses. By the late 1990s, Lasik surgery had taken care of the glasses, and "he resolved to get in fighting trim. [He] began lifting weights and dropped sixty-five pounds in a number of months. He... started using a hair-growth drug" to deal with his baldness. "At the age of forty-three, he'd never looked better."[14] He was positioning himself to take over from Lay, whose flabby intellect and lack of commitment to the operations of the company had made him increasingly irrelevant. On February 12, 2001, Skilling reached the top of the greasy pole at last. He replaced Lay as Enron's chief executive officer. He brought Fastow along with him, making him chief financial officer in 1998. From 1997 to 2000, Skilling's charismatic "incandescent brilliance" was rewarded by what to him was the fairest of indicators, the market. Quarter after quarter, Enron met its earnings estimates. And everyone was happy.

Here is one method the company used to perform so well. This is selected not because it is exceptional but because it is typical, and unlike the mind-numbing schemes Fastow usually cooked up, this is easy to understand.

As the fourth quarter of 1999 was coming to a close, Enron found itself owning three gigantic power plants floating on barges off the coast of Nigeria. Don't ask for details. The company knew that if it did not unload these assets, it would miss quarterly earnings and the house of cards would collapse.

Enron pressured one of its investment bankers, Merrill Lynch, to buy the tankers, promising to repurchase them after the quarter. This left Merrill Lynch with a dilemma. "If the buyback guarantee were real, the sale was a sham... [I]f Enron wasn't really guaranteeing the buyback, Merrill was risking $7 million on an asset—Nigerian barges?—that no one there wanted to own."[15] With some—but apparently not much—soul-searching, Merrill Lynch went along with the proposition. It worked out. On January 18, 2000, Enron announced that it had met Wall Street's expectations.

Multiply this story by dozens, and you have a good idea of how Enron ran its business. This sort of scheming was sure to fail if and when a bad quarter could not be covered over. As happened to all the companies that rose on the dot-com bubble but lacked the fundamentals of solid revenue and real profits, 2001 brought disaster. Enron was unusual chiefly in its magnitude.

The collapse was swift. From Wikipedia: "Enron shareholders filed a $40 billion lawsuit after the company's stock price, which achieved a high of $90.75 per share in mid-2000, plummeted to less than $1.00 by the end of November 2001. The... Securities and Exchange Commission... began an investigation, and rival Houston competitor Dynegy offered to purchase the company at a very low price. The deal failed, and on December 2, 2001, Enron filed for bankruptcy under Chapter 11 of the United States Bankruptcy Code."[16]

A collapse of the size of the Enron bankruptcy has consequences that go beyond disappointment into tragedy. Cliff Baxter was a graduate of New York University who served in the air force from 1980 to 1985 and left with the rank of captain. He earned his MBA from Columbia, joined Enron in

1991, and worked his way up to chief strategy officer. After the bankruptcy in December 2001, he was scheduled to testify before congressional committees the following February.

Baxter was being sued for $30 million after the walls had come tumbling down. Skilling did not have many friends. Baxter was one of them. In the midst of the uproar after the bankruptcy, he said to Skilling, "[T]hey're calling us child molesters. That will never wash off." On January 25, 2002, parked in his black Mercedes S 500, Baxter shot himself in the head.[17]

On July 7, 2004, Ken Lay was indicted on eleven counts of securities and wire fraud and making false statements. On May 25, 2006, the jury found him guilty of six counts of conspiracy and fraud. In a separate trial, Judge Simeon T. Lake III found him guilty of four counts of fraud and false statements. During the night of July 5, 2006, in Aspen, Colorado, Lay got out of bed at one o'clock to go to the bathroom. He dropped dead of a heart attack.[18] More than a dozen other top managers were criminally convicted.

Enron employees, more than twenty thousand of them, suffered the consequences of the malfeasance at the top. They lost their jobs. A lot of personal tragedies resulting from irresponsible and illegal behavior on the top floor of Enron's gleaming tower in Houston will never be publicly aired. In addition to Enron, Arthur Andersen, Enron's complicit auditor, also imploded, and with its collapse almost thirty thousand jobs disappeared. What about Jeff Skilling? What happened to him?

On August 14, 2001, Skilling announced that he was resigning from Enron. The only explanation he offered for taking this startling step was "personal reasons."[19] He had been complaining that he was not having fun anymore. He wanted to take vacations with his children rather than put up with the daily grind of running a huge company.

We do not know the real reason that Skilling quit after only six months on a job he had lusted after for years. It is true that he seemed sufficiently depressed to worry those around him. His first marriage had ended in divorce in 1997. He had three children with his first wife (two boys and a girl) and was not married again until 2002. So home was not a haven in a heartless world. Nevertheless, "personal reasons" sounds unlike the arrogant Skilling the world had come to know and to fear and to dislike.

Here is what McLean and Elkind have to say: "If indeed there was one specific personal reason, no one... knew what it was." But they also doubt the obvious possibility that Skilling was a rat deserting a sinking ship. "It is difficult to find evidence that Skilling—who once told *BusinessWeek* that he had 'never not been successful at work or business, ever'—has ever admitted that he failed at Enron. Not even to himself."[20]

The same day that Skilling resigned, an accountant named Sherron Watkins delivered a letter to Ken Lay, who assumed once again the position of CEO upon Skilling's abandonment of it. In this letter, Watkins wrote, "I am incredibly nervous that we will implode in a wave of accounting scandals."[21] If she knew this, Skilling would have had to be deeply in denial not to know it also.

On the other hand, Skilling's capacity for denial should not be underestimated. After the bankruptcy, when questioned under oath by then representative Ed Markey, he said, "Congressman, I can just say it again. On the day I left, I absolutely unequivocally thought the company was in good shape."[22] This is an astonishing statement. The witness was either a fool or a liar.

McLean and Elkind believe that the real reason Skilling left was the decline in the price of Enron's stock. "[N]o matter what the real condition of Enron's business, if the stock had continued to climb, Skilling would not have quit. Skilling wasn't lying when he said he was leaving for personal reasons—the stock's steep fall was personal. For Jeff Skilling, Enron's stock was one of the most deeply personal things in his life."[23]

Skilling's departure will remain a mystery. We do know that putting Ken Lay back in charge was a comically inadequate response to a desperate business situation. In any event, Skilling's flight from Enron when it needed him most says all that needs to be said about the man's character. Many people had placed their faith in him. He betrayed their trust while making off with tens of millions of dollars for himself.

Enron was indeed about to "implode in a wave of accounting scandals." The accounting issues gave unstoppable momentum to the legislative reform known as Sarbanes-Oxley, a complex bipartisan effort to bar the practices that Enron used so promiscuously. But the rise and fall of Enron is not just an accounting story. It is the story of a grandiose, overestimated, charismatic business leader in Jeffrey Skilling who had constructed a business model that could only succeed if the stock price continued to climb rapidly, without pause or downturn, forever. That does not happen in the real world of business. Warren Buffett famously said that it is only when the tide goes out that you discover who has been swimming naked. The tide went out. Skilling was revealed to be as naked as the day he was born. He did not possess "incandescent brilliance." He was simply a phony.

The wages of sin were a dozen years in jail. The jury found him guilty of conspiracy, insider trading, making false statements to auditors, and securities fraud. While he was serving his time, both his parents died. His youngest child, John Taylor "JT" Skilling, died of a drug overdose at the age of twenty. He was a communications major at Chapman College in Orange, California. Was this a suicide? The weight of the evidence is that it was an accidental overdose. But in the words of a psychologist, "In the case of a young man whose father was essentially guilty of a heinous crime and he admired and looked up to his father, it can be a severe psychological blow..."[24]

Baxter died. Lay died. JT died. But Skilling is very much alive. He is planning to go back into business. This plan must give the reader pause.

Can charisma be faked? Indeed it can. The business world today needs charisma so much that the opportunity to fake it looms large. Skilling had the ability to attract followers in large numbers but faked the business. Our next story is one of a person who extended fakery from personality to product.

Elizabeth Holmes idolized Steve Jobs and did her best to copy him. Holmes graced the cover of *Fortune*'s June 12, 2014, issue. She was the founder and CEO of a company called Theranos. She gazes out at the reader from the cover with big, blue, arresting eyes. She was dressed in black, including the trademark Jobs turtleneck.[25]

She imitated Jobs's aggression as well. The cover announced, "This CEO Is Out for Blood."[26] The title was a play on the business of Theranos. Holmes proposed to save lives through a revolutionary development in blood testing that promised early diagnosis, giving patients greater control over their health care and enabling doctors to move more quickly against illness. Like Jobs at Apple, Holmes was strictly secretive about her product development. But unlike Jobs, she announced her successes, not only through *Fortune* but through the whole media world, before she had anything to sell.

Holmes's only stock in trade was her imitative, spurious charisma. She pretended to be someone other than who she was, and she promoted a product that existed exclusively in her imagination.

Theranos blood tests did not generate reliable results. Her company was valued at $9 billion in 2014 and bankrupt in 2018. She stands before the world today as a con artist and proof of the danger of charisma. How did this happen?

The subtitle on *Fortune*'s cover was "Elizabeth Holmes and Her Secretive Company, Theranos, Aim to Revolutionize Health Care." *Fortune* was the first publication to feature Holmes. The article could not have been more fawning. Theranos (the name is a combination of *therapy* and *diagnosis*) employed five hundred people at the time and had raised more than $400 million from investors. Holmes is quoted as saying that Theranos "is about being able to do good." Later she used a line that she repeated often: "I genuinely don't believe anything else matters more than when you love someone so much and you have to say goodbye too soon." These two quotations show her making meaning rather than making money. Theranos was building a "testing infrastructure" that would deliver blood test results immediately to patients as well as doctors and therefore save lives.[27]

Following *Fortune* was *Forbes*. The magazine ran an article about Holmes entitled "Bloody Amazing." She was described as "the youngest woman to become a self-made billionaire."[28] With a fortune estimated at $4.5 billion, she made the *Forbes* 400, ranked number 110, and was on the cover of the magazine for that issue. To the left of her photograph was "The Freshman: Elizabeth Holmes Leads the Class of 2014." Soon thereafter, Holmes was featured on the cover of *Inc.* with the headline: "The Next Steve Jobs..." According to *Inc.*, Theranos was now valued at $10 billion.[29]

The year 2014 was simply terrific for Holmes. Interviews for magazines, newspapers, radio, and television. Anointed by *Time* magazine as one of the hundred most influential people in the world. Invited to join the Harvard Medical School's board of fellows. Appointed by President Barack Obama as an American ambassador for global entrepreneurship. What would be next?

Elizabeth Anne Holmes was born in Washington, DC, on February 3, 1984, about two weeks after the airing of Apple's famed Super Bowl advertisement. Her father is Christian Rasmus Holmes IV. He was a vice president at Enron, and after its implosion, he held a number of high-ranking jobs in the federal government. Her mother, Noel Anne (Daoust) Holmes, was a congressional staffer whose father was a West Point graduate who held high-ranking positions in the Pentagon. On her father's side, Holmes's great-great-grandfather was Charles Louis Fleischmann, a Hungarian Jew who founded Fleischmann's Yeast. At his death in 1897, Fleischmann was one of the richest men in the United States. His children and grandchildren lived the high life and frittered away their fortune.

Holmes's parents were not super-rich but certainly not poor. They could afford to send her to a tony prep school in

Houston. They paid for a tutor in Mandarin, in which Holmes became fluent. The family eventually moved to Woodside, California, one of the most expensive towns in Silicon Valley, and Holmes enrolled in Stanford in the fall of 2001.

When she was nine, Holmes wrote a letter to her father in which she said, "Dear Daddy, What I want out of life is to discover something new, something that mankind didn't even know was possible..."[30] At about the same time, one of her relatives asked Holmes what she wanted to be when she grew up. "Without skipping a beat, Elizabeth replied, 'I want to be a billionaire.'"[31] Did she have in the back of her mind Charles Fleischmann's fortune, and did she cherish the desire to recapture the lavish life of days gone by? Or did she really want to create a new future for the world? These objectives are not necessarily mutually exclusive. Did she want both?

Who was—and is—Elizabeth Holmes? Is she an example of what has been called "noble cause corruption"? John Carreyrou, the dauntless *Wall Street Journal* reporter whose articles put an end to Theranos, used this term when interviewed by Jim Cramer on *Mad Money* on August 22, 2018.[32]

Holmes dropped out of Stanford in the middle of her sophomore year. Silicon Valley charisma stories often have as part of their origin a college dropout. If she had finished college, she might never have recovered from that mark of normally estimable success. She wanted to be abnormally successful. Step one was to create the riches-to-riches story of a Valley wunderkind.

Step two was to start a company. She called hers Real-Time Cures, but she got rid of that because she felt the word *cure* would invite skepticism and require results. She wanted her company to be situated so far in the future that the present did not matter. She changed the name to Theranos, which sounded like a god's name. The company was founded in 2003. Only in September of 2018 did it cease operations.

High tide was 2014, when the avalanche of publicity exploded upon the public scene. The board of directors in that year was composed of George Shultz, former secretary of state; Gary Roughead, former admiral in the United States Navy; William Perry, former secretary of defense; Sam Nunn, former United States senator; James Mattis, former general in the United States Marine Corps who became Donald Trump's first secretary of defense; William Frist, former United States senator who is also a surgeon; Henry Kissinger, former everything; Richard Kovacevich, former CEO of Wells Fargo; Riley P. Bechtel, chairman of the board of the Bechtel group; and William H. Foege, former director of the Centers for Disease Control and Prevention. It hardly needs saying that this is quite a distinguished group.

Also on the board was Ramesh "Sunny" Balwani, the company's chief operating officer. Sunny—and never was a nickname less appropriate; he was despised by almost... almost... everyone who dealt with him—was thirty-seven years old when he met Elizabeth, who was eighteen or nineteen (it is unclear) at the time. The two began living together in July of 2005.[33] He joined Theranos in 2009. He had a background in software as well as an MBA but no training in medical devices. Holmes and Balwani never disclosed publicly or to the board that they were living together. They broke up in the spring of 2016. Holmes got married in 2019 in a secret wedding to twenty-seven-year-old William "Billy" Evans, described as the heir to the Evans Hotel Group, a hotel chain in

California.[34] Perhaps she has found true love at last. She is about to go on trial and faces the potential of twenty years in prison.[35]

The chair of the Theranos board was, of course, Holmes. James "Mad Dog" Mattis said of her, "She really does want to make a dent in the universe—one that is positive." (That last clause seems superfluous.) "The strength of the leader's vision in the military," Mattis explained, "is seen as the critical element in that unit's performance. I wanted to be around something again that had that sort of leadership."[36]

The obvious question is: How on earth did Theranos not only survive but prosper for fifteen years? The company was a complete fraud. Its technology never worked. It never could have worked. Nevertheless, Theranos raised, by some estimates, a billion dollars in investments. The biggest investor was none other than Rupert Murdoch, who put $125 million into the company. Irony is piled upon irony when one realizes that the *Wall Street Journal*'s reporting finally put Theranos out of business and that Murdoch owns the paper.

A necessary if not sufficient explanation for the phenomenon of Theranos is the charisma of Elizabeth Holmes. She conjured up her charismatic image in a number of ways.

First, Holmes never gave a straight answer. When dubious people put direct questions to her, she could bob and weave like the greatest of boxers.

Second, Holmes could turn on the charm. Especially susceptible were older men. Look at her board in 2014. George Shultz was ninety-four that year, Henry Kissinger ninety-one. Avie Tevanian, whom we met when he worked with Steve Jobs at NeXT and Apple, joined the Theranos board in 2006. He asked too many questions and was told to leave the board the following year. In 2006, Tevanian was forty-five years old, less than half the age of Shultz and Kissinger in 2014.

The first person to see through Holmes was a woman. Phyllis Gardner is a professor at Stanford Medical School who also is experienced in the world of venture capital. She has during the course of her career pushed for the advancement of women in science and served as a mentor. Holmes came to Gardner in 2002 with an idea for a skin patch that would scan the body for infections and automatically deliver the appropriate antibiotics. Gardner told her that this idea would not and could never work. Holmes saw her a second time. She refused to listen when Gardner told her that what she was proposing was impossible. When Theranos was founded, Gardner was not reluctant to tell people that Holmes could not be trusted.

"It was very tough for me all those years, and part of it was that women were idolizing her. I didn't like that they were idolizing a fraud."[37] In March of 2019, Gardner said, "I just want her convicted. All I want is to see her in an orange jumpsuit with a black turtleneck accent. [She] put people in danger. I don't forgive that."[38]

The third contributing factor to Holmes's charisma was that she could turn off the charm as quickly as she could turn it on. When questioned in a way she felt denoted a lack of perfect loyalty, she transformed herself from charming to rejecting, even menacing, in an instant.

Holmes did not look back, and she did not have a conscience. In 2005, she hired an experienced biochemist, Ian Gibbons, as chief scientist at Theranos. By all accounts a fine man, Gibbons did what he could to craft technical solutions to the endless problems with the product Theranos was trying to build. He became progressively more frustrated in his efforts. Holmes and Balwani became progressively more frustrated with him.

In May of 2013, Gibbons was subpoenaed to testify in a patent suit. If he told the truth, he would be forced to expose what appeared to be the unfixable problems Theranos was facing. It was not in him to lie. He became depressed. Just prior to his deposition, he committed suicide on May 23, 2013. His widow contacted Holmes's office to inform her. Holmes had a company attorney email his widow, instructing her to return all Theranos-related material. Holmes herself never contacted Mrs. Gibbons.

The fourth factor was Holmes's remarkable ability to lie. When Carreyrou's articles about Theranos began appearing in the *Wall Street Journal*, she was asked about them more than once. On October 16, 2015, she appeared on Jim Cramer's CNBC show *Mad Money*. He asked her, while holding the *Wall Street Journal* in his hands, "What do you think is going on here?" She responded, smiling and without blinking an eye, "This is what happens when you work to change things. First they think you're crazy. Then they fight you. And then all of a sudden you change the world." The nine-and-a-half-minute interview was a bravura performance. Holmes did not give an inch and projected supreme self-confidence.[39]

Winston Churchill, who was, of course, as charismatic as anybody and well familiar with telling the truth and not doing so, wrote in 1952, "In wartime, truth is so precious that she should always be attended by a bodyguard of lies."[40] There was no truth at the core of Theranos, where it was always wartime, but this nullity was surrounded by quite an impressive bodyguard of lies nevertheless. The leader of the pack was Holmes. Beside her was her boyfriend, Balwani. And at their command were security people, private detectives, and lawyers whose specialty was browbeating adversaries. Not a pretty picture.

The last piece of the puzzle of Holmes's charisma was her physical self-presentation. In Carreyrou's book and in the innumerable articles about her, this is invariably mentioned. The features upon which reporters endlessly focus are the way she dresses, the way she speaks, and the way she looks at the people with whom she is conversing. To begin with, there was the ubiquitous black turtleneck.

She also cultivated a baritone voice. When she spoke to anyone about work, she spoke an octave lower than her natural voice. This, it is said, endowed her statements with a gravitas they would not otherwise have had. Then there were her eyes. She has big, bright-blue eyes, and all that is written about her says that she blinks less often than others.

Like Jobs, she induced in many people a near-hypnotic state. This was her version of the reality distortion field. There was something about her that made you want to believe her. What precisely was it? It was some combination of what has just been discussed. You wanted to believe her because it was easier than not believing her. And she was the person that Silicon Valley wanted. In a world often criticized for being dominated by men, she was a woman who was not only successful—other women have been as well—but she was a founder and CEO of a multibillion-dollar company. This was front-page news.

The net effect of her self-presentation was not sexual. Rather, there seems to have been something akin to a state she induced in some (certainly not all) of the people with whom she interacted that prompted a willing suspension of disbelief. She had a power pose that worked.

And this is one of the great lessons of the fiasco that is the career of Elizabeth Holmes. Charisma works. Not necessarily indefinitely, depending on the situation. You can fool some of the people... A good deal of serious academic work supports this assertion. And charisma can work for ill as well as for good. Because it distorts reality, charisma is dangerous.

We cannot know what was going on in Holmes's mind during the long years in which she represented the company's successes in a way that now clearly bears no relationship to reality. Was she as much a victim of her charisma as were her investors, board members, employees, and enchanted followers?

Why tell these two stories in the same chapter? On the face of it, they are quite different.

The systematic looting of Enron by those with fiduciary responsibility to keep it healthy is not new in the history of American business. What Jeff Skilling, Ken Lay, Andy Fastow, and their gang did does not seem so different from the Erie War of the 1860s when Daniel Drew, Jim Fisk, and Jay Gould fought for control of the Erie Railroad against Cornelius Vanderbilt. When Gould, Fisk, and Drew had stolen what they could, Drew observed, "There ain't nothing more in Erie."[41] There was nothing more in Enron when Skilling was finished with it.

The nineteenth-century "economic dinosaurians"[42] were more colorful than their twenty-first-century counterparts. Drew, for example, introduced a new financial instrument for his time—"watered stock"—to Wall Street. This was to him what special purpose entities were to Enron. Watered stock was stock that had an artificially inflated value, which of course Enron specialized in. The term has a charming pedigree. Before he went into high finance, Drew was in the cattle business. Apparently, he would deprive his cattle of water, then lead them to a salt lick, then have them drink water to increase their weight before they were sold. Drew was also a pioneer in short selling. He wisely warned that "He who sells what isn't his'n, must buy it back or go to pris'n."[43] The Enron crowd was less poetic but every bit as dishonest.

Superficially, Theranos was different. Captained by a charismatic, captivating young woman who was still in her teens when she founded the company, Theranos presented itself as being in business for the good of humankind. Holmes claimed to have chosen business rather than, say, setting up a nonprofit organization, because business was supposedly a better vehicle for the achievement of its virtuous goals. And as Holmes said more than once, Theranos "is about being able to do good."

The financial fraud that characterized Enron is as old as finance itself. But the black box of technology—Theranos's Edison blood-testing device—was presented as being all about the future. Breakthrough engineering would solve problems incumbent blood testing laboratories would never solve because they were doing too well with the status quo.

Some of the things that Skilling did—publicly calling an analyst who asked a perfectly reasonable question an "asshole,"[44] glorying in what he viewed as a world driven by the survival of the fittest, terrifying those who he claimed were too stupid to "get it" (a phrase he endlessly repeated) about his business—were for the most part alien to Holmes. She was all about ingratiating herself.

That said, these two stories have a lot in common.

Both Enron and Theranos attached themselves to people with big names. Both had star-studded boards of directors. Enron had Bill Kristol and Paul Krugman visit twice a year to discuss the future. They were paid $25,000 a visit. The company's closeness to the Bush family was no secret. Recipients of the Enron Prize for Distinguished Public Service included Nelson Mandela, Colin Powell, Mikhail Gorbachev, and Alan Greenspan. Greenspan received the award in 2001. There was no award the next year. The members of the Theranos board were a Who's Who of big shots. And the roster of famous people who praised Holmes, including among many others Bill Clinton, would fill a book. In both cases, the association with well-known people helped inoculate the companies from the prying eyes of regulators and from those among their own employees who held on to their consciences and knew something was not right.

The second trait these two people and their companies have in common is that they vividly illustrate the dangers of deregulation and the critical role of public oversight of private business. Deregulation of business in the United States began in a serious way in the 1970s. Wall Street deregulation was in full swing by 1975. Airline deregulation followed later in the decade. In Ronald Reagan's first inaugural address, he famously said, "[G]overnment is not the solution to our problem; government is the problem."[45] In June of 2000, Lay delivered a speech in London about the wonders of deregulation. If anyone needed proof, the appreciation of Enron's stock by a factor of nine in the preceding decade provided it. "We'll do it again this coming decade," Lay predicted.[46]

This prediction turned out to be wrong. If the run-up of the price of the stock made the case for deregulation, did its opposite make the case for more regulation? The federal government thought so. The Sarbanes-Oxley Act of 2002 was designed "To protect investors by improving the accuracy and reliability of corporate disclosures made pursuant to the securities laws..."[47] And of course the debacle of 2008 demonstrated that under certain circumstances, government was the only solution. Unregulated private greed was the problem.

The only reason that Theranos was able to inaugurate its partnership with Walgreens in Arizona in 2015 was that the state enacted a law allowing its citizens to order their blood tests without a doctor's involvement. John Carreyrou describes this as "a bill Theranos had practically written itself and heavily lobbied for."[48] If that bill had not been enacted, the health of Arizonans, which was endangered by Theranos, would have been better protected.

Holmes suggested in a coy manner to reporters that Theranos's blood analyzers were being used for American soldiers in Afghanistan. In fact, they never were. The reason is that the army demanded certification from the Food and Drug Administration that the devices performed as represented. This certification Theranos never even tried to produce because its technology never performed. There is a lesson here. The next time you hear someone say that government is the problem, think twice.

Finally, Holmes and Skilling belong together because they both show that in our modern age, after all the corporate chicanery we have seen, we can successfully be lied to. They were both very good liars. Indeed, staggeringly good. Good enough to fool a lot of smart people. But not forever.

Many charismatic leaders have done great things. How can we sort out the fakes from the genuine articles, to discern the difference between charisma as con and charisma as true leadership? When is charisma productive? When is it real? When are the followers glad that they followed? How can you tell before the fact that behind the public presentation of the charismatic leader is an attainable vision worth striving for?

The fundamentals of business will sooner or later apply. The products have to work. People must buy them. Early investors must want to sell their stock, and later investors must want to buy. The distortion field disappears, and reality will have its day. For Holmes and Skilling, the outcome was disaster.

From the Department of Eternal Verities, we have recourse to Benjamin Franklin's best-selling essay of 1758, "The Way to Wealth": "Trusting too much to others' care is the ruin of many; for in the affairs of this world, men are saved, not by faith, but by the want of it."[49]

CHAPTER 15

CHARISMA IN AMERICAN BUSINESS HISTORY: YESTERDAY AND TODAY

The thesis of this book can be simply stated. Speaking generally, charisma played only a minor part in American business during the first of the three periods into which this discussion is divided—from 1945 to the mid-1970s. The representative CEO of this era is Harlow Curtice. Charisma was not necessary during these years because the United States dominated the world economy. The CEOs were administrators, men in gray flannel suits.

The example of a notable exception is Edwin Land, a charismatic CEO who created a new technology, instant photography. Much admired by Steve Jobs, who is the leading exemplar of charisma in American business, Land's personality was magnetic, a product of his vision, his mastery of technology, and his showmanship.

During the second period, from the mid-1970s to the mid-1990s, we begin to encounter an increasing number of charismatic businesspeople. These include Lee Iacocca, Sam Walton, Mary Kay Ash, Michael Milken, and Sir James Goldsmith.

Lee Iacocca saved Chrysler when the company appeared to be in a hopeless situation. His autobiography was the best-selling book of its kind at that time.

Sam Walton showed what charisma could do in retailing. Faced with what appeared to be dominant competition—Kmart and Sears especially—he demonstrated how a new look at an old industry could overwhelm competitors who assumed that next year would be like last year and that they could coast uphill forever on the basis of their past dominance.

Mary Kay Ash showed how a member of an out-group, women, could create a successful new company. She marketed not only cosmetics. She marketed herself. What I have done, she communicated to the women who contracted with her company, you can do, too.

During this period, the general narrative of American business history is the transition from managerial capitalism to investor capitalism. This narrative may be a bit exaggerated, but there is some truth to it. We see that truth when we meet Michael Milken and Sir James Goldsmith, who were not formally CEOs but might as well have been. Milken weaponized junk bonds and attracted a fanatical following. Goldsmith was the model for Sir Lawrence Wildman (that last name was doubtless not chosen by accident) in the 1987 movie *Wall Street*.[1] Goldsmith's raid on Goodyear shows how activist investors could attack traditionally managed companies. The business world was beginning to look for charisma in its CEOs during this era.

The third period into which the book is divided begins in 1995. August of that year marked two of the most important events in the history of technology. One was Microsoft's release of Windows 95. The other was Netscape's IPO, demonstrating that the internet was a power to be reckoned with. From that time, we enter into the era of the charismatic CEO. This era has been characterized by the rise of technology and the ability of a corporate CEO to touch consumers.

We return to the Steve Jobs story in the first chapter of this section. NeXT, his computer start-up, failed. Pixar, his "side bet," turned into a startling success. It was during the dozen years from 1985 to 1997 when he was absent from Apple that he grew up and learned how to use his charisma to transform a company flirting with bankruptcy into the Apple we know today.

In our next chapter, we discuss Oprah Winfrey's rise to preeminence. Her journey has been as spectacular as it has been unlikely. The most charismatic African American woman in the history of American business, she created a new model for power and influence in every communications medium to which she turned her attention.

We then move on to Elon Musk, an immigrant from South Africa by way of Canada. This book began by discussing the automobile industry in the age of Harlow Curtice and the glory days of General Motors. Musk is revolutionizing the industry with Tesla. The car is impressive, but Musk's highly unorthodox conduct has generated unforced errors in its development.

The chapter that follows completes the Steve Jobs story by illustrating the magic he worked at Apple.

We can think of this historical development in terms of three phases:

PHASE 1–ADMINISTRATION VERSUS CHARISMA

The first phase of the postwar history of charisma can be called the "gray flannel suit" phase. This was a world in which a job had a man rather than a man having a job. Its symbol was the organization chart, perfected by Alfred P. Sloan Jr. of General Motors. It was a comfortable environment for the millions of veterans returning from military service during the war. This lasted from the end of World War II to the mid-1970s.

This phase offered a structure and caste of mind that suited big business in manufacturing. One thing led to another. Events took place in order. The goal was to fit in rather than to think out of the box. This was right for the economy, for the culture, and for the experience of the former officer who was now a vice president of, say, public relations. Charisma was not in demand. Business did not need it. Phase One was the phase of anti-charisma in favor of down-to-earth, routine administration.

PHASE 2–THE TRANSITION

The workforce coming of age in the mid-1970s had quite a different experience of life from their parents. Far fewer people had led the regimented life of the armed forces. A large number of people had experience with the drug culture, which differed in important ways from the alcohol culture. The former was mind-altering. The latter mind-numbing.

Ideas about patriotism had been deeply shaken by the defining experiences of Vietnam and Watergate. The desire for inclusiveness was expanding. All-male educational institutions were becoming coeducational. The historic wrongs done to African Americans were more generally recognized by the educated segment of society. Demography and history demanded that a place be made for people who were not White males of Anglo-Saxon heritage.

The young people rioting in the streets of Chicago during the Democratic National Convention in the summer of 1968 were junior executives a decade later. In an economic climate of stagflation, they wanted something different from what their parents had strived for. They were a little more daring and a lot less patient.

Microsoft was founded in 1975 and Apple the following year, both by college dropouts. Both rejected the military mindset of IBM. Indeed, it is difficult to imagine a public company with a name like Apple being founded in the 1950s. Technology was to be democratized, and its headquarters were moved from the East and the Midwest to the West. The world of Harlow Curtice, which celebrated established procedure and straight lines, was in the process of being transformed into the world of Steve Jobs, which insisted upon seeing around corners.

At the same time, finance was attracting a new breed of entrepreneur, who lived not for the system—known derisively as "working for the man"—but off it. Think of Michael Milken in his X-shaped secretive office in Beverly Hills, showing up each day at four thirty in the morning, doing mysterious deals and making a fortune at an early age. The idea of a Sloan-like organization chart would have been ridiculous to him. It would have been nothing more than just so much overhead. Milken needed charisma, not hierarchy, to make his operation work.

Milken was the enabler of a new approach to corporate life in the United States. Companies that had existed for decades and had become institutions in the communities in which they were located were suddenly "in play." Financiers using new financial instruments created a market for corporate control the like of which had not been seen since the great railroad wars of the nineteenth century.

PHASE 3—THE NEW RULES

By the mid-1990s, the seeds planted in Phase Two came into full flower. Venture capital began to play a greater role in private enterprise than ever before. Venture capital has been around for a long time. A recently written history traces it back to whaling in the 1830s.[2] Note that the word *venture* was at its birth "adventure."[3] And adventure was what the young, smart people were looking for in the age of the internet.

The internet age quickly became the age of information and of social media. By the early twenty-first century, top executives of headline companies are all public figures, whether they want to be or not.

Satya Nadella, CEO of Microsoft as of 2014, is a good example. The capitalist system that we all enjoy "will fundamentally be in jeopardy," he recently said, if companies do not take action on climate change. When Nadella talks about the future, he is informed, optimistic, and convincing. And executives of companies as powerful as Microsoft are expected to take positions on issues of public policy.[4]

We know a great deal about Steve Jobs not just because he is the subject of more than half a dozen biographies but because one of his first lovers and their child together have both written books about him. The racy texts Jeff Bezos, the wealthiest person in history, sent to his lover are available on the internet now. There is no place to hide for the superstar CEO.

In Phase Three of charisma, we encounter a profoundly new world. It demands that the CEO show a public face. Charisma is in high demand. Some aspects of it can be taught. Other aspects cannot.

The truly charismatic business leader has been touched by genius. Often, unfortunately, with that genius comes deficits. Empathy and simple human decency cannot be allowed to get in the way of the ambition of a charismatic business leader who is out to—for example—save the human race and populate Mars. A world that so passionately values charisma is a world characterized by uncertainty and demanding flexibility. It is an open question how much of that uncertainty a society can sustain.

The word *charisma* is used all the time these days in articles and books about business executives. Indeed, companies are sometimes described as charismatic. This was not true in the 1950s. Then, the job of the executive was taken to be what Alfred P. Sloan Jr. described it as being. It was to increase the return on the investment of the shareholders because it was their capital that was at risk, "and it is in their interests first of all that the corporation is supposed to be run."

Charisma plays no part in Sloan's autobiography. That is among the reasons that he has exercised little influence upon the leading figures in the American business world today. General Motors in Sloan's era had something close to monopoly power. Today, we live in a world of global competition.

The issue with the approach of Sloan is not that his advice is irrelevant today. Businesses still have to make money. The problem is that profit alone is an insufficient raison d'être. Modern executives must—to be true leaders—do more than make money. They are also responsible for making meaning. They must inspire. It is in this endeavor that charisma plays such an important role. The charismatic leader lives on the edge of history, bringing the future to the present. The ability to be an inspirational leader is in part a gift, as Saint Paul and, nineteen centuries later, Max Weber said. Charisma concerns itself with creating a version of chaos—disrupting expectations and motivating people to head in a new direction—based more on hope than on reason or experience.

If a person is endowed with the gift of charisma, it has to be polished. Charisma is a social construct. No one becomes charismatic by themselves. Steve Jobs is the perfect example. In his first stint at Apple, he was a diamond in the rough. After twelve years of polishing by Ed Catmull, by Laurene Powell Jobs, and by life, he returned to Apple—and the rest is history.

We have seen that charisma can be faked. The business world today needs charisma so much that the opportunity to fake it looms large. Elizabeth Holmes and Jeffrey Skilling took advantage of this need.

Having established what this book is, a word is in order about what it is not. This book is about general trends. There are exceptions to the generalizations, and it has not been my intention to list every one of them. Edwin Land was an exception to the common CEO of his era. Walt Disney (1901–1966) was also an exception, and if this book were a compendium, he would merit a chapter.

This book deals with CEOs, many of whom are company founders. Charismatic leaders also exist within companies, but for reasons of space, they have been omitted.

There are also exceptions to the current mania for charisma. Paramount among them is Mark Zuckerberg. At first blush, he seems to check all the boxes. He has founded a fabulously successful company and become personally wealthy beyond imagining. In a get-big-fast industry, Facebook got big fast. Yet no one would call him charismatic. He did visit the same ashram in India where Steve Jobs stayed before founding Apple. If Zuckerberg hoped that charisma would rub off, he left disappointed.[5]

An illustration of Zuckerberg's lack of charisma was on display when he testified at a hearing of the Financial Services Committee of the House of Representatives on October 23, 2019.[6] Nancy Pelosi, Speaker of the House, has labeled Facebook a "shameful" company that thrives on "misleading the American people."[7] To the outside world, he is without charisma. Inside Facebook, I am informed, he is viewed differently, with charisma aplenty.

Although one doubts that Zuckerberg will ever have trouble putting food on the table, Facebook may yet be damaged by his clumsy and inept self-presentation and more seriously by what appears to be his lack of understanding of the impact of his company's services, including, for example, monetizing hatred, disseminating lies, bullying, and so forth. Wikipedia has a very long entry entitled "Criticism of Facebook." *Vanity Fair* recently published an article describing Zuckerberg as "the most reviled man in tech."[8]

Zuckerberg illustrates that charisma is one lever of leadership, but it is one among many. If you do not have it and cannot develop it (which in Zuckerberg's case is yet to be seen), you must rely more heavily on the other levers. These include industry position made possible by first-mover advantage, dictatorial control of your company made possible by dysfunctional corporate governance, and the help of other executives in your company who are charismatic. If your products or services are sufficiently magnetic—as Facebook (and Instagram and WhatsApp, which Facebook owns)—are to billions of people, the CEO can apparently borrow the charisma of what he or she is selling.

A case can be made that charismatic authority is unsustainable. Charismatic authority demands a denial of "fine-grained and complex" problems in favor of "vision." It is correct that charismatic leadership is about "smashing limits."

If Elon Musk were constrained by convention, there would be no Teslas on the road today. That company has already made a major contribution to the electrification of transportation. Unless cars, trucks, and buses are weaned from fossil fuel, the battle against climate change will be lost. Nothing less than species survival is at stake. The creation of Tesla is the accomplishment of a man who, after striking it rich at PayPal, could have spent his whole life throwing parties for himself. So far, his contributions to society appear to outweigh his shortcomings.

When discussing the sustainability of charismatic leadership, the problem of passing it along from one person to the next asserts itself as exceptionally difficult. Most institutions fail at the task of charismatic succession and by default become bureaucracies managed in accord with rational characteristics.

With a secular institution like a corporation, the problem of charismatic succession is acute. Some companies manage it, at least for a time. Arthur Rock, who provided some of the seed money for Intel, said that "Intel needed [Robert] Noyce, [Gordon] Moore, and [Andy] Grove. And it needed them in that order."[9] The accomplishments of these men were remarkable. The men who have succeeded them have not been charismatic, nor have they been as successful.

General Electric provides a more severe and stark example of the succession problem involving charismatic leadership. GE's CEO from 1981 to 2001 was Jack Welch. In 1999, *Fortune* named him the best manager of the twentieth century. [10] Welch said that "My success will be determined by how well my successor grows it [i.e., GE] in the next twenty years."

According to the *New York Times*, "Mr. Welch brought much needed energy and charisma to the chief executive's job and streamlined GE's bloated bureaucracy. Had he stayed on through the financial crisis, perhaps he would have recaptured the growth that eluded Mr. [Jeffrey] Immelt. [Immelt was Welch's handpicked successor.]

"But hardly anyone considers Mr. Welch... a management role model anymore, and the conglomerate model he championed at GE—that with strict discipline, you could successfully manage any business as long as your market share was first or second—has been thoroughly discredited..." According to an NYU Business School professor, "It's always tough to follow a legend." Because of the failure of GE during the Immelt years, no one looks at Welch as a legend any longer. [11]

It is worth mentioning that governmental restrictions on corporate activity have not developed in a straight line. In the years after the Civil War, corporations were remarkably free of governmental restraint. During the Progressive Era, roughly 1900 to 1918, the government, especially on the federal level, became far more active than it had been previously in regulating corporations, even to the point of regulating the prices the railroad industry, the nation's most important at the time, could charge.

Coincident with the rise of government regulation was the decline of charismatic business leadership. Names such as Rockefeller, Carnegie, Morgan, Stanford, and Vanderbilt—famously labeled "robber barons" by journalist Matthew Josephson—are far better known than their successors in the early twentieth century. "As the barons of the nineteenth-century business retired," in the words of one historian, "their successors appeared to have come from a smaller mold. No one ranked William C. Brown of the New York Central with the Vanderbilts, or George Gould and John D. Rockefeller Jr. with their fathers; nor did the fastidious Elbert Gary of US Steel compare as a public personality... with Andrew Carnegie... The emphasis in business was shifting from the man to the company, from ingenuity to training, from an ideal of competition to a matter-of-fact belief in cooperation and stabilized profits."[12]

It is true that charisma is much in demand in the modern American corporation. The question being raised here is that just as charisma has given way to bureaucracy in the past, could something similar happen in the future? Max Weber said charisma could not exist in a bureaucratic environment. Perhaps that will prove true in the future, and corporate leaders two decades from now will resemble Harlow Curtice more than Steve Jobs.

Elizabeth Holmes is but the latest example of the spectacular failure of a charismatic leader in business. Two decades ago, the charismatic CEO of the day was Jeffrey Skilling, CEO of Enron. His charisma led to a bankruptcy of monumental proportions. There would be no difficulty in assembling an impressive list of charismatic failures between Skilling and Holmes.

A case can be made for returning to the mores of Curtice's era. No one would call him charismatic. But he was an honest man. The numbers he signed off on were real. People were not hurt by him the way they have been by Holmes, Skilling, and others like them.

Despite all this, I believe that demand for charismatic CEOs is going to increase.[13] I say this as a historian, which means I am no better at predicting the future than anybody else, but my belief is based not only on the work on this particular book but also on a half century of studying American business history.

What can the charismatic CEO do that the plain-vanilla CEO cannot? Three areas of potential accomplishment assert themselves.

First, the charismatic CEO can personally breach barriers erected by society that keep out-groups from attaining the commanding heights of corporate success. We have seen in previous chapters how Oprah Winfrey and Mary Kay Ash achieved this goal. Tim Cook has as well by being a spectacularly successful CEO of Apple who is also openly gay.

Second, there is every reason to believe that the world is going to be more technologically complex in the future. Let us look at the past for what may serve as a guide to this assertion. The electro-mechanical household refrigerator came on the market in the United States about nine decades ago. Everyone knew what it was for. Everyone knew how to operate it. Nobody had to be told anything. When the personal computer hit the market, its usefulness was not at all clear. The future holds more computers and fewer refrigerators. It will take a charismatic business leader to develop the stories and the metaphors that unleash the power of consumer technology in the future. Steve Jobs said the computer was "a bicycle for our minds."[14] Metaphors such as this contributed to his charisma.

The third reason suggesting the increasing importance of charismatic CEO leadership in the future is the need to align the incentives of those who work in the corporation with the aims of the corporation itself. As robots take over assembly lines, the people working—especially in technology companies—will be knowledge workers. These people will have options to work at other firms.

It will be an important part of the job of the CEO to bind these workers to his or her firm. This goal can be achieved through vision. Steve Jobs always believed that the computer was meant to be a product for the mass market. It was to be presented to consumers rather than pushed upon them. Consumers would bond with it because it came combined, as Jobs insisted, with aesthetic considerations privileged. Beauty with functionality. "On the first day I got my iPod," a twelve-year-old girl reported, "I kissed it good night."[15] One would not kiss an ugly product. Design has always played a key role at Apple.

Jobs intuitively understood that engineers should feel like artists. Remember how he had everyone involved sign the Mac? That desire to combine technology with the liberal arts comes from the top at Apple and still suffuses the company. If it is sacrificed, not only will the products be less appealing, the meaning of working at Apple will be put at risk.

In "Self-Reliance," his immortal 1841 essay, Ralph Waldo Emerson wrote, "An institution is the lengthened shadow of one man..."[16] Any good thesis is worth a good overstatement, which this is. But when you see a corporation in crisis, this statement is worth thinking about.

This book has provided numerous such stories. Mary Kay founding her company in spite of the sudden death of her husband, and Lee Iacocca breathing new life into a moribund Chrysler are but two examples. In his definition of charisma, Iacocca emphasized the importance of trust in creating it.

Some people believe the word *charisma* is inapplicable to business. John Kotter, an emeritus professor at the Harvard Business School who has written extensively about business leadership, insists that there is nothing "mystical" about it. Leadership in business, he believes, "has nothing to do with having 'charisma' or other exotic personality traits."[17] Iacocca disagreed with him.

Recall that when Weber wrote of charisma, he referred to people with "supernatural, superhuman, or at least specifically exceptional qualities." "Supernatural" and "superhuman" are a stretch when dealing with the secular world. However, over the course of centuries, charisma has undergone "a transformation from religious idea to sociological concept to general usage." Read about business today, and one sees the word constantly.

Reference has been made to the three phases of charisma. The first was the world John Kotter describes. Charisma in business was hard to find. In the second phase, one finds it, but it is still more the exception than the rule. In the third phase, people have come to demand it.

Among the forces driving this transformation are changes in communications technology. How could Harlow Curtice have become widely known? The media infrastructure for business stardom we have today was not in place in the 1950s. Network news from the end of World War II to the 1960s was only fifteen minutes in length each weekday evening. Even then, the only business news was the stock market, the rise and fall of which was broken down into three categories: industrials, rails, and utilities. There were few, if any, programs devoted specifically to business news. There was no business analogue to *Modern Farmer*, which aired very early on Saturday mornings from 1950 to 1958.

Businesses were bureaucratic institutions. The cult of personality was discouraged. It would have been considered in very bad taste for Curtice to put himself forward as a charismatic leader. In fact, it might have cost him his job.

By Phase Two, the reluctance of businesspeople to position themselves as leaders who were at least implicitly charismatic was diminishing. In her realm, Mary Kay Ash was unquestionably charismatic. In his realm, Sam Walton was, too. He became nationally known because of the omnipresence of his stores and because the fantastic success of his company made him fabulously wealthy.

Lee Iacocca solved the problem of becoming a public figure by putting himself on television commercials and by writing a very well-crafted best-selling autobiography. In that book, he not only told his story his way, he also advertised Chrysler and in the process managed to wrap himself in the American flag.

By the 1980s, mass media was coming to recognize that there was quite a large commercial market for stories about charismatic business leaders. The world of the media also underwent a revolution with the coming of cable. Ted Turner founded CNN in 1980. This network operated twenty-four hours a day, seven days a week. It needed stories. Business could provide them.

By Phase Three, cable channels such as CNBC were devoting themselves exclusively to business. *Mad Money*, starring—and that is the word—Jim Cramer, premiered in 2005. Cramer's infotainment program features not only business commentary but interviews with important business figures. A program like this is unimaginable in 1995, never mind 1955. Cramer comes on like a carnival barker, but he is no fool and not inexperienced on Wall Street. A graduate of Harvard College and the Harvard Law School, he has worked for Goldman Sachs and managed his own hedge fund in addition to being a best-selling author.

Cramer interviewed Elizabeth Holmes for *Mad Money* twice. The second of these interviews, on October 16, 2015, has already been referred to. The first took place five and a half months earlier on April 27. This April 27 interview is worth seeing, because it brings to the fore an important question—how do you spot a fraud?

Cramer interviewed Holmes in San Francisco with the Golden Gate Bridge as a backdrop. He described Theranos as a "revolutionary diagnostics company that allows individuals to take better control of their own bodies while at the same time upending the existing pattern in this costly, inefficient, and painful for the client—namely you—[system]. This is a revolutionary company that threatens to change health care the same way that Amazon changed retail or Intel and Microsoft changed computing or Apple, yes, changed the cell phone. It could be that huge."[18] With this kind of publicity, how do you give free play to your own judgment about how real Holmes's "technology" was?

The confidence man, or in this case woman, is nothing new. Historian Daniel J. Boorstin has written about the "booster spirit," which played an important role in enticing Europeans to migrate to the American West. This spirit "called for an ever greater willingness to take risks... No wonder that in their enthusiasm [i.e., the enthusiasm of boosters], they sometimes confused the vision and the reality, that (as one early [newspaper] editor put it) they 'sometimes represented things that have not yet gone through the formality of taking place.'"[19]

This is by no means a strictly American phenomenon. "The Emperor's New Clothes" is a Hans Christian Andersen story published in Denmark in 1837. It is about a vain emperor who is sold a new suit of clothes that is magnificent but invisible to stupid people. The suit, of course, does not exist at all.[20] This is the Enron story. Critics of the company were dismissed as too stupid to "get it." They were mocked as "assholes."

The birth of the computer industry was characterized by marketing endless possibility. As one early Microsoft engineer put it, "we could sell a promise and pull it off... And virtually everything we sold was not a product when we sold it. We sold promises."[21]

The term *vaporware* was coined by a Microsoft engineer in 1982. Vaporware has been defined as a good idea incompletely implemented, or not implemented at all. Microsoft presently has a market capitalization of over $1.88 trillion. How do you tell the truth from a promise that will not be fulfilled? Is Tesla the automobile of the future, or is it vaporware? How do you draw the line between skepticism and cynicism?

There is no easy answer to these questions. Bethany McLean has said she looks to "outsiders—people who aren't part of the system." She believes short sellers are more likely to read footnotes carefully than others and "play an important role in policing the system." Of course, they are biased, too. They want the price of the stock to drop. But she believes the fact that "they are biased in the opposite direction" is an important counterweight to those who are boosting the stock.[22] Short sellers did play an important role in exposing Enron. They could play no part with regard to Theranos, because the company was never publicly traded.

One can offer all the usual advice. Show special care if you want too much for something to be true. Try to get beyond the hype. Look at a company with fresh eyes. Remember that the person who unmasked the scam in "The Emperor's New Clothes" was a child who was unafraid of being called ignorant or unworthy. And so forth.

Unfortunately, when all is said and done, there is no silver bullet for detecting fraud. Enron and Theranos will happen again. Perhaps every time an investor or an employee looks at a charismatic leader, he or she should not stop by saying this could be the next Elon Musk or Steve Jobs. What should also be said is this could be the next Jeffrey Skilling or Elizabeth Holmes.

If you, the reader, want to be a leader, charisma is a tool that can help you immeasurably. Charisma turns a market exchange—you work and I pay you—into a social exchange—follow me and you will be a more fulfilled human being. You will do the best work of your life (Jobs); you will revolutionize transportation and colonize Mars (Musk); you will lower the cost of living for everyone (Walton); you will transform women into the beautiful creatures God intended them to be (Ash); and so on.

You, the acolyte, may not believe the goal is probable or even possible (colonize Mars?!). The charismatic leader asks you to believe in him or her and not to limit yourself with doubts, however reasonable your doubts might be. The charismatic leader says, "Trust me. I know you can do it." "It" is whatever assignment you have been given to contribute to the achievement of the goal of the charismatic individual in question. "You can do it!" is what Mary Kay's mother constantly told her. The central dilemma of charisma is that people endowed with it can lead (Walton) or mislead (Holmes). Indeed, they can mislead at one time (Jobs at NeXT) and lead at another (Jobs at Apple after 1997).

Charisma permits the believer to put his or her reason on the shelf and follow the leader. It is inspiring, seductive, and dangerous.

From the historical narrative presented in these pages, a number of suggestions emerge. First, an aspiring leader who is not charismatic should learn how to change that situation. Some of the components of charisma can be taught. Knowing that you are not charismatic and desiring to be is an important step to take. What to do?

No primer will be offered here. For a place to start, I suggest the *Harvard Business Review* article by John Antonakis and colleagues entitled "Learning Charisma."[23] It is accessible and easily digested.

Charisma should be looked at not as a binary phenomenon (that is, either you have it or you don't) but rather as a continuum. A set of common-sense measures such as proposed in the Antonakis article won't make you Steve Jobs, but they will help you distance yourself from Mark Zuckerberg, which in this particular is a good thing. Get more charismatic. That is suggestion number one.

Suggestion number two is don't believe what you read or hear in the media. An important part of moving in the right direction on the charismatic continuum is manipulating your messaging and your public image. When people think of Elon Musk, they think of creativity unchained. When they think of Tim Cook, they think of integrity. Neither of these thoughts have come into our minds by accident.

The management of public relations is difficult. You have your own agenda. Reporters and commentators have theirs. If you succeed, you will be reading what you want to read and hearing what you yourself have sold. Don't forget it. Jeffrey Skilling and Elizabeth Holmes did.

Suggestion number three is never forget that the truth will eventually be known. Find out what the truth is. In order to do so, you have to make it crystal clear that you really want to know it. The higher you climb on the leadership ladder, the further removed you are from the facts on the ground.

As Andy Grove pointed out, snow melts at the periphery. The charismatic businessperson spends a lot of time on the borders of the business. If this book had been a study of businesspeople who failed, time and again it would have been apparent that "the CEO was the last to know." The business leader can only be charismatic if he or she somehow manages to be omnipresent.

A daunting challenge. But the results of success make it all worthwhile to a select set of intrepid souls.

ACKNOWLEDGMENTS

Many people helped me in writing this book, and it is a pleasure to express my gratitude. As in every research project that I have undertaken since 1978, the research services of Baker Library at Harvard Business School have proven invaluable. Jeff Cronin and Kathleen Ryan supplied vital and sometimes difficult-to-access data. Repeated requests were met with timely assistance. Their help was made possible by the Division of Research at Harvard Business School, which also funded the purchase of books and the use of other libraries.

At the Harvard Business School Senior Faculty Center, Luz Velazquez was generous in her explanation of the workings of Mary Kay. Also invariably helpful was Luz's colleague, Paula Alexander.

Arthur Klebanoff, the CEO of RosettaBooks, showed unwavering confidence in this project. He read the complete manuscript and made innumerable suggestions for improvement. My thanks also to Brian Skulnik of RosettaBooks and to my editor Mina Samuels.

Robert M. Sussman read the complete manuscript and wrote a lengthy and valuable critique. A lifelong friend, Bob is also acknowledged in the first book that I published back in 1980. Walter A. Friedman, lecturer at Harvard Business School and co-editor of the *Business History Review*, read the entire manuscript and provided numerous helpful suggestions. Walter also encouraged me to publish a review article of biographies of Steve Jobs in the *Business History Review*.

Tom Nicholas, William J. Abernathy Professor of Business Administration at Harvard Business School, was a terrific thought companion in the preparation of this book. His new cases on Edwin Land, for example, are as outstanding as his teaching ratings. His history of venture capital is the standard by which all other such studies are now measured. I would also like to express my gratitude to Robert J. Dolan, Baker Foundation professor at Harvard Business School, for his guidance on some particularly difficult passages in the book. Bob has been a leading expert on marketing for decades, and his generosity in sharing that expertise has benefitted me enormously.

I would also like to thank my friends Michael Dearing and David Ruben. Michael, an exceptionally successful entrepreneur, helped me understand the inner workings of a world that I could only read about. David's sharp eye enabled me to access sources I otherwise would have missed.

My greatest debt is to Reed E. Hundt. Reed's insight into the issues with which this book deals have been outstanding. A sympathetic yet blunt critic, Reed's combination of business experience, training as a litigator, years in corporate board rooms, and love for the liberal arts, made this a much more sophisticated book than it otherwise would have been. I owe him a lot (and not only for his help on this book).

Also thank you to Nathanial Hundt, and Julia and Mike Roberts.

I want to acknowledge the thousands of students it has been my honor and pleasure to teach over the decades. I have been teaching business history to MBAs and executives since 1979. During these years, I learned far more from them than they did from me. This book is a token of my gratitude.

Young, handsome, ambitious to make a dent in the universe —**Steve Jobs** in his early twenties.

Jobs with what is arguably the most important product of the century—so far.

The master presenter—show, don't tell. **Jobs** holding the feather-light MacBook Air on his fingertips.

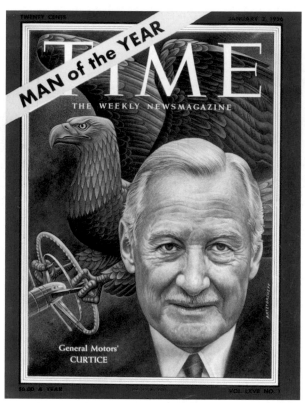

The perfect example of a CEO in the pre-charismatic era. Like almost all corporate figures in the 1950s, **Harlow Curtice** was unknown to the general public.

Changing times—**Lee Iacocca** and the beginning of the CEO as superstar. Master of the Chrysler turnaround, star of television commercials, best-selling author.

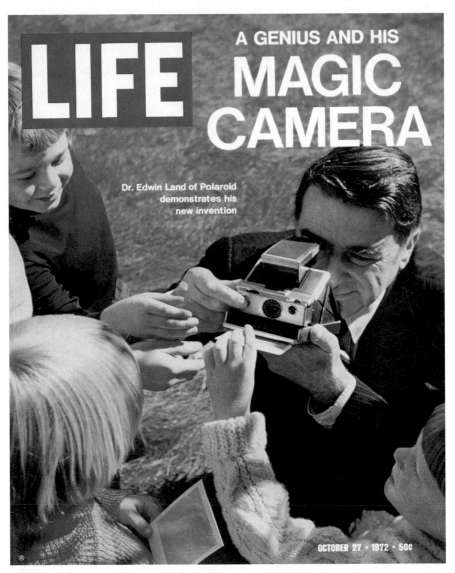

The progenitor of the era of the charismatic CEO. **Edwin Land**—a genius who makes magic.

Sam Walton with President George H.W. Bush on the day he received the Presidential Medal of Freedom—March 17, 1992.

Greatest retailer of his era. **Walton** was idolized by some and hated by others, but known to everyone.

Mary Kay—her name was her brand. Aspirational. Inspirational. A path-breaking woman in the business world.

Oprah Avoided politics until the Obama campaign. He awarded her the Presidential Medal of Freedom on November 20, 2013.

Oprah Winfrey—the "Queen of All Media." Known all over the world, she is the first female African American multibillionaire.

Elon Musk and the automobile he summoned into being through genius, force of will, and charisma—the Tesla.

Michael Milken—junk bond king. The evil genius of financial capitalism.

Sir James Goldsmith—corporate raider. Welcome guest at Milken's "Predators' Ball."

Elizabeth Holmes with her Jobs-like turtleneck. Her unblinking stare was her trademark. The charismatic leader as fraud.

"Theranos Chairman, CEO and Founder Elizabeth Holmes at TechCrunch Disrupt on September 8, 2014 (14996937900).jpg," *Wikimedia Commons*.

BIBLIOGRAPHY

I. BOOKS

Amelio, Gil, and William L. Simon. *On The Firing Line: My 500 Days At Apple*. New York: HarperBusiness, 1998.

Ash, Mary Kay. *Mary Kay*. New York: Harper & Row, 1987.

_____. *The Mary Kay Way: Timeless Principles from America's Greatest Woman Entrepreneur*. Hoboken: Wiley, 2008.

Barnouw, Erik. *A Tower in Babel*. New York: Oxford University Press, 1966.

_____. *The Golden Web*. New York: Oxford University Press, 1968.

_____. *The Image Empire*. New York: Oxford University Press, 1970.

_____. *Tube of Plenty*. New York: Oxford University Press, 1975.

Bernstein, Irving. *Turbulent Years*. Boston: Houghton Mifflin, 1971.

Bonanos, Christopher. *Instant: The Story of Polaroid*. New York: Princeton Architectural Press, 2012.

Boorstin, Daniel J. *The Americans: The National Experience*. New York: Knopf, 1965.

Brennan, Chrisann. *The Bite in the Apple*. New York: St. Martin's Press, 2013.

Brennan-Jobs, Lisa. *Small Fry*. New York: Grove Press, 2018.

Brown, Jackie. *Ask Me About MARY KAY: The Story Behind The Bumper Sticker on the Pink Cadillac*. Durham: Strategic, 2010.

Bruchey, Stuart W. *Robert Oliver: Merchant of Baltimore*. Baltimore: The Johns Hopkins University Press, 1956.

Bruck, Connie. *The Predators' Ball: The Inside Story of Drexel Burnham and the Rise of the Junk Bond Raiders*. New York: Simon & Schuster, 1988.

Bryman, Alan. *Charisma & Leadership in Organizations*. London: Sage, 1992.

Butcher, Lee. *Accidental Millionaire: The Rise and Fall of Steve Jobs at Apple Computer*. New York: Paragon House, 1988.

Carreyrou, John. *Bad Blood: Secrets and Lies in a Silicon Valley Startup.* New York: Knopf, 2018.

Carroll, Paul. *Big Blues: The Unmaking of IBM.* New York: Crown, 1993.

Catmull, Ed. *Creativity, Inc.: Overcoming the Unseen Forces that Stand in the Way of True Inspiration.* New York: Random House, 2014.

Cervantes, Miguel de. *Don Quixote.* London: Sovereign, 2014.

Chandler, Jr., Alfred D., Thomas K. McCraw, and Richard S. Tedlow. *Management Past and Present: A Casebook on the History of American Business* Cincinnati: South-Western, 1996.

Cheit, Earl F., Ed. *The Business Establishment.* New York: Wylie, 1964.

Collier, Peter and David Horowitz, *The Fords: An American Epic.* New York: Summit, 1987.

Collins, Jim. *Good to Great.* New York: HarperCollins, 2001.

Collins, Jim, and Morten T. Hansen, *Great by Choice.* New York: Harper-Collins, 2011.

Doctorow, E.L. *Ragtime.* New York: Bantam, 1976.

Dougan, Michael B. *Arkansas Odyssey: The Saga of Arkansas from Prehistoric Times to Present.* Little Rock: Rose Publishing, 1994.

Douglass, Frederick. *The Complete Works of Frederick Douglass.* Madison & Adams Press, 2018.

Du Bois, W.E.B. *The Souls of Black Folk.* New York: Dover, 1994.

Eastman, Joel W. *Styling vs. Safety: The American Automobile Industry and the Development of Automotive Safety, 1900–1966.* Lanham: University Press of America, 1984.

Emerson, Ralph Waldo. *Essays – First Series.* 1882.

Erikson, Erik H. *Gandhi's Truth: On the Origins of Militant Nonviolence.* New York: Norton, 1970.

Fierstein, Ronald K. *A Triumph of Genius: Edwin Land, Polaroid, and the Kodak Patent War.* Chicago: Ankerwyke, American Bar Association, 2015.

Foster, Lawrence G. *Robert Wood Johnson: The Gentleman Rebel.* State College: Lillian Press, 1999.

Friedman, Milton. *Capitalism and Freedom.* Chicago: University of Chicago Press, 1962.

Galbraith, John Kenneth. *American Capitalism: The Concept of Countervailing Power.* Boston: Houghton Mifflin, 1952.

Grove, Andrew S. *Only the Paranoid Survive: How to Exploit the Crisis Points that Challenge Every Company*. New York: Doubleday, 1996.

Halberstam, David. *The Fifties*. New York: Open Road Integrated Media, 2012.

Hammond, Bray. *Banks and Politics in America*. Princeton: Princeton University Press, 1957.

Hickman, W. Braddock. *Corporate Bond Quality and Investor Experience*. Princeton: Princeton University Press, 1958.

Hounshell, David A., and John Kenley Smith, Jr. *Science and Corporate Strategy: Du Pont R&D, 1902–1980*. Cambridge England: Cambridge University Press, 1988.

Hutchins, Chris and Dominic Midgley, *Goldsmith: Money, Women, and Power*. London: Neville Ness House, 2015.

Iacocca, Lee. *Iacocca: An Autobiography*. New York: Bantam, 1984.

_____. *Talking Straight*. New York: Bantam, 1988.

_____. *Where Have All the Leaders Gone?* New York: Scribner's, 2007.

Illouz, Eva. *Oprah Winfrey and the Glamour of Misery: An Essay on Popular Culture*. New York: Columbia University Press, 2003.

Isaacson, Walter. *Steve Jobs*. New York: Simon & Schuster, 2011.

Johnson, James Weldon. *God's Trombones: Seven Negro Sermons in Verse*. New York: Penguin, 2008.

Josephson, Matthew. *The Robber Barons: The Great American Capitalists, 1861–1901*. New York: Harcourt, Brace & World, 1934.

Joyce, James. *Ulysses*. London: 1922; Project Gutenberg, 2003. https://www.gutenberg.org/ebooks/4300.

Kahney, Leander. *Tim Cook: The Genius Who Took Apple to the Next Level*. New York: Penguin, 2019.

Kelley, Kitty. *Oprah: A Biography*. New York: Random House, 2011.

Keynes, John Maynard. *The Economic Consequences of the Peace*. New York: Harcourt, Brace & Howe, 1920.

Khurana, Rakesh. *Searching for a Corporate Savior: The Irrational Quest for Charismatic CEOs*. Princeton: Princeton University Press, 2002.

Kocienda, Ken. *Creative Selective: Inside Apple's Design Process during the Golden Age of Steve Jobs*. New York: St. Martin's Press, 2018.

Lawrence, D.H. *Studies in Classic American Literature.* 1923. https://en.wikisource.org/wiki/Studies_in_Classic_American_Literature/Chapter_1.

Lebergott, Stanley. *The Americans: An Economic Record.* New York: Norton, 1984.

Levy, Lawrence. *To Pixar and Beyond: My Unlikely Journey with Steve Jobs to Make Entertainment History.* Boston: Mariner, 2017.

Levy, Steven. *Facebook: The Inside Story.* New York: Penguin, 2020.

_____. *The Perfect Thing.* New York: Simon & Schuster, 2006.

Lewis, David L. *The Public Image of Henry Ford: An American Folk Hero and His Company.* Detroit: Wayne State University Press, 1976.

Livesay, Harold C. *American Made: Shapers of the American Economy.* Boston: Pearson, 2012.

Love, Steve, and David Geffels. *Wheels of Fortune: The Story of Rubber in Akron.* Akron: University of Akron Press, 1999.

Manes, Stephen, and Paul Andrews. *Gates.* New York: Simon & Schuster, 1994.

McCraw, Thomas K. *American Business: 1920–2000: How It Worked.* Wheeling, Illinois: Harlan Davidson, 2000.

_____, ed. *Creating Modern Capitalism: How Entrepreneurs, Companies, and Countries Triumphed in Three Industrial Revolutions.* Cambridge, MA: Harvard University Press, 1995.

McElheny, Victor K. *Insisting on the Impossible: The Life of Edwin Land.* Cambridge: Perseus, 1988.

McLean, Bethany, and Peter Elkind. *The Smartest Guys in the Room: The Amazing Rise and Scandalous Fall of Enron.* New York: Penguin, 2013.

Mitchard, Jacquelyn. *The Deep End of the Ocean.* New York: Penguin, 1996.

Morris, Charles. *Tesla: How Elon Musk and Company Made Electric Cars Cool and Remade the Automotive and Energy Industries.* Charles Morris, 2017.

Nader, Ralph. *Unsafe at Any Speed.* New York: Grossman, 1965.

Nathan, John. *Sony.* Boston: Houghton Mifflin, 1999.

Nevins, Allan, and Frank Ernest Hill. *Ford: The Times, the Man, the Company.* New York: Scribner's, 1954.

Newcomer, Mabel. *The Big Business Executive; The Factors that Made Him.* New York: Columbia University Press, 1955.

Nicholas, Tom. *VC: An American History*. Cambridge: Harvard University Press, 2019.

Nilsen, Sarah, and Sarah E. Turner. *The Colorblind Screen: Television in Post-Racial America*. New York: New York University Press, 2014.

Ortega, Bob. *In Sam We Trust*. New York: Random House, 1998.

Poe, Edgar Allan. *The Complete Poems of Edgar Allan Poe*. e-books.Adelaide.edu.au.

Potts, John. *A History of Charisma*. London: Palgrave Macmillan, 2009.

Rattansi, Ali. *Racism: A Very Short Introduction*. London: Oxford University Press, 2020.

Riesman, David. *The Lonely Crowd: A Study of the Changing American Character*. New Haven: Yale University Press, 1961.

Roazen, Paul. *Freud: Political and Social Thought*. New Brunswick: Transaction Publishers, 1999.

Rosenzweig, Phil. *The Halo Effect*. New York: Free Press, 2014.

Schlender, Brent, and Rick Tetzeli. *Steve Jobs: The Evolution of a Reckless Upstart into a Visionary Leader*. New York: Crown, 2015.

Sculley, John. *Odyssey: Pepsi to Apple . . . A Journey of Adventure, Ideas, and the Future*. New York: Harper & Row, 1987.

Sloan, Jr., Alfred P. *My Years with General Motors*. New York: Doubleday, 1963.

Sobel, Robert. *Dangerous Dreamers: The Financial Innovators from Charles Merrill to Michael Milken*. Washington, D.C.: Beard Books, 2001.

Stobaugh, Robert, and Daniel Yergin, Eds. *Energy Future*. New York: Random House, 1979.

Stone, Brad, *Amazon Unchained: Jeff Bezos and the Invention of a Global Empire*. New York: Simon & Schuster, 2021.

_____. *The Everything Store: Jeff Bezos and the Age of Amazon*. New York: Little, Brown, 2014.

Stross, Randall E. *Steve Jobs & the NeXT Big Thing*. New York: Macmillan, 1993.

Tedlow, Richard S. *Andy Grove: The Life and Times of an American Business Icon*. New York: Penguin, 2006.

_____. *Denial: Why Business Leaders Fail to Look Facts in the Face – and What to Do about It*. New York: Penguin, 2011.

_____. *Giants of Enterprise: Seven Business Innovators and the Empires They Built.* New York: HarperBusiness, 2001.

_____. *New and Improved: The Story of Mass Marketing in America.* New York: Basic Books, 1990.

_____. *The Rise of the American Business Corporation.* Chur: Harwood Academic Publishers, 1991.

Travis, Trysh. *The Language of the Heart: A Cultural History of the Recovery Movement from Alcoholics Anonymous to Oprah Winfrey.* Chapel Hill: University of North Carolina Press, 2013.

Vance, Ashlee. *Elon Musk: Tesla, SpaceX, and the Quest for a Fantastic Future.* New York: HarperCollins, 2015.

Vance, Sandra E., and Roy V. Scott. *Wal-Mart: A History of Sam Walton's Retail Phenomenon.* New York: Twayne, 1994.

Vogelstein, Fred. *Dogfight.* New York: Farrar, Straus and Giroux, 2013.

Walton, Sam, and John Huey. *Made in America: My Story.* New York: Bantam, 1993.

Watkins , Julian Lewis. *The 100 Greatest Advertisements: Who Wrote Them and What They Did.* New York: Dover, 1959.

Weber, Max. *Economy and Society: An Outline of Interpretive Sociology.* Edited by Guenther Roth and Claus Wittich. Berkeley: University of California Press, 1978.

_____. *The Protestant Ethic and the Spirit of Capitalism.* New York: Scribner's, 1958.

Wensberg, Peter C. *Land's Polaroid: A Company and the Man Who Invented It.* Boston: Houghton Mifflin, 1987.

White, Lawrence J. *The Automobile Industry Since 1945.* Cambridge: Harvard University Press, 1971.

Whyte, William H. *The Organization Man.* Philadelphia: University of Pennsylvania Press, 2002.

Wiebe, Robert H. *Businessmen and Reform: A Study of the Progressive Movement.* Chicago: Quadrangle, 1962.

Wilson, Bryan R. *The Noble Savages: The Primitive Origins of Charisma and Its Contemporary Survival.* Berkeley: University of California Press, 1975.

Wilson, Sloan. *The Man in the Gray Flannel Suit.* Cambridge: Perseus, 1955.

Winfrey, Oprah. *The Path Made Clear: Discovering Your Life's Direction and Purpose.* New York: Flatiron Books, 2019.

_____. *What I Know for Sure*. New York: Flatiron Books, 2014.

Woodward, Bob, and Carl Bernstein. *The Final Days*. New York: Simon & Schuster, 1976.

Young, Jeffrey S., and William L. Simon. *iCon: Steve Jobs, The Greatest Second Act in the History of American Business*. New York: Wiley, 2005.

II. ARTICLES

"A Genius and His MAGIC CAMERA," *Life*, October 27, 1972.

"A Million Little Lies: Exposing James Frey's Fiction Addiction," *The Smoking Gun*, January 4, 2006. http://www.thesmokinggun.com/documents/celebrity/million-little-lies.

Alfred, Randy, "April 3, 1973: Motorola Calls AT&T ... by Cell," *Wired*, https://dynallc.com/april-3-1973-motorola-calls-att-by-cell-wired-april-2008/.

Amadeo, Kimberly, "Mark-to-Market Accounting; How It Works, and Its Pros and Cons," https://www.thebalance.com/mark-to-market-accounting-how-it-works-3305942.

Andersen, Hans Christian, "The Emperor's New Clothes," H.C. Andersen Centre, Andersen.sdu.dk, https://andersen.sdu.dk/vaerk/hersholt/TheEmperorsNewClothes_e.html.

"Andrew Grove: Man of the Year," *Time*, December 29, 1997.

Anastakis, Dimitry, "Lee Iacocca Saves Chrysler, 1978-1986," *Business and Economic History* online, Vol. 5 (2007), https://thebhc.org/sites/default/files/anastakis_0.pdf.

Antonakis, John, Marika Fenley, and Sue Liechli, "Can Charisma Be Taught? Tests of Two Interventions," *Academy of Management Learning and Education*, Vol. 10, No. 3 (2011), https://journals.aom.org/doi/10.5465/amle.2010.0012.

Antonakis, John, Nicolas Basterdoz, Philippe Jacquart, and Boas Shamir, "Charisma: An ill-defined and ill-measured gift," *Annual Review of Organizational Psychology and Organizational Behavior*, Vol. 3:293-319, March, 2016, https://www.annualreviews.org/doi/abs/10.1146/annurev-orgpsych-041015-062305.

Antonakis, John, Marika Fenley, and Sue Liechti, "Learning Charisma," *Harvard Business Review*, June, 2012.

Askew, Tim, "The Generalist and The Entrepreneur ... And Steve Jobs,"

Inc., April 30, 2018, https://www.inc.com/tim-askew/the-generalist-entrepreneur-steve-jobs.html.

Baila, Morgan, "Phyllis Gardner warned everyone about Elizabeth Holmes—but no one listened," Refinery29, March 19, 2019, https://www.refinery29.com/en-us/2019/03/226452/phyllis-gardner-elizabeth-holmes-professor-interview-the-inventor.

Barnes, Bart, "Auto Industry Giant Henry Ford II Dies," *Washington Post*, September 30, 1987.

Bell, Daniel, "The Company He Keeps," *New York Review of Books*, March 19, 1964.

Bell, David A., *Men on Horseback: The Power of Charisma in the Age of Revolution* (New York: Farrar, Straus and Giroux, 2020).

Bell, Emma, and Scott Taylor, "Vernacular mourning and corporate memorialization in framing the death of Steve Jobs," https://journals.sagepub.com/doi/10.1177/1350508415605109.

Beschloss, Michael, "Changing the Market in an Instant," *New York Times,* July 5, 2015.

Biddle, Sam, "Samsung Exposes Blatant iPhone Jealousy," *Gizmodo*, August 7, 2012, https://gizmodo.com/474052195.

"'Big Bill' Knudsen turned Chevrolet into a powerhouse: His crosstown move after a clash with Henry Ford turned out to be a windfall for GM," *Automotive News*, October 31, 2011, https://www.autonews.com/article/20111031/CHEVY100/310319979/big-bill-knudsen-turned-chevrolet-into-a-powerhouse.

"Bill Gates on making 'one of the greatest mistakes of all time,'" TechCrunch.com. June 22, 2019, https://techcrunch.com/2019/06/22/bill-gates-on-making-one-of-the-greatest-mistakes-of-all-time/.

"Bill Gates says his 'greatest mistake ever' was failing to create Android at Microsoft," www.aol.com/article/finance/June 24, 2019.

Bilton, Nick, "'He's F---king Destroyed This Town': How Mark Zuckerberg Became the Most Reviled Man in Tech," *Vanity Fair*, November 6, 2019, https://www.vanityfair.com/news/2019/11/how-mark-zuckerberg-became-the-most-reviled-man-in-tech.

Blumberg, Peter, "Elizabeth Holmes Loses Request to Throw Out Criminal Charges," Bloomberg.com, October 13, 2020, https://www.bloomberg.com/news/articles/2020-10-13/elizabeth-holmes-loses-request-to-throw-out-criminal-charges.

Boffey, Daniel, "Apple admits Briton DID invent iPod, but he still not getting any money," *Daily Mail*, September 8, 2008, https://www.dailymail.co.uk/news/article-1053152/Apple-admit-Briton-DID-invent-iPod-hes-getting-money.html.

Bowles, Nellie, "In 'Small Fry,' Steve Jobs Comes Across as a Jerk. His Daughter Forgives Him. Should We?" *New York Times*, August 23, 2018.

Brandom, Russell, "If Tesla goes up in smoke, it won't be because Elon Musk bet a blunt: executive departures are a bigger problem than a little weed smoke," *The Verge*, September 17, 2018. https://www.theverge.com/2018/9/7/17832154/elon-musk-blunt-tesla-stock-problems-executive-retention.

Brown, Mike, and Jake Kleinman, "SpaceX Mars City," *Inverse*, November 20, 2020, https://www.inverse.com/innovation/spacex-mars-city-werner-herzog.

Cakebread, Caroline, "People will take 1.2 trillion digital photos this year—thanks to smart phones," *Business Insider*, August 31, 2017, https://www.businessinsider.com.au/12-trillion-photos-to-be-taken-in-2017-thanks-to-smartphones-chart-2017-8.

Capretta, Lisa, "Oprah and Her Audience Losing It Over an iPod in 2003 Is Pure Magic," *OWN*, April 28, 2016, *HuffPost*, https://www.huffpost.com/entry/oprah-audience-ipod-2003_n_57213a28e4b0f309baefb140.

Carr, David, "A Triumph of Avoiding the Traps," *New York Times*, November 22, 2009.

_____, "How Oprahness Trumped Truthiness," *New York Times*, January 30, 2006.

_____, "Oprah Puts Her Brand on the Line," *New York Times*, December 24, 2007.

Chokshi, Niraj, "Elon Musk Says Tesla Share Price Is Too High," *New York Times*, May 1, 2020.

"Chrysler aid cleared in final day's session," *CQ Almanac*, 1979, in CQ Almanac 1979, 35th ed. Washington, DC: Congressional Quarterly, 1980. http://library.cqpress.com.ezp-prod1.hul.harvard.edu/cqalmanac/cqal79-1185075.

Clifford, Tyler, "Capitalism 'will fundamentally be in jeopardy' if business does not act on climate change, Microsoft CEO Satya Nadella says," CNBC, January 16, 2020.

Colvin, Geoffrey, "The Ultimate Manager," *Fortune*, November 22, 1999.

Costello, Sam, "How Many iPhones Have Been Sold Worldwide," Lifewire, December 27, 2019, https://www.lifewire.com/how-many-iphones-have-been-sold-1999500.

_____, "This is the number of iPods sold all-time," *Lifewire*, December 13, 2019, https://www.lifewire.com/number-of-ipods-sold-all-time-1999515.

Crandall, Robert W., "The Effects of U.S. Trade Protection for Autos and Steel," Brookings Papers on Economic Activity, 1:1987, https://www.brookings.edu/wp-content/uploads/1987/01/1987a_bpea_crandall.pdf.

Decker, Jeffrey Lewis, "Saint Oprah," *Modern Fiction Studies*, Vol. 52, No. 1 (spring, 2006) p. 169, https://www.jstor.org/stable/26286927.

Defree, Suzanne, "Apple IPO makes instant millionaires, December 12, 1980" *EDN*, December 12, 2019, https://www.edn.com/apple-ipo-makes-instant-millionaires-december-12-1980/.

Dormehl, Luke, "Apple introduced iTunes store 13 years ago today," April 28, 2016, https://www.cultofmac.com/425543/apple-introduced-itunes-store-13-years-ago-today/.

Drucker, Peter F., "Why *My Years with General Motors* is 'must' reading," in Sloan, *My Years with General Motors*.

Dvorsky, George, "Humans Will Never Colonize Mars," *Gizmodo*, July 30, 2019, https://gizmodo.com/humans-will-never-colonize-mars-1836316222.

Elliott, Stuart, "The Media Business: Advertising; A New Ranking of the '50 best Television Commercials' Ever Made," *New York Times*, March 14, 1995.

Ellis, Blake, "Apple topples Microsoft's throne," CNN money, May 27, 2010.

"Elon Musk," *Esquire.com*, October 1, 2008, https://classic.esquire.com/article/2008/10/1/elon-musk.

"Elon Musk's 'Evil' Father," *The Sunday Times*, March 15, 2019, https://www.driving.co.uk/news/elon-musks-evil-father-baby-stepdaughter/.

Fernandez, Alexia, "Who is Sunny Balwani," *People*, March 27, 2019.

"Flamboyant Goldsmith Dies of Heart Attack," BBC, "Politics 97," http://www.bbc.co.uk/news/special/politics97/news/07/0719/goldsmith.shtml.

Franklin, Benjamin, "The Way to Wealth, as clearly shown in the Preface of an old Pennsylvania Almanack, entitled Poor Richard Improved," reprinted in Alfred D. Chandler, Jr., Thomas K. McCraw, and Richard S. Tedlow, *Management Past and Present: A Casebook on the History of American Business*. Cincinnati: South-Western, 1996.

Franklin, Eric, "The $200 iPod Touch now has some legit competition," CNET, July 13, 2019, https://www.cnet.com/news/200-ipod-touch-has-some-legit-competition/.

Franzen, Carl, "The History of the Walkman: 35 Years of Iconic Music Players, *The Verge*, July 1, 2014, https://www.theverge.com/2014/7/1/5861062/sony-walkman-at-35.

Gavenas, Mary Lisa, "Ash, Mary Kay," https://doi.org/10.1093/anb/9780198606697.article.1002284.

Glass, Andrew, "Supreme Court orders Du Pont to divest itself of GM stock," June 3, 1957 reproduced in Politico, June 3, 2018, https://www.politico.com/story/2018/06/03/supreme-court-order-du-pont-divest-itself-of-gm-stock-june-3-1957-615544.

"Goldsmith talks back; Sir James Goldsmith challenges Lee Iacocca's book," *The Sunday Times*, July 17, 1988.

"Sir James Goldsmith," *telegraph.co.uk* obituaries 7720479, https://www.telegraph.co.uk/news/obituaries/7720479/Sir-James-Goldsmith.

"Sir James Goldsmith," *The Telegraph*, July 21, 1997.

Gordon, John Steele, "The Ordeal of Charlie Wilson," *American Heritage*, Vol. 46, Issue 1 (February-March, 1995).

Greenspan, Aaron, "Reality Check: Tesla, Inc.," *PlainSite*, January 7, 2020, https://www.plainsite.org/realitycheck/tsla.pdf.

Grub, Jeff, "How games helped make Elon Musk the real-Life Tony Stark," *venturebeat.com*, April 17, 2015, https://venturebeat.com/2015/04/07/how-games-helped-make-elon-musk-the-real-life-tony-stark/.

Gurman, Mark, and Dana Hull, "Former chief Tesla engineer Doug Field returns to Apple," *Bloomberg*, August 10, 2018, https://www.bloomberg.com/news/articles/2018-08-10/former-chief-tesla-vehicle-engineer-doug-field-returns-to-apple.

"Harlow H. Curtice is dead at 69; Retired Head of General Motors," *New York Times*, November 4, 1962.

Hartmans, Avery and Kat Tenbarge, "How to pronounce 'X Æ A-Xii,' the name Elon Musk and Grimes gave their new baby," *Business Insider*, May, 2020, https://www.businessinsider.com/how-to-pronounce-x-ae-a-12-elon-musk-grimes-baby-name-2020-5.

Healy, Paul M., and Krishna Palepu, "The Fall of Enron," *Journal of Economic Perspectives*, Vol. 17, No. 2 (spring, 2003), https://www-jstor-org.ezp-prod1.hul.harvard.edu/stable/3216854?seq=1#metadata_info_tab_contents.

Heilbron, Johan, Jochem Verheul, and Sander Quak, "The Origins and Early Diffusion of 'Shareholder Value' in the United States," *Theory and Society*, October 12, 2013, https://link.springer.com/article/10.1007/s11186-013-9205-0.

Hernandez, Bryan Anthony, "California Declares Oct. 16 Steve Jobs Day, "*Mashable*, October 14, 2011, https://mashable.com/2011/10/14/steve-jobs-day-california-october-16-stanford/.

Hicks, Jonathan P., "Goodyear Buys Out Goldsmith," *New York Times*, November 21, 1986.

Higgins, Bill, "Oprah's First Show: How She Became Who She Is Today," *The Hollywood Reporter,* May 19, 2011, https://www.hollywoodreporter.com/news/oprah-s-first-show-how-190319.

Higgins, Tucker, "Democratic Presidential Candidates Disown Biden's Comments about Segregationist Senators in Personal Terms," CNBC, June 19, 2019, https://www.cnbc.com/2019/06/19/democrats-slam-biden-over-comments-on-segregationist-senator.html.

Hodgson, Godfrey, "William H. White Obituary," *The Guardian*, January 15, 1999.

Hollandsworth, Skip, "Hostile Makeover," *Texas Monthly,* November, 1995.

Hormby, Tom, "The Rise and Fall of Apple's Gil Amelio," *Low End Mac*, August 10, 2013, https://lowendmac.com/2013/the-rise-and-fall-of-apples-gil-amelio/.

Hunter, Marjorie, "James O. Eastland Is Dead at 81; Leading Senate Foe of Integration," *New York Times*, February 20, 1986.

Iacocca, Lee, "Lee Iacocca on Chrysler's Bankruptcy," *Newsweek*, April 29, 2009.

"Inquest Held Unlikely in Curtice Kill; Canadian Crown Attorney Maintains Shooting 'Accident,'" *Palm Springs Desert Sun,* November 19, 1959, p.2.

Irfan, Umair, "Elon Musk's tweet about taking Tesla private has triggered a federal lawsuit," *Vox,* September 28, 2018, https://www.vox.com/2018/9/27/17911826/elon-musk-tesla-sec-twitter-lawsuit.

James, Susan Donaldson, "John Taylor Skilling, Ex-Enron Chief's Son, Dies of Possible Overdose," ABC News, February 4, 2011.

James, William to H. G. Wells, September 11, 1906, https://wist.info/james-william/5715/.

"John Riccardo, Chrysler CEO Who Helped Recruit Iacocca, Dies at 91," *Automotive News*, February 14, 2016, https://www.autonews.com/article/20160214/OEM02/160219923/john-riccardo-chrysler-ceo-who-helped-recruit-iacocca-dies-at-91/.

Judge, Paul C., "Selling Autos by Selling Safety," *New York Times*, January 26, 1990.

Junod, Tom, "Triumph of His Will," *Esquire*, November 15, 2012, https://www.esquire.com/news-politics/a16681/elon-musk-interview-1212/.

Kayama, Hayley Tsu, "Steve Jobs Dies: Reaction to His Death," *Washington Post*, October 15, 2011.

Kim, Sung Ho, "Max Weber," *The Stanford Encyclopedia of Philosophy* (Winter 2019 Edition), Edward N. Zalta (ed.), https://plato.stanford.edu/archives/win2019/entries/weber/.

Kurylko, Diana T., "Ford had a better idea in 1956, but found that safety didn't sell," *Automotive News*, June 26, 1996, https://www.autonews.com/article/19960626/ANA/606260836/ford-had-a-better-idea-in-1956-but-it-found-that-safety-didn-t-sell.

Le Tran, Anne, "The History of the Car Radio: from Morse Code to Mixtapes," https://esurance41.rssing.com/chan-11821666/latest.php.

Lee, Felicia R., "Cosby Defends His Remarks About Poor Blacks' Values," *New York Times*, May 22, 2004.

Lehrer, Jonah, "Steve Jobs, 'Technology Alone Is Not Enough,'" *The New Yorker*, October 7, 2011.

Leskin, Paige, "Theranos founder Elizabeth Holmes has reportedly gotten married in a secret wedding," *Business Insider*, June 17, 2019, https://www.businessinsider.com/elizabeth-holmes-theranos-everything-about-fiance-william-billy-evans-2019-3.

_____, "Watch a high schooler be completely unimpressed when Amazon CEO Jeff Bezos shows up to his computer-science class," *Business Insider*, October 21, 2019.

Levy, Steven, "An Oral History of Apple's Infinite Loop," *Wired*, https://www.wired.com/story/apple-infinite-loop-oral-history.

Lohr, Steve, "Apple, a Success at Stores, Bets Big on Fifth Avenue," *New York Times*, May 19, 2006.

Luce, Henry R., "The American Century," *Life*, February 17, 1941.

"Man of the Year: First among Equals," *Time*, January 2, 1956.

Markovits, Daniel, "How McKinsey Destroyed the Middle Class," *Atlantic*, February 3, 2020.

Marsal, Katie, "iPod: How big can it get?" *AppleInsider*, May 24, 2006, http://www.appleinsider.com/articles/06/05/24/ipod_how_big_can_it_get.html.

Marshall, Aarian, and Alex Davies, "Tesla is (finally!) Selling the Model 3 for $35,000," *Wired*, February 28, 2019, https://www.wired.com/story/tesla-model-3-35000-price-autopilot-self-driving-stores-closing/.

Masters, Kim, "John Lasseter's Pattern of Alleged Misconduct Detailed by Disney/Pixar Insiders," *The Hollywood Reporter*, November 21, 2017, http://www.hollywoodreporter.com/news/john-lasseters-pattern-al-leged-misconduct-detailed-by-disney-pixar-insiders-1059594.

Matousek, Mark, "Elon Musk slammed one of Tesla's founders by calling him the worst person he's ever worked with," *Business Insider*, February 10, 2020, https://www.businessinsider.com/elon-musk-tesla-cofounder-worst-person-hes-worked-with-2020-2.

Max, D. T., "The Oprah Effect," *New York Times*, December 26, 1999.

McCracken, Harry, "Polaroid's SX-70: The Art and Science of the Nearly Impossible," *technologizer.com*, https://www.technologizer.com/2011/06/08/polaroid/.

McDowell, Edwin, "Publishing: 'Iacocca' Reaches Millionth Copy," *New York Times*, December 14, 1984.

Mcfadden, Robert D., "Lee Iacocca, Visionary Automaker Who Led Both Ford and Chrysler, Is Dead at 94," *New York Times*, July 2, 2019.

McPherson, James M., "Parchman's Plantation," *New York Times*, April 28, 1996.

Miller, Mike, "Smith Barney Sues Goodyear, Goldsmith, Charging Buyback Broke Securities Law," *Wall Street Journal*, December 8, 1986.

Morrison, Toni, "Comment," *The New Yorker*, October 5, 1998.

Moss, Caroline, "Former Apple CEO Is Being Sued By Ex-Wife For Allegedly Hiding $25 Million During Divorce," *Business Insider*, January 26, 2015, https://www.businessinsider.in/Former-Apple-CEO-John-Sculley-Is-Being-Sued-By-Ex-Wife-For-Allegedly-Hiding-25-Million-During-Divorce/articleshow/46022442.cms.

Moss, J. Jennings, "Tesla co-founder J.B. Straubel steps down as CTO," *Silicon Valley Business Journal*, https://www.bizjournals.com/sanjose/news/2019/07/24/tesla-co-founder-jb-straubel-steps-down-as.html.

Musk, Justine Wilson, "'I Was a Starter Wife': Inside America's Messiest Divorce," *Marie Claire*, September 10, 2018, https://www.marieclaire.com/sex-love/a5380/millionaire-starter-wife/.

Ngo, Sheireso, "The Sickening Reason Why Elon Musk Called His Father a 'Terrible Human Being,'" *Showbiz Cheat Sheet*, June 11, 2013, https://www.cheatsheet.com/health-fitness/the-sickening-reason-why-elon-musk-called-his-father-a-terrible-human-being.html/.

O'Kane, Sean, "Play the PC game Elon musk wrote as a pre-teen," *The Verge*, June 19, 2015, https://www.theverge.com/2015/6/9/8752333/elon-musk-blastar-pc-game.

Parloff, Roger, "This CEO Is Out for Blood," *Fortune*, June 12, 2014.

Peck, Janice, "Oprah Winfrey: Cultural Icon of Mainstream (White) America," in Sarah Nilsen and Sarah E. Turner, *The Colorblind Screen: Television in Post-Racial America*. New York: New York University Press, 2014.

_____, "Talk about Racism: Framing a Popular Discourse of Race on Oprah Winfrey," *Cultural Critique*, No. 27 (Spring, 1994), https://www.jstor.org/stable/1354479?seq=1.

Mcfadden, Robert D., "Lee Iacocca, Visionary Automaker Who Led Both Ford and Chrysler, Is Dead at 94," *New York Times*, July 2, 2019.

"Polaroid's Land: Here Come Those Great New Cameras," *Time*, June 26, 1972.

"Politics: Industrialist Who Led Anti-Europe Crusade," http://www.bbc.co.uk/news/special/politics97/news/07/0719/obit.shtml.

Poss, Jane, "Edwin Land dead at 81; Polaroid chief left image on industry," *Boston Globe*, March 2, 1991.

Ramsey, Lydia, "The Stanford professor who rejected one of Elizabeth Holmes early ideas explains what it was like to watch the rise and fall of Theranos," *Business Insider*, March 18, 2019, https://www.businessinsider.in/the-stanford-professor-who-rejected-one-of-elizabeth-holmess-early-ideas-explains-what-it-was-like-to-watch-the-rise-and-fall-of-theranos/articleshow/68468364.cms.

Roberts, Ken, "Insult to Injury: Foreign Manufacturers Now Making More Cars in U.S. than U.S. Companies," *Forbes*, January 22, 2018.

Scales, Delia, *Medium*, July 29, 2018, https://medium.com/@wikihospitals/who-is-the-young-stanford-grad-with-long-blond-hair-a-tight-body-in-clinging-black-dresses-red-2509680200e8.

Sheetz, Michael, "SpaceX valuation rises to $33.3 billion as investors look to satellite opportunity," CNBC, May 31, 2019, https://www.cnbc.com/2019/05/31/spacex-valuation-33point3-billion-after-starlink-satellites-fundraising.html.

Shiel, Jr., MD, William C., "Medical Definition of Cachectic," medterms medical dictionary, medicinenet, https://www.medicinenet.com/cachectic/definition.htm.

"Sir James Goldsmith," *The Telegraph*, https://www.telegraph.co.uk/news/obituaries/7720479/Sir-James- Goldsmith.

Smith, Henry Nash, "The Search for a Capitalist Hero: Businessmen in American Fiction," in Earl F. Cheit, Ed. *The Business Establishment*. New York: Wylie, 1964.

Spiegel, Mark, "Tesla No Longer Even A Growth Company; Going Bankrupt: Shortseller," *Yahoo! Finance*, July 4, 2020, https://www.yahoo.com/now/tesla-no-longer-even-growth-121604978.html.

Stevens, Matt, and Matthew Haag, "Jeffrey Skilling; Former Enron Chief, Released after 12 Years in Prison," *New York Times*, December 22, 2019.

Stewart, James B., and Philip Revzin, "Sir James Goldsmith, As Enigmatic as Ever, Bales Out of Goodyear," *Wall Street Journal*, November 21, 1986.

Stewart, James B., "Did Jack Welch Model Sew Seeds of G.E. Decline?" *New York Times*, June 15, 2017.

Strauss, Neil, "Elon Musk: The Architect of Tomorrow," *Rolling Stone*, November 15, 2017, https://www.rollingstone.com/culture/culture-features/elon-musk-the-architect-of-tomorrow-120850/.

Sull, Donald N., Richard S. Tedlow, and Richard S. Rosenbloom, "Managerial Commitments and Technological Change in the U.S. Tire Industry," *Industrial and Corporate Change* Vol. 6, No. 2 (1997).

Tedlow, Richard S., "The Sky above and the Mud below: Two Books about Steve Jobs," *Business History Review* 94, no. 4 (Winter 2020): 835–852.

"Tesla's Elon Musk says tweet that led to $20 million fine 'worth it,'" Reuters, October 27, 2018, https://mobile.reuters.com/article/amp/ca/idUSKCN1N10K2.

Thatcher, Margaret, "Speech celebrating the memory of Sir James Goldsmith," November 13, 1997, Margaret Thatcher Foundation.

"The Fall of Enron," Bloomberg, December 26, 2001, https://www.bloomberg.com/news/articles/2001-12-16/the-fall-of-enron.

"The Mackintosh Mouse, Making the Macintosh: Technology and Culture in Silicon Valley," https://web.stanford.edu/dept/SUL/library/mac/.

"The Power of a Book Club to Boost Sales," http://alinefromlinda.blogspot.com/2015/04/the-power-of-book-club-to-boost-sales.html.

Tripsas, Mary and Giovanni Gavetti, "Capabilities, Cognition, and Inertia: Evidence from Digital Imaging," *Strategic Management Journal*, Vol. 21 (2000).

Urban, Tim, "The Elon Musk Blog Series," *Wait But Why*, Kindle edition, 2015.

"Veda Anderson, widow of former GM labor chief, recalls her husband's tragic death," https://baggyparagraphs.wordpress.com/2012/02/20/veda-anderson/.

Villasanta, Arthur, "Elon Musk 'Too Embarrassed' To Put His Tiny Invention In A Tesla," *International Business Times*, November 18, 2019, https://www.ibtimes.com/elon-musk-too-embarrassed-put-his-tiny-invention-tesla-2868829.

Waldman, Katy, "'Small Fry' Reviewed: Lisa Brennan-Jobs's Mesmerizing Discomfiting Memoir," *The New Yorker*, September 16, 2018.

Ward, John William, "The Meaning of Lindbergh's Flight," *American Quarterly*, Vol. 10, No. 1 (spring, 1958).

Warner, Stuart, "25 years ago: Driving back the raider at the gates of Goodyear Tire and Rubber Co.," *Cleveland.com*, November 27, 2011; updated January 12, 2019, https://www.cleveland.com/business/2011/11/25_years_ago_driving_back_the.html.

Weisul, Kimberly, "How Playing the Long Game Made Elizabeth Holmes a Billionaire," *Inc.*, https://www.inc.com/magazine/201510/kimberly-weisul/the-longest-game.html.

White, Theodore H., "The Danger from Japan," *New York Times*, July 28, 1985.

"Why Steve Jobs said meeting the founder of Polaroid was 'like visiting a shrine,'" *The Economist*, March 29, 2015.

Whyte, William H., "Patrolling Guadalcanal," February 16, 2010., history.net from Whyte's *A Time of War*, https://www.historynet.com/patrolling-guadalcanal.htm.

Wired staff, "Straight dope on the iPod's Birth," https://www.wired.com/2006/10/straight-dope-on-the-ipods-birth/.

Zeltchik, Steven, "Oprah Winfrey's Prince Harry and Meghan interview netted her $7 million and 17 million viewers. It also validated her larger business strategy," *Washington Post*, March 8, 2021.

Zoglin, Richard, "Oprah Winfrey: Lady with a Calling," *Time*, August 8, 1988.

III. OTHER SOURCES

A variety of other sources were used in researching this book. These include cases distributed by Harvard Business School Publishing and a remarkable array of material on the internet. YouTube proved exceptionally useful. Vimeo was also helpful. Wikipedia used cautiously can be quite valuable. Other sources, such as manuals for the use of products discussed, have been uploaded by individual collectors. When the internet is used with care in a book such as this, it is invaluable.

ENDNOTES

PART 1: The Great Transformation

1 William H. Whyte, The Organization Man (Philadelphia: University of Pennsylvania Press, 2002 – originally published in 1956) p. 224.

Chapter 1

1 "Remembering Steve Jobs," Apple.com, https://www.apple.com/stevejobs/.

2 Lisa Brennan-Jobs, Small Fry (NY: Grove Press, 2018).

3 Bryan Anthony Hernandez, "California Declares Oct. 16 Steve Jobs Day," Mashable, October 14, 2011, mashable.com/2011/10/14/steve-jobs-day-california-october-16-stanford; Hayley Tsu Kayama, "Steve Jobs Dies: Reaction to his Death," Washington Post, October 15, 2011.

4 Brent Schlender and Rick Tetzeli, Steve Jobs: The Evolution of a Reckless Upstart into a Visionary Leader (NY: Crown, 2015).

5 Steve Jobs's 2005 Stanford commencement address is available on YouTube: youtube.com/watch?v=Hd_ptbiPoXM.

6 Walter Isaacson, Steve Jobs (NY: Simon & Schuster, 2011).

7 Schlender and Tetzeli; Isaacson.

8 Chrisann Brennan, The Bite in the Apple (NY: St. Martin's Press, 2013).

9 Ibid.

10 Suzanne Defree, "Apple IPO makes instant millionaires December 12, 1980," EDN, December 12, 2019, edn.com/apple-ipo-makes-instant-millionaires-december-12-1980; Isaacson, 213-214.

11 Silicon Valley Historical Association, "From the Documentary Film Steve Jobs: Secrets of Life," youtube.com/watch?v=kYfNvmF0Bqw.

12 Paul Carroll, Big Blues: The Unmaking of IBM (NY: Crown, 1993), 363.

13 John Sculley, Odyssey: Pepsi to Apple: A Journey of Adventure, Ideas, and the Future (NY: Harper & Row, 1987), 56–76.

14 Ibid., 36.

15 Ibid., 56.

16 Ibid., 57.

17 Ibid., 61.

18 Ibid., 77.

19 Ibid., 8, 74–75.

20 Ibid., 49.

21 Ibid., 136.

22 Ibid., 49.

23 Ibid., 433.

24 Isaacson; Sculley, 90, 100.

25 Sculley, 131.

26 Sculley, 196; Isaacson.

27 Ibid.

28 Sculley, 248-249.

29 Ibid., 167.

30 Ibid., 198.

31 Schlender and Tetzeli.

32 "Jobs on Sculley," YouTube, February 11, 2017, youtube.com/watch?v=IuMyBAvRjL0.

33 "John Sculley on How Steve Jobs Lost His Job," YouTube, October 24, 2013, https://www.youtube.com/watch?v=YlNh1O-paG8.

34 Sculley, 133.

35 Isaacson.

36 Sculley, 166.

37 Isaacson.

38 Ibid.

39 Ibid.

40 The advertisement is on YouTube. "Apple 1984 Super Bowl Commercial Introducing Macintosh Computer," October 8, 2011, https://www.youtube.com/watch?v=zIE-5hg7FoA.

41 Isaacson.

42 See note 40 above.

43 Schlender and Tetzeli.

44 Isaacson.

45 Sculley, 178. Sculley writes that "we had spent nearly $1.6 million on a single sixty-second commercial."

46 Stuart Elliott, "The Media Business: Advertising; A New Ranking of the '50 Best Television Commercials' Ever Made," New York Times, March 14, 1995. See also "Top Ten Super Bowl Commercials," https://www.youtube.com/watch?v=HPR3PB_VGVs.

47 Isaacson.

48 Ibid.

49 Sculley, 257-258.

50   Caroline Moss, "Former Apple CEO Is Being Sued By Ex-Wife For Allegedly Hiding $25 Million During Divorce," Business Insider, January 26, 2015, https://www.businessinsider.com/john-sculley-sued-for-hiding-assets-2015-1.

51   Isaacson.

52   Schlender and Tetzeli provide the authoritative discussion.

53   Isaacson; "Steve Jobs," Wikipedia.

54   Paul Roazen, Freud: Political and Social Thought (New Brunswick, NJ: Transaction Publishers, 1999), 276. The ancient Greek to whom this observation is ascribed is Herclitus. His quotation is sometimes rendered as "character is destiny."

Chapter 2

1   Rakesh Khurana, Searching for a Corporate Savior: The Irrational Quest for Charismatic CEOs (Princeton: Princeton University Press, 2002), 153, 260.

2   "Charisma," Wikipedia.

3   Max Weber, Economy and Society: An Outline of Interpretive Sociology, Edited by Guenther Roth and Claus Wittich (Berkeley: University of California Press, 1978), 246–254. The literature which this book has spawned is immense. A good introduction to Weber and his often difficult-to-understand oevre is Kim, Sung Ho, "Max Weber", The Stanford Encyclopedia of Philosophy (Winter 2019 Edition), Edward N. Zalta (editor.), plato.stanford.edu/archives/win2019/entries/weber.

4   Alan Bryman, Charisma & Leadership in Organizations (London: Sage, 1992), 24.

5   Geertz quoted in David A. Bell, Men on Horseback: The Power of Chaisma in the Age of Revolution (New York: Farrar, Straus and Giroux, 2020); John Potts, A History of Charisma (London: Palgrave Macmillan, 2009), 3.

6   John Antonakis, Nicolas Basterdoz, Philippe Jacquart, and Boas Shamir, "Charisma: An ill-defined and ill-measured gift," Annual Review of Organizational Psychology and Organizational Behavior, Vol. 3: 293–319, March, 2016, annualreviews.org/doi/abs/10.1146/annurev-orgpsych-041015-062305.

7   John Antonakis, Marika Fenley, and Sue Liechli, "Can Charisma Be Taught? Tests of Two Interventions," Academy of Management Learning and Education, Vol. 10, No. 3 (2011), journals.aom.org/doi/10.5465/amle.2010.0012. In an altogether different but enticingly revealing context, see Erik H. Erikson's treatment of Mahatma Gandhi's charisma, his response to his "inner voice," and his relationship to the "charisma-hungry masses" in Gandhi's Truth: On the Origins of Militant Nonviolence (New York: Norton, 1970).

8   Antonakis et al., "Charisma: An ill-defined...." The 13 attributes the authors list are:
   1. Quality, ability, gift of the leader
   2. Exceptional, extraordinary, exemplary individual
   3. Defined in terms of an outcome
   4. Vision, ideology, values, morals, beliefs, mission, symbols of leader
   5. Followers' attribution (including group prototypicality of leader)
   6. Social process (interaction, relationship)
   7. Divine related
   8. Emotion-based
   9. Leader's behaviors and actions
   10. Followers' characteristics (need, motives, background, self-esteem)
   11. Expressive communication
   12. Any contextual circumstances (crisis, social situation)
   13. Leader trait (e.g., self-confidence, persistence, passion, optimism, honest, reliable)

9   Bryman, 41.

10   John Adams, "From George Eliot to Neo-Nazi Skinheads: The Chaotic Cult of Richard Wagner," review of Wagnerism, by Alex Ross. New York Times, September 16, 2020.

11   Jacobellis v. Ohio, 378 US at 197 (Stewart, J., concurring).

12   Neil Strauss, "Elon Musk: The Architect of Tomorrow," Rolling Stone, November 15, 2017, rollingstone.com/culture/culture-features/elon-musk-the-architect-of-tomorrow-120850.

13   Schlender and Tetzeli.

14   Isaacson.

15   Randall E. Stross, Steve Jobs & the NeXT Big Thing (NY: Macmillan, 1993).

16   Ibid.

17   Bell, Horseback. In his discussion of the role of charisma in politics during the age of democratic revolutions—roughly 1770 to 1820—Professor David A. Bell of Princeton emphasizes the importance of the "media revolution" underway during that era.

18   Paige Leskin, "Watch a high schooler be completely unimpressed when Amazon CEO Jeff Bezos shows up to his computer-science class," Business Insider, October 21, 2019, businessinsider.com/jeff-bezos-amazon-

dunbar-high-school-student-reaction-video-2019-10.

Chapter 3
1 "USS Missouri," Wikipedia.
2 Theodore H. White, "The Danger from Japan," New York Times, July 28, 1985.
3 Henry R. Luce, "The American Century," Life, February 17, 1941, 61–65.
4 Pearl Harbor, of course, was attacked on December 7, 1941, and two Aleutian Islands were occupied by Japan. However, neither Hawaii nor Alaska were states in what was a forty-eight-state union until 1959.
5 Roosevelt used this phrase in a radio broadcast on December 19, 1940.
6 Richard S. Tedlow, Giants of Enterprise: Seven Business Innovators and the Empires They Built (New York: HarperBusiness, 2001), 181–182; Thomas K. McCraw, American Business: 1920–2000: How It Worked (Wheeling, Illinois: Harlan Davidson, 2000), 67–102.
7 John Kenneth Galbraith, American Capitalism: The Concept of Countervailing Power (Boston: Houghton Mifflin, 1952), chapter VI.
8 Stanley Lebergott, The Americans: An Economic Record (New York: Norton, 1984), 470.
9 Ibid., 471–476.
10 Tedlow, Giants, 227.
11 Richard S. Tedlow, The Rise of the American Business Corporation (Chur, Switzerland: Harwood Academic Publishers, 1991), 1–2.
12 Robert Cuff, "Organizational Capabilities and US War Production: The Controlled Materials Plan of World War II," Harvard Business School Case # 9-390-166; Rev. August 1, 1997.
13 "Charles E. Wilson," Wikipedia; John Steele Gordon, "The Ordeal of Charlie Wilson," American Heritage, Vol. 46, Issue 1 (February-March, 1995).
14 "Man of the Year: First among Equals," Time, January 2, 1956.
15 The preceding material is from ibid.
16 "Harlow H. Curtice Is Dead at 69; Retired Head of General Motors," New York Times, November 4, 1962.
17 Lawrence J. White, The Automobile Industry since 1945 (Cambridge, Massachusetts: Harvard University Press, 1971), 290–306.
18 General Motors Annual Report, 1955.
19 Daniel Bell, "The Company He Keeps," New York Review of Books, March 19, 1964.
20 Alfred Sloan, Jr., My Years with General Motors (New York: Doubleday, 1963).
21 Irving Bernstein, Turbulent Years (Boston: Houghton Mifflin, 1971), 513.
22 Sloan, 213.
23 Milton Friedman, Capitalism and Freedom (Chicago: University of Chicago Press, 1962).
24 Andrew Glass, "Supreme Court orders Du Pont to divest itself of GM stock," June 3, 1957 reproduced in Politico, June 3, 2018, politico.com/story/2018/06/03/supreme-court-order-du-pont-divest-itself-of-gm-stock-june-3-1957-615544; United States v. E. I. Dupont de Nemours & Co. 353 US 586 (1957).
25 Peter F. Drucker, "Why My Years with General Motors is 'must' reading" in Sloan, xii.
26 Mabel Newcomer, The Big Business Executive; The Factors that Made Him (New York: Columbia University Press, 1955), 7.
27 Sloan, 406.
28 Diana T. Kurylko, "Ford had a better idea in 1956, but found that safety didn't sell," Automotive News, June 26, 1996, autonews.com/article/19960626/ANA/606260836/ford-had-a-better-idea-in-1956-but-it-found-that-safety-didn-t-sell; Paul C. Judge, "Selling Autos by Selling Safety," New York Times, January 26, 1990. The advertisement is in the Henry Ford Museum and is online: thehenryford.org/collections-and-research/digital-collections/artifact/366079.
29 Ralph Nader, Unsafe At Any Speed (New York: Grossman, 1965).
30 Ken Roberts, "Insult to Injury: Foreign Manufacturers Now Making More Cars in US than US Companies," Forbes, January 22, 2018.
31 Andrew S. Grove, Only the Paranoid Survive: How to Exploit the Crisis Points That Challenge Every Company (New York: Doubleday, 1996).
32 Sloan, 149.
33 Jeffrey R. Bernstein, "Toyota Automatic Looms and Toyota Automobiles" in Thomas K. McCraw, editor., Creating Modern Capitalism: How Entrepreneurs, Companies, and Countries Triumphed in Three Industrial Revolutions (Cambridge, MA: Harvard University Press, 1995), 428 and 398–438 passim.
34 Jim Collins, Good to Great (New York: HarperCollins, 2001).
35 Sloan, 162.
36 Ibid., 165.
37 Ibid., 162.

38   Bell, 6.

39   Joel W. Eastman, Styling vs. Safety: The American Automobile Industry and the Development of Automotive Safety, 1900-1966 (Lanham, Maryland: University Press of America, 1984), 41.

40   See Howard H. Stevenson, "A Perspective on Entrepreneurship," Harvard Business School Case # 9-384–131; Rev. April 13, 2006.

41   "Harlow H. Curtice Is Dead at 69," New York Times, November 4, 1962.

42   "Inquest Held Unlikely in Curtice Kill; Canadian Crown Attorney Maintains Shooting 'Accident,'" Palm Springs Desert Sun - November 19, 1959.

43   "Veda Anderson, widow of former GM labor chief, recalls her husband's tragic death," posted February 20, 2012 on baggy-paragraphs, baggyparagraphs.wordpress.com/2012/02/20/veda-anderson.

Chapter 4A

1   Sloan Wilson, The Man in the Gray Flannel Suit (Cambridge, MA: Perseus, 1955).

2   David Halberstam, The Fifties, (New York: Open Road Integrated Media, 2012).

3   Wilson, "Afterword" to the 1983 addition of Suit.

4   D.H. Lawrence, Studies in Classic American Literature (1923) Chapter 1, en.wikisource.org/wiki/Studies_in_Classic_American_Literature/Chapter_1.

5   Wilson.

6   Nunnally Johnson, The Man in the Gray Flannel Suit, screenplay (1955). I watched the movie a number of times. Script available at: scriptcity.com/all-scripts/movie-scripts/man-in-the-gray-flannel-suit-detail?utm_source=scriptsonscreen&utm_medium=referral&utm_campaign=solo.

7   "Success" was famously referred to as a "bitch-goddess" by William James in a letter to H. G. Wells, September 11, 1906, wist.info/james-william/5715.

Chapter 4B

1   Godfrey Hodgson, "William H. White Obituary," The Guardian, January 15, 1999.

2   Whyte, Organization, 353.

3   Ibid., 112–119.

4   Ibid., 117.

5   Ibid., 117, 119.

6   William H. Whyte, "Patrolling Guadalcanal," February 16, 2010., history.net from Whyte's A Time of War, historynet.com/patrolling-guadalcanal.htm.

7   Ibid.

8   For "repressive tolerance," see Herbert Marcuse's essay by that title in Robert Paul Wolff, Barrington Moore, Jr., and Herbert Marcuse, A Critique of Pure Tolerance (Boston: Beacon Press, 1969), 96-137.

Chapter 5

1   "Polaroid's Land: Here Come Those Great New Cameras," Time, June 26, 1972.

2   "A Genius and His MAGIC CAMERA," Life, October 27, 1972.

3   Victor K. McElheny, Insisting on the Impossible: The Life of Edwin Land (Cambridge, MA: Perseus, 1988), 341.

4   Ibid., 16.

5   Ibid., 17–18.

6   Time in 1961, quoted in McElheny, 200.

7   Harold C. Livesay, American Made: Shapers of the American Economy (Boston: Pearson, 2012), 181.

8   Ibid., 176.

9   "Edwin Land," Wikipedia.

10   "Why Steve Jobs said meeting the founder of Polaroid was 'like visiting a shrine,'" The Economist, March 29, 2015.

11   Christopher Bonanos, "The Man Who Inspired Jobs," New York Times, October 7, 2011; idem., Instant: The Story of Polaroid (New York: Princeton Architectural Press, 2012), 15, 18; Ronald K. Fierstein, A Triumph of Genius: Edwin Land, Polaroid, and the Kodak Patent War (Chicago: Ankerwyke, American Bar Association, 2015).

12   Tim Askew, "The Generalist and The Entrepreneur... And Steve Jobs," Inc., April 30, 2018, inc.com/tim-askew/the-generalist-entrepreneur-steve-jobs.html.

13   Fierstein.

14   McElheny, 16.

15   Ibid., 41.

16   Ibid., 82.

17   Ibid., 163.

18   Ibid., 21.

19   Jane Poss, "Edwin Land dead at 81; Polaroid chief left image on industry," Boston Globe, March 2, 1991.

20   Forbes, May 4, 1987, quoted in American Chemical Society, "Edwin Land and Polaroid Photography," acs.org/content/acs/en/education/whatischemistry/landmarks/land-instant-photography.html.

21   American Chemical Society, "Edwin Land and Polaroid Photography."

22   Polaroid Originals, "10 Magical Moments in Edwin Land's Life that Paved the Way for Polaroid Originals," Polaroid originals.com, us.polaroid.com/blogs/news.

23   Livesay, 184.

24 McElheny, 192.

25 Livesay, 183.

26 Michael Beschloss, "Changing the Market in an Instant," New York Times, July 5, 2015.

27 Ibid.

28 McElheny, 400; see also Peter C. Wensberg, Land's Polaroid: A Company and the Man Who Invented It (Boston: Houghton Mifflin, 1987), 184–185 for slightly different numbers.

29 McElheny, 379.

30 Ibid.

31 Harry McCracken, "Polaroid's SX-70: The Art and Science of the Nearly Impossible," technologizer.com, technologizer.com/2011/06/08/polaroid.

32 Tedlow, Giants, 72-113.

33 The manual is online at: cameramanuals.org/polaroid_pdf/polaroid_20.pdf.

34 Mary Tripsas and Giovanni Gavetti, "Capabilities, Cognition, and Inertia: Evidence from Digital Imaging," Strategic Management Journal, Vol. 21 (2000).

35 McCracken; Wensberg, 168–171.

36 McCracken.

37 Ibid.

38 McElheny, 384, 399-400.

39 Ibid., 403.

40 Ibid., 420.

41 Mitchell Lynch, "Polaroid Tries to Get Itself into Focus," New York Times, May 15, 1983.

42 David Riesman, The Lonely Crowd: A Study of the Changing American Character (New Haven: Yale University Press, 1961), 25.

43 Tom Nicholas, Christopher T. Stanton, and Matthew T. Preble, "Edwin Land: The Art and Science of Innovation," HBS Case # 9-817-107; Rev.: May 25, 2018.

PART II: 1975 to 1995: The Transitional Era

1 Bob Woodward and Carl Bernstein, The Final Days (New York: Simon & Schuster, 1976).

2 Robert W. Crandall, "The Effects of U.S. Trade Protection for Autos and Steel," Brookings Papers on Economic Activity, 1:1987, 276, brookings.edu/wp-content/uploads/1987/01/1987a_bpea_crandall.pdf.

3 Robert Stobaugh and Daniel Yergin, Editors, Energy Future (NY: Random House, 1979), 3.

Chapter 6

1 Henry Nash Smith, "The Search for a Capitalist Hero: Businessmen in American Fiction" in Earl F Cheit, Editor, The Business Establishment (New York: Wylie, 1964), 112. For a contrary view, see Jack Cashill, "Capitalism's Hidden Heroes: The Literary Establishment Contrives to Ignore the Business Giants in the American Novel," Fortune, February 18, 1985.

2 Lee Iacocca, Iacocca: An Autobiography (New York: Bantam, 1984).

3 Edwin, McDowell, "Publishing: 'Iacocca' Reaches Millionth Copy," New York Times, December 14, 1984.

4 HR 5860.

5 "Chrysler aid cleared in final day's session," CQ Almanac, 35th ed., (Washington, DC: Congressional Quarterly, 1979) 285–292, library.cqpress.com.ezp-prod1.hul.harvard.edu/cqalmanac/cqal79-1185075.

6 Iacocca, Iacocca. All the quotations up to the next endnote are from this book.

7 "'Big Bill' Knudsen turned Chevrolet into a powerhouse: His crosstown move after a clash with Henry Ford turned out to be a windfall for GM," Automotive News, October 31, 2011, autonews.com/article/20111031/CHEVY100/310319979/big-bill-knudsen-turned-chevrolet-into-a-powerhouse.

8 Iacocca, Iacocca; Peter Collier and David Horowitz, The Fords: An American Epic (New York: Summit, 1987) p. 342.

9 Robert D. McFadden, "Lee Iacocca, Visionary Automaker Who Led Both Ford and Chrysler, Is Dead at 94," New York Times, July 2, 2019.

10 Collier and Horowitz, 339.

11 Ibid., 342.

12 Iacocca, Iacocca. All the quotations up to the next endnote are from this book.

13 Bart Barnes, "Auto Industry Giant Henry Ford II Dies," Washington Post, September 30, 1987.

14 Iacocca.

15 Ibid.

16 "John Riccardo, Chrysler's CEO Who Helped Recruit Iacocca, Dies at 91," Automotive News, February 14, 2016, https://www.autonews.com/article/20160214/OEM02/160219923/john-riccardo-chrysler-ceo-who-helped-recruit-iacocca-dies-at-91.

17 Iacocca, Iacocca. All the quotations up to the next endnote are from this book.

18 Julian Lewis Watkins, The 100 Greatest Advertisements: Who Wrote Them and What They Did (New York: Dover, 1959), 108–111.

19 Iacocca, Iacocca.

20 Lee Iacocca, Where Have All the Leaders Gone? (New York: Scribner's, 2007), 18.

21 Collins.

22 David Phillips, "Lee Iacocca, Mustang mastermind and tireless Chrysler savior, dies at 94," Automotive News Europe, July 2, 2019.
23 As of 2021, Musk has talked a lot about moving the company to Texas.
24 Julie Halpert, "Lee Iacocca on Chrysler's Bankruptcy," Newsweek, April 29, 2009.

Chapter 7
1 Sam Walton with John Huey, Made in America: My Story (NY: Bantam, 1993), 186. Two other biographies of Walton are worth reading: Bob Ortega, In Sam We Trust (New York: Random House, 1998) and Sandra E. Vance and Roy V. Scott, Wal-Mart: A History of Sam Walton's Retail Phenomenon (New York: Twayne, 1994). Ortega published his book in 1998. Walton died six years earlier, and Wal-Mart had become a different company. Nevertheless his critical perspective is valuable. Particularly enlightening is his C-Span appearance: https://www.c-span.org/video/?116778-1/in-sam-trust.
See also Judith Newman, "Attention, Shoppers," New York Times, November 15, 1998, and Ortega's letter in response, December 6, 1998. My purpose is to discuss Walton in the context of charisma, and the Walton/Huey book is outstanding for that goal. I have used it extensively. Harvard Business School Case Services contains a wealth of cases, teaching notes, and other reading material on Walton and Walmart. See, for example, Stephen Bradley and Pankaj Ghemawat, "WalMart Stores, Inc." 9-794-024, Rev. November 6, 2002 accompanied by Stephen Bradley "Wal-Mart Stores, Inc., Teaching Note," 5-395-225; Michael E. Porter and Jorge Ramirez-Vallejo, "Walmart: Navigating a Changing Retail Landscape," 9-717-474, Rev. July 23, 2019; John R. Wells and Gabriel Ellsworth, "The Inexorable Rise of Walmart? 1988–2016" 9-716-426, May 11, 2016; and Jenny Mead and R. Edward Freeman, "Wal-Mart in 2005 (A)" UV 1346.
2 Stone, The Everything Store. Stone, Amazon Unchained.
3 Walton, 189.
4 Tedlow, Giants, 346–347.
5 Walton, 12–13. All the quotations up to the next endnote are from this book.
6 "Kingfisher, Oklahoma," Wikipedia.
7 Walton, 5. All the quotations up to the next endnote are from this book.
8 Michael B. Dougan, Arkansas Odyssey: The Saga of Arkansas from Prehistoric Times to Present (Little Rock: Rose Publishing, 1994), 573.
9 Walton, 31. All the quotations up to the next endnote are from this book.

10 Tedlow, Giants, 88–89.
11 Walton. All the quotations up to the next endnote are from this book.
12 "Sam Walton Receives the Medal of Freedom," YouTube, July 9, 2012, https://www.youtube.com/watch?v=DgqoRzj62dY.
13 Benjamin Franklin, "The Way to Wealth, as clearly shown in the Preface of an old Pennsylvania Almanack, entitled Poor Richard Improved" reprinted in Alfred D. Chandler, Jr., Thomas K. McCraw, and Richard S. Tedlow, Management Past and Present: A Casebook on the History of American Business (Cincinnati: South-Western, 1996), 1–11.
14 Walton.

Chapter 8
1 Mary Kay Ash, Mary Kay (New York: Harper & Row, 1987), 1-10.
2 Mary Lisa Gavenas, "Ash, Mary Kay," doi.org/10.1093/anb/9780198606697.article.1002284.
3 Ash, Mary, 17, 55.
4 Nicole Wolseley Biggart, Charismatic Capitalism: Direct Selling Organizations in America (Chicago: University of Chicago Press, 1989), 42–44; Ash, Mary, 50.
5 Biggart, 43.
6 Ash, Mary, 19.
7 Ibid., 106.
8 John Kotter, "Mary Kay Cosmetics, Inc." HBS Case # 9-481-126; January 1, 1981. Mary Kay doubtless told this story more than once. See, for example, Ash, Mary, 106.
9 Ash, Mary, 4, 26-27; www.biography.com, Mary Kay Ash.
10 Ash, Mary, 26.
11 Ibid., 4.
12 Mary Kay Ash, The Mary Kay Way: Timeless Principles from America's Greatest Woman Entrepreneur (Hoboken, NJ: Wiley, 2008).
13 Ash, Mary, 5–6.
14 Ibid., 7.
15 Ibid., 62.
16 Ibid.
17 Ash, Mary Kay Way.
18 Mary Kay, interview on 60 Minutes, July 25, 1982, youtube.com/watch?v=nrWz_MzKAMk.
19 Max Weber, The Protestant Ethic and the Spirit of Capitalism (New York: Scribner's, 1958).
20 The Rockefeller quotation can be found at azquotes.com.
21 Enid Nemy, "Mary Kay Ash, Who Built a

Cosmetics Empire and Adored Pink, Is Dead at 83," New York Times, November 23, 2001.

22 Ash, Mary Kay Way.

23 Tedlow, Giants, 247; Kathy Peiss, Hope in a Jar: The Making of America's Beauty Culture (New York: Henry Holt, 1998).

24 Ash, Mary Kay Way.

25 Ash, Mary, 41.

26 60 Minutes, Mary Kay.

27 "Advance," July 1, 2019 – June 30, 2020. This is a brochure published and copywritten by Mary Kay Inc. in 2020.

28 John A. Quelch, "Mary Kay Cosmetics, Inc." HBS Case # 9-383-068; Rev. June 25, 1985; Doretha Dingler, In Pink (Scottsdale, AZ: Bevin, 2012).

29 Ash, Mary, 32.

30 Ibid., 31.

31 Ibid., 23, 27.

32 Mary Kay Ash, You Can Have It All: Lifetime Wisdom from America's Foremost Woman Entrepreneur, (Prima, 1995).

33 Quelch, "Mary Kay."

34 60 Minutes, Mary Kay.

35 Ash, Mary, 158.

36 Ibid., 57–58, 84.

37 60 Minutes, Mary Kay.

38 Ash, Mary.

39 Dingler.

40 Ash, Mary Kay Way.

41 Ash, Mary, 57–58.

42 Ibid.

43 Ibid., 56–59.

44 Ash, Mary, 67, 141.

45 "Walton... Medal of Freedom."

46 Dingler.

47 A poster with this quotation is reproduced on the Library of Congress website, loc.gov.

48 Dingler.

49 Ibid.

50 Jackie Brown, Ask Me About MARY KAY: The Story Behind the Bumper Sticker on the Pink Cadillac (Durham, CT: Strategic, 2010).

51 Ibid.

52 This observation was made by Dalene White. Skip Hollandsworth, "Hostile Makeover," Texas Monthly (November, 1995).

53 Brown.

Chapter 9

1 John Maynard Keynes, The Economic Consequences of the Peace (New York: Harcourt, Brace and Howe, 1920).

2 Bray Hammond, Banks and Politics in America (Princeton: Princeton University Press, 1957), 273–275.

3 E.L. Doctorow, Ragtime (NY: Bantam, 1976), 158–159.

4 W. Braddock Hickman, Corporate Bond Quality and Investor Experience (Princeton: Princeton University Press, 1958).

5 Robert Sobel, Dangerous Dreamers: The Financial Innovators from Charles Merrill to Michael Milken (Washington, D.C.: Beard Books, 2001). See also Tom Nicholas and Matthew G. Preble, "Michael Milken: The Junk Bond King," HBS Case # 9-816-050; Rev. March 25, 2018, for an excellent brief treatment of Milken's rise and fall.

6 Sobel.

7 Ibid.

8 Ibid.

9 Ibid.

10 "John D Rockefeller," en.wikiquote.org.

11 James B. Stewart, Den of Thieves (New York: Simon & Schuster, 1992).

12 Connie Bruck, The Predators' Ball: The Inside Story of Drexel Burnham and the Rise of the Junk Bond Raiders (New York: Simon & Schuster, 1988).

13 Data developed by Kathleen Ryan, Information Research Specialist, Harvard Business School. See also Johan Heilbron, Jochem Verheul, and Sander Quak, "The Origins and Early Diffusion of 'Shareholder Value' in the United States," Theory and Society, October 12, 2013, link.springer.com/article/10.1007/s11186-013-9205-0.

14 Richard S. Tedlow, New and Improved: The Story of Mass Marketing in America (New York: Basic Books, 1990), 335.

15 Ibid., 332–335.

16 "Louis Wolfson," Wikipedia.

17 See, for example, Steve Love and David Geffels, Wheels of Fortune: The Story of Rubber in Akron (Akron, Ohio: University of Akron Press, 1999).

18 Donald N. Sull, Richard S. Tedlow, and Richard S. Rosenbloom, "Managerial Commitments and Technological Change in the U.S. Tire Industry," Industrial and Corporate Change Vol. 6, No. 2 (1997), 461–500; Richard S. Tedlow, Denial: Why Business Leaders Fail to Look Facts in the Face—and What To Do About It (New York: Penguin, 2011), 39-56; Timothy A. Luehrman, "The All American Pipeline," HBS Case # 9-292-040; September 13, 1991; idem., "Goodyear Tire and Rubber Company, 1986," HBS Case # 9-295-033, Rev. January 8, 2007; idem., "Goodyear Tire and Rubber Company, 1988," HBS Case # 9-290-016, Rev. March 27, 1995.

19 Sull et al, 470.

20 Tedlow, Denial, 44–45.

21 Luehrman, "Goodyear, 1986."

22 Ibid.

23 Robert Mercer, interview with David Lieberth, 2001, vimeo.com/312981353.

24 Paul Asquith, "Goodyear Restructuring," HBS Case # 9-288-046; 3/18/88. See also Stuart Warner, "25 years ago: Driving back the raider at the gates of Goodyear Tire and Rubber Co.," Cleveland.com, November 27, 2011; updated January 12, 2019, cleveland.com/business/2011/11/25_years_ago_driving_back_the.html.

25 Mercer, interview with David Lieberth.

26 Asquith, "Goodyear Restructuring,"

27 Mercer, interview with David Lieberth.

28 Chris Hutchins and Dominic Midgley, Goldsmith: Money, Women, and Power (London: Neville Ness House, 2015).

29 "Industrialist Who Led Anti-Europe Crusade," BBC, bbc.co.uk/news/special/politics97/news/07/0719/obit.shtml.

30 "Goldsmith," Wikipedia; "Sir James Goldsmith," The Telegraph, July 21, 1997.

31 Love and Geffels, 245.

32 Goldsmith was an international playboy and bon vivant who had considerable success as a raider in Europe before turning his attention to the United States. His lifestyle was lavish and gauche. For the mansion on East 80th Street in Manhattan, see Hutchins and Midgley.

33 Mercer, interview with David Lieberth.

34 Love and Geffels, 245.

35 Ibid.

36 Mercer, interview with David Lieberth; Love and Geffels, 254.

37 Asquith.

38 Love and Geffels, 252.

39 Lee Iacocca, Talking Straight (New York: Bantam, 1988), 95; Jonathan Hicks, "Goodyear Buys Out Goldsmith," New York Times, November 21, 1986; Hutchins and Midgley.

40 Iacocca, Straight, 95.

41 Love and Geffels, 246

42 Lawrence G. Foster, Robert Wood Johnson: The Gentleman Rebel (State College, PA: Lillian Press, 1999), 277–287, insert between 454–455, 639–647.

43 Love and Geffels, 246.

44 Asquith.

45 James B. Stewart and Philip Revzin, "Sir James Goldsmith, As Enigmatic as Ever, Bales Out of Goodyear," Wall Street Journal, November 21, 1986.

46 Mike Miller, "Smith Barney Sues Goodyear, Goldsmith, Charging Buyback Broke Securities Law," Wall Street Journal, December 8, 1986.

47 "Flamboyant Goldsmith Dies of Heart Attack," BBC.co.uk. See also Margaret Thatcher, "Speech celebrating the memory of Sir James Goldsmith," November 13, 1997; Margaret Thatcher Foundation and "Goldsmith talks back; Sir James Goldsmith challenges Lee Iacocca's book," The Sunday Times, July 17, 1988.

PART III: The Rise of the Superstar CEO

1 For an outstanding discussion of charisma and the CEO search process at the turn of the century, see Khurana. Professor Khurana's point of view is different from the one put forward in this book.

2 Carter, "Crisis of Confidence: Energy and National Goals," msu.edu, msu.edu/~jdowell/135/JCarter.html.

3 Reagan, Brainyquote.com.

4 "Tear Down This Wall!," Wikipedia.

5 "Andrew Grove: Man of the Year," Time, December 29, 1997.

6 "Oprah Winfrey," Wikipedia.

7 Toni Morrison, "Comment," The New Yorker, October 5, 1998.

Chapter 10

1 "Frederic W. Maitland," azquotes.com.

2 Ed Catmull, Creativity, Inc.: Overcoming the Unseen Forces that Stand in the Way of True Inspiration (New York: Random House, 2014).

3 This is the title of Chapter 5 of Schlender and Tetzeli.

4 Isaacson.

5 Ibid.

6 Schlender and Tetzeli.

7 Stross.

8 Ibid.

9 Ibid.

10 Ibid.

11 Ibid.

12 Schlender and Tetzeli.

13 Ibid.

14 Ibid.

15 Lawrence Levy, To Pixar and Beyond: My Unlikely Journey with Steve Jobs to Make Entertainment History (Boston: Mariner, 2017).

16 Stross.

17 Schlender and Tetzeli.

18 Bryan R. Wilson, The Noble Savages: The Primitive Origins of Charisma and Its Contemporary Survival (Berkeley: University of California Press, 1975), 7.

19 Jonah Lehrer, "Steve Jobs, 'Technology Alone Is Not Enough,'" The New Yorker, October 7, 2011.

20 Catmull.

21 Ibid.

22 Ibid.

23 Ibid.

24 Ibid.

25 Ibid.

26 Ibid.

27 Lawrence Levy.

28 Catmull.

29 Ibid.

30 Schlender and Tetzeli.

31 Schlender and Tetzeli; Miguel de Cervantes, Don Quixote (London: Sovereign, 2014); Catmull.

32 Catmull.

33 Ibid.

34 Ibid.

35 Lawrence Levy.

36 Schlender and Tetzeli.

37 Lawrence Levy.

38 Catmull.

39 Ibid.

40 Brennan.

41 Ibid.

42 Ibid.

43 Ibid.

44 Ibid.

45 Ibid.

46 Ibid.

47 Ibid.

48 Ibid.

49 Ibid.

50 Ibid.

51 Isaacson; "Laurene Powell Jobs," Wikipedia.

52 Isaacson; "Laurene Powell Jobs," Wikipedia.

53 Brennan.

54 Katy Waldman, "'Small Fry' Reviewed: Lisa Brennan-Jobs's Mesmerizing Discomfiting Memoir," The New Yorker, September 16, 2018. See also Nellie Bowles, "In 'Small Fry,' Steve Jobs Comes Across as a Jerk. His Daughter Forgives Him. Should We?" New York Times, August 23, 2018.

55 Bowles.

Chapter 11

1 Marjorie Hunter, "James O. Eastland Is Dead at 81; Leading Senate Foe of Integration, New York Times, February 20, 1986; Tucker Higgins, "Democratic Presidential Candidates Disown Biden's Comments about Segregationist Senators in Personal Terms," CNBC, June 19, 2019, cnbc.com/2019/06/19/democrats-slam-biden-over-comments-on-segregationist-senator.html.

2 Oprah Winfrey, What I Know for Sure (New York: Flatiron Books, 2014). See also James M. McPherson, "Parchman's Plantation," New York Times, April 28, 1996.

3 Winfrey, Sure; 347 U.S. 483 (1954).

4 Rev. Martin Luther King, Jr., "I Have A Dream," Speech, delivered at the 'March on Washington,'" 1963, archives.gov.

5 "Oprah Winfrey," Academy of Achievement interview, achievement.org, achievement.org/achiever/oprah-winfrey/.

6 Ibid. The reference to James Weldon Johnson's sermons is to God's Trombones: Seven Negro Sermons in Verse (New York: Penguin, 2008).

7 Eva Illouz, Oprah Winfrey and the Glamour of Misery: An Essay on Popular Culture (New York: Columbia University Press, 2003); Kitty Kelley, Oprah: A Biography (New York: Random House, 2011), 98–102. Illouz states that Winfrey was first raped when she was twelve but later in her book uses the age of nine. She also writes that "Winfrey reported on these events in contradictory ways."

8 Kelley.

9 "What It Takes: Oprah Winfrey, Part 1," learningenglish.voa.news, September 1, 2017, learningenglish.voanews.com/a/what-it-takes-oprah-winfrey-1/3993224.html.

10 Aureliee Corinthios, "Oprah Winfrey Reveals the Name She Chose for the Premature Baby Boy She Lost at Age 14," People, December 2, 2015, https://people.com/tv/oprah-winfrey-reveals-name-of-premature-baby-she-lost-at-age-14/.

11 Kelley, 185, 197–198. See also Academy of Achievement, "Oprah Winfrey, Academy Class of 1989, Full Interview," youtube.com/watch?v=PEZIjUA6u_U. For Vernon Winfrey, see nationalbarbermuseum.org/about/hall-of-fame/98-2016-vernon-winfrey. See also "Oprah's Hometown Trip to Visit Her Father"; The Oprah Winfrey Show; OWN, YouTube, October 15, 1919, youtube.com/watch?v=cyg6OtU42uQ, and Oprah Winfrey, The Path Made Clear: Discovering Your Life's Direction and Purpose (New York: Flatiron Books, 2019).

12 Winfrey has told the story of the "Miss Fire Prevention" contest a number of times. She has said she was not only the first African American woman but the first woman

who did not have red hair to win. See "Meet the Man Who Discovered Oprah," The Oprah Winfrey Show, OWN, May 8, 2015, youtube.com/watch?v=5benh0Dft_Q. There is a remarkable video of Winfrey's audition singing "Sometimes I feel like a motherless child," "Oprah Winfrey-Miss Fire Prevention Audition (1971)," December 14, 2017, youtube.com/watch?v=L_XjqBava4M.

13 "Oprah Winfrey, Academy Class of 1989, Full Interview."

14 Ibid.; Kelley.

15 Kelley.

16 "Oprah Winfrey, Academy Class of 1989, Full Interview."

17 W.E.B. Du Bois, The Souls of Black Folk (NY: Dover, 1994).

18 Kelley.

19 Ibid.

20 Ibid.

21 Ibid.

22 Ibid.

23 Ibid.

24 Ibid.

25 Ibid.

26 Ibid.

27 "Early Oprah | Baltimore TV Years (1978–1981)," https://www.youtube.com/watch?v=3dv7RGIWUxE.

28 Frederick Douglass, Life and Times of Frederick Douglass in The Complete Works of Frederick Douglass (Madison & Adams Press, 2018).

29 Kelley.

30 Ibid.; Phil Donahue, interviewed by on Oprah Winfrey, July 13, 2016, interviews.televisionacademy.com/interviews/phil-donahue; "Oprah on Her Early Career: They Told Me I Couldn't Beat Phil Donahue," youtube.com/watch?v=YXUwQbK3z8A.

31 Jeffrey Lewis Decker, "Saint Oprah," Modern Fiction Studies, Vol. 52, No. 1 (spring, 2006), jstor.org/stable/26286927. For Del Shields, see also "Night Call, 1968–1969," soundtheology.org/nightcall-1968-69.

32 Erik Barnouw, The Golden Web (New York: Oxford University Press, 1968), 297.

33 Erik Barnouw, The Image Empire (New York: Oxford University Press, 1970), 223–224, 239–241.

34 Janice Peck, "Oprah Winfrey: Cultural Icon of Mainstream (White) America" in Sarah Nilsen and Sarah E. Turner, The Colorblind Screen: Television in Post-Racial America (New York: New York University Press, 2014).

35 TV Guide's Top 25, Oprah Winfrey Network, "#3 Exclusive: Where Did Oprah Get 67 Pounds of Fat?" https://www.youtube.com/watch?v=xoVmIyzNn-8.

36 Trysh Travis, The Language of the Heart: A Cultural History of the Recovery Movement from Alcoholics Anonymous to Oprah Winfrey (Chapel Hill: University of North Carolina Press, 2013).

37 Peck, "Icon."

38 Ibid., 85.

39 Janice Peck, "Talk about Racism: Framing a Popular Discourse of Race on Oprah Winfrey," Cultural Critique, No. 27 (Spring, 1994), jstor.org/stable/1354479?seq=1.

40 Peck, "Icon."

41 See, for example, Cosby's famous–or infamous–"pound cake speech," youtube.com/watch?v=Gh3_e3mDQB, and Felicia R. Lee, "Cosby Defends His Remarks About Poor Blacks' Values," New York Times, May 22, 2004.

42 Marcia Clark, interview by Oprah Winfrey, The Oprah Winfrey Show, May 1997, https://www.youtube.com/watch?v=5rdO-JeVs7tM.

43 Peck, "Icon."

44 Ibid.

45 Winfrey, Path.

46 "Meet the SuperSoul100: The World's Biggest Trailblazers in One Room," Oprah.com, www.oprah.com/spirit/supersoul100-the-worlds-biggest-trailblazers-in-one-room.

47 "Holding Onto History, You Could Lose Your Destiny | Oprah's Lifeclass | Oprah Winfrey Network," https://www.youtube.com/watch?v=AXIGlL8b0y8.

48 Ibid.

49 James Joyce, Ulysses, Project Gutenberg e-book.

50 David Carr, "A Triumph of Avoiding the Traps," New York Times, November 22, 2009.

51 Ibid.

52 Steven Zeltchik, "Oprah Winfrey's Prince Harry and Meghan interview netted her $7 million and 17 million viewers. It also validated her larger business strategy," Washington Post, March 8, 2021. For Harvard Business School cases on Winfrey, see Bill George and Andrew N. McLean, "Oprah!" 9-405-087, Rev. April 11, 2007 and Nancy F. Koehn, Erica Helms, Katherine Miller, and Rachel K. Wilcox, "Oprah Winfrey," 9-809-068, Rev. May 13, 2009.

53 Richard Zoglin "Oprah Winfrey: Lady with a Calling", Time, August 8, 1988. See also Bill Higgins, "Oprah's First Show: How She Became Who She Is Today," The Holly-

wood Reporter, May 19, 2011, hollywoodreporter.com/news/oprah-s-first-show-how-190319.zou.

54 Illouz, Winfrey.

55 Kelley.

56 David Carr, "Oprah Puts Her Brand on the Line," New York Times, December 24, 2007.

57 D. T. Max, "The Oprah Effect," New York Times, December 26, 1999.

58 Jacquelyn Mitchard, The Deep End of the Ocean (NY: Penguin, 1996).

59 Max.

60 Kelley.

61 "The Power of a Book Club to Boost Sales," http://alinefromlinda.blogspot.com/2015/04/the-power-of-book-club-to-boost-sales.html.

62 "A Million Little Lies: Exposing James Frey's Fiction Addiction," The Smoking Gun, January 4, 2006, thesmokinggun.com/documents/celebrity/million-little-lies. See also http://cpb-us-w2.wpmucdn.com/blogs.cofc.edu/dist/8/455/files/2011/11/Frey-sample-bibliography-entry.pdf.

63 "Oprah Endorses Barack on Larry King," youtube.com/watch?v=_atVBYMW0AY.

64 Costas Panagopoulos, "Obama Supporter Oprah Takes a Big Dive," Politico, April 7, 2008, politico.com/story/2008/04/obama-supporter-oprah-takes-a-big-dive-009427.

65 "So Much for One Person One Vote," freakonomics, August 6, 2008 freakonomics.com/2008/08/06/so-much-for-one-person-one-vote/.

66 The complete story of Oprah Winfrey, race, and wealth is yet to be told. When visiting Zurich for Tina Turner's wedding, Winfrey went into an upscale store and asked to see a handbag. The saleswoman obviously did not know who Winfrey was. She refused to show her the handbag, explaining that "It's too expensive.... I don't want to hurt your feelings." "Now," Oprah asked an interviewer, "why did she do that? Why did she do that?" She did not buy the handbag (which cost $38,000). She made a point of not mentioning the store's name but did not let the matter rest. She brought it to the attention of Zurich Tourism. Christian Trottman, representative of Zurich Tourism, was taped saying "This incident with Oprah Winfrey is very regrettable. Zurich Tourism does regret this incident.... We are known as an open-minded city, and this incident does not really help that[?] image." youtube.com/watch?v=5ATBCT8sq9k. Ali Rattansi, Racism: A Very Short Introduction (London: Oxford University Press, 2020), 419-420.

Chapter 12

1 Ashlee Vance, Elon Musk: Tesla, SpaceX, and the Quest for a Fantastic Future (NY: HarperCollins, 2015).

2 Mark Matousek, "Elon Musk slammed one of Tesla's founders by calling him the worst person he's ever worked with," Business Insider, February 10, 2020, https://www.businessinsider.com/elon-musk-tesla-cofounder-worst-person-hes-worked-with-2020-2.

3 Charles Morris, Tesla: How Elon Musk and Company Made Electric Cars Cool and Remade the Automotive and Energy Industries (Smashwords, 2017). For Eberhard and Tarpenning's discussion of the founding and early years of Tesla, see the following excellent video: https://www.cnbc.com/2021/02/06/tesla-founders-martin-eberhard-marc-tarpenning-on-elon-musk.html.

4 "Joe Rogan Experience #1169 - Elon Musk," youtube.com/watch?v=ycPr5-27vSI.

5 Mark Spiegel, "Tesla No Longer Even a Growth Company; Going Bankrupt: Shortseller," Yahoo! Finance, July 4, 2020, yahoo.com/now/tesla-no-longer-even-growth-121604978.html.

6 Vance.

7 Ibid.

8 Ibid.

9 Ibid.

10 Ibid.

11 Ibid.; Neil Strauss, "Elon Musk: The Architect of Tomorrow," Rolling Stone, November 15, 2017, rollingstone.com/culture/culture-features/elon-musk-the-architect-of-tomorrow-120850/.

12 Sheireso Ngo, "The Sickening Reason Why Elon Musk Called His Father a 'Terrible Human Being,'" Showbiz Cheat Sheet, June 11, 2013, cheatsheet.com/health-fitness/the-sickening-reason-why-elon-musk-called-his-father-a-terrible-human-being.html/; "Elon Musk's 'Evil' Father," The Sunday Times, March 15, 2019, driving.co.uk/news/elon-musks-evil-father-baby-step-daughter.

13 Vance.

14 Ibid.

15 Jeff Grub, "How Games helped make Elon Musk the real-Life Tony Stark," venturebeat.com, April 17, 2015, venturebeat.com/2015/04/07/how-games-helped-make-elon-musk-the-real-life-tony-stark/.

16 Ibid.

17 Ibid.

18 Vance; Arthur Villasanta, "Elon Musk 'Too Embarrassed' to Put His Tiny Invention in a Tesla," International Business Times, November 18, 2019, ibtimes.com/elon-musk-too-embarrassed-put-his-tiny-invention-tesla-2868829; Sean O'Kane, "Play the PC Game Elon musk wrote as a pre-teen," The Verge, June 19, 2015, theverge.com/2015/6/9/8752333/elon-musk-blastar-pc-game.

19 Vance.

20 Edgar Allan Poe, "Alone," poetryfoundation.org. This poem was written in 1829 but not published until 1875. The Complete Poems of Edgar Allan Poe, e-books. Adelaide. edu.au.

21 Vance; Tim Urban, "The Elon Musk Blog Series," Wait But Why, Kindle edition, 2015.

22 Vance.

23 Ibid.

24 Ibid.

25 Justine Wilson Musk, "'I Was a Starter Wife: Inside America's Messiest Divorce," Marie Claire, September 10, 2018, marieclaire.com/sex-love/a5380/millionaire-starter-wife/

26 Ibid.; Tom Junod, "Triumph of His Will," Esquire, November 15, 2012, esquire.com/news-politics/a16681/elon-musk-interview-1212/.

27 Wilson Musk, "Starter Wife."

28 "California laws about naming a baby stipulate that the name can include only the 26 letters of the English alphabet," Avery Hartmans and Kat Tenbarge, "How to pronounce 'X Æ A-Xii,' the name Elon Musk and Grimes gave their new baby," Business Insider, May, 2020, businessinsider.com/how-to-pronounce-x-ae-a-12-elon-musk-grimes-baby-name-2020-5.

29 Strauss.

30 Vance.

31 "X.com," Wikipedia.

32 Tom Nicholas, VC: An American History (Cambridge, MA: Harvard University Press, 2019). Nicholas's book contains a wealth of information about the successes and failures of the venture capital world in the years since 1990.

33 "Elon Musk," Esquire.com, October 1, 2008, classic.esquire.com/article/2008/10/1/elon-musk.

34 George Dvorsky, "Humans Will Never Colonize Mars," Gizmodo, gizmodo.com/humans-will-never-colonize-mars-1836316222.

35 "The Boring Company," Wikipedia; "The future we're building—and boring," TED, May 3, 2017, ted.com/talks/elon_musk_the_future_we_re_building_and_boring/transcript?language=en.

36 Faiz Siddiqui, "Elon Musk moved to Texas and embraced celebrity. Can Tesla run on Autopilot?" Washington Post, February 23, 2021.

37 Allan Nevins and Frank Ernest Hill, Ford: The Times, The Man, The Company (New York: Scribner's, 1954), 576–577.

38 Morris.

39 "Car of the Century," Wikipedia.

40 David L. Lewis, The Public Image of Henry Ford: An American Folk Hero and His Company (Detroit: Wayne State University Press, 1976), 43, 494–495, n.14.

41 For Tesla in 2017, see Frank T. Rothaermel, "Tesla, Inc." HBS Case MHE-FTR-049, 12599272628, Rev: October 6, 2017.

42 Aarian Marshall and Alex Davies, "Tesla Is (Finally!) Selling the Model 3 for $35,000," Wired, February 28, 2019, wired.com/story/tesla-model-3-35000-price-autopilot-self-driving-stores-closing/.

43 Khan Academy, "Elon Musk - CEO of Tesla Motors and SpaceX," youtube.com/watch?v=vDwzmJpI4io; "Sal Khan," en.wikipedia.org/wiki/Sal_Khan.

44 See, for example, Russell Brandom, "If Tesla Goes Up in Smoke, It Won't Be Because Elon Musk Bet a Blunt: Executive Departures Are a Bigger Problem Than a Little Weed Smoke," The Verge, September 17, 2018, theverge.com/2018/9/7/17832154/elon-musk-blunt-tesla-stock-problems-executive-retention; Mark Gurman and Dana Hull, "Former chief Tesla engineer Doug Field returns to Apple," Bloomberg, August 10, 2018, bloomberg.com/news/articles/2018-08-10/former-chief-tesla-vehicle-engineer-doug-field-returns-to-apple; and J. Jennings Moss, "Tesla co-founder J.B. Straubel steps down as CTO," Silicon Valley Business Journal, bizjournals.com/sanjose/news/2019/07/24/tesla-co-founder-jb-straubel-steps-down-as.html. For executive departures, see especially Aaron Greenspan, "Reality Check: Tesla, Inc.," PlainSite, 45–50, January 7, 2020, plainsite.org/realitycheck/tsla.pdf.

45 Vance.

46 The tweet was on August 7, 2018; Umair Irfan, "Elon Musk's Tweet About Taking Tesla Private Has Triggered a Federal Lawsuit," Vox, September 28, 2018, vox.com/2018/9/27/17911826/elon-musk-tesla-sec-twitter-lawsuit.

47 Ibid.

48 Ibid.

49 "Tesla's Elon Musk says tweet that led to $20 million fine 'Worth it,'" Reuters, October 27, 2018, https://www.reuters.com/article/us-tesla-musk-tweet/teslas-elon-musk-says-tweet-that-led-to-20-million-fine-worth-it-idUSKCN1N10K2.

50 Niraj Chokshi, "Elon Musk Says Tesla Share Price Is Too High," New York Times, May 1, 2020.

51 Michael Sheetz, "SpaceX valuation rises to $33.3 billion as investors look to satellite opportunity," CNBC, May 31, 2019, cnbc.com/2019/05/31/spacex-valuation-33point3-billion-after-starlink-satellites-fundraising.html.

52 Jeffrey Kluger, "SpaceX CEO Elon Musk on the next giant leap for mankind," CBS News, July 21, 2019, https://www.cbsnews.com/news/spacex-ceo-elon-musk-on-the-next-giant-leap-for-mankind/.

53 Vance.

54 George Dvorsky, "Humans Will Never Colonize Mars"; Mike Brown and Jake Kleinman, "SpaceX Mars City: Werner Herzog Issues a Stark Warning to Elon Musk," Inverse, November 20, 2020, inverse.com/innovation/spacex-mars-city-werner-herzog.

55 Dvorsky.

Chapter 13

1 Gil Amelio and William L. Simon, On the Firing Line: My 500 Days at Apple (New York: HarperBusiness, 1998), 185–202.

2 Schlender and Tetzeli.

3 Amelio and Simon, 32.

4 Ibid., 159. For a sympathetic account of the Amilio story, see Tom Hormby, "The Rise and Fall of Apple's Gil Amelio," Low End Mac, August 10, 2013, lowendmac.com/2013/the-rise-and-fall-of-apples-gil-amelio/.

5 Schlender and Tetzeli; Steve Jobs and Bill Gates interviewed by Gina Smith, 2007, https://www.youtube.com/watch?v=kveOixeuD5w.

6 Steve Jobs and Bill Gates interviewed by Gina Smith.

7 Schlender and Tetzeli.

8 Amelio and Simon, 268.

9 Jeffrey S. Young and William L. Simon, iCon: Steve Jobs, The Greatest Second Act in the History of American Business (New York: Wiley, 2005), 334.

10 Schlender and Tetzeli.

11 Ibid.

12 "Steve Jobs Apple Product Matrix Strategy 1997," youtube.com/watch?v=VkVs4ZqWgN8.

13 Robert J. Dolan, "iPod: The Perfect Thing?" HBS Case # 520-097, rev. July 2020; April 27, 2020, in process.

14 Leander Kahney, Tim Cook: The Genius Who Took Apple to the Next Level (New York: Penguin, 2019), 174–178.

15 Ibid., 176.

16 Ibid., 178.

17 Steven Levy, "An Oral History of Apple's Infinite Loop," wired.com/story/apple-infinite-loop-oral-history.

18 Schlender and Tetzeli.

19 Ibid.

20 Ibid.; Blake Ellis, "Apple topples Microsoft's throne," CNN money, May 27, 2010.

21 Schlender and Tetzeli.

22 Mark Gurman, "Apple Director Millard Drexler to retire, replacement yet to be named," 9to5Mac, January 22, 2015, 9to5mac.com/2015/01/22/apple-director-millard-drexler-to-retire-replacement-yet-to-be-named/.

23 Steve Lohr, "Apple, a Success at Stores, Bets Big on Fifth Avenue," New York Times, May 19, 2006.

24 Schlender and Tetzeli.

25 Ibid.

26 Sam Costello, "This Is the Number of iPods Sold All-Time," Lifewire May 6, 2019, lifewire.com/number-of-ipods-sold-all-time-1999515.

27 Anne Le Tran, "The History of the Car Radio: From Morse Code to Mixtapes," esurance41.rssing.com/chan-11821666/latest.php.

28 "Motorola," Wikipedia.

29 Steven Levy, The Perfect Thing (New York: Simon & Schuster, 2006), 16–49; Sam Costello, "This is the number of iPods sold all-time," Lifewire, December 13, 2019, lifewire.com/number-of-ipods-sold-all-time-1999515; Carl Franzen, "The History of the Walkman: 35 Years of Iconic Music Players", The Verge, July 1, 2014, theverge.com/2014/7/1/5861062/sony-walkman-at-35; John Nathan, Sony (Boston: Houghton Mifflin, 1999), 150–155; Katie Marsal, "iPod: How big can it get?" AppleInsider, May 24, 2006, archive.vn/20120604184947/appleinsider.com/articles/06/05/24/ipod_how_big_can_it_get.html.

30 "Unveiling the Digital Hub Strategy Macworld San Francisco," January 9, 2001, youtube.com/watch?v=lmvmtmqqbeI.

31 Ibid.

32 "The Mackintosh Mouse, Making the Macintosh: Technology and Culture in Sil-

icon Valley," web.stanford.edu/dept/SUL/library/mac/.

33 Isaacson.

34 Daniel Boffey, "Apple admits Briton DID invent iPod, but he still not getting any money," Daily Mail, September 8, 2008, dailymail.co.uk/news/article-1053152/Apple-admit-Briton-DID-invent-iPod-hes-getting-money.html.

35 "Straight dope on the iPod's Birth," Wired, October 17, 2006, https://www.wired.com/2006/10/straight-dope-on-the-ipods-birth/.

36 Ibid.; Isaacson. Schlender and Tetzeli write that in January 2001, Rubinstein asked "some former Newton engineers to begin work in earnest on some sort of portable audio device around the Toshiba micro-drive." Since it appears that Rubenstein did not learn of this drive until February, there is obviously a problem with dating.

37 Schlender and Tetzeli.

38 "Straight Dope," Wired.

39 Levy, "Oral History."

40 Isaacson.

41 Steve Jobs, "Apple - Steve Jobs introduces the iPod - 2001," October 10, 2001, youtube.com/watch?v=Mc_FiHTITHE.

42 Isaacson.

43 Schlender and Tetzeli.

44 Ibid.

45 Ibid.

46 Ibid. For iPod pricing, See Dolan, "iPod."

47 Lisa Capretta "Oprah and Her Audience Losing It Over an iPod in 2003 Is Pure Magic," OWN, April 28, 2016, HuffPost, huffpost.com/entry/oprah-audience-ipod-2003_n_57213a28e4b0f309baefb140; Levy, Perfect.

48 Isaacson.

49 Ibid.

50 Ibid.

51 Ibid.; "Steve Jobs introduces iTunes for windows - Apple special event 2003," youtube.com/watch?v=MvCJ613HORA.

52 Eric Franklin, "The $200 iPod Touch now has some legit competition," CNET, July 13, 2019, cnet.com/news/200-ipod-touch-has-some-legit-competition/.

53 Levy, Perfect, 365–366.

54 Schlender and Tetzeli.

55 Luke Dormehl, "Apple introduced iTunes store 13 years ago today," April 28, 2016, cultofmac.com/425543/apple-introduced-itunes-store-13-years-ago-today/.

56 "Oprah's First iPod: 'How Does the Music Get in There?!'" Oprah.com, youtube.com/watch?v=Wp8EjmmVHew, April 7, 2016.

57 Randy Alfred, "April 3, 1973: Motorola Calls AT&T... by Cell," Wired, dynallc.com/april-3-1973-motorola-calls-att-by-cell-wired-april-2008/.

58 Sam Costello, "How Many iPhones Have Been Sold Worldwide," Lifewire, December 27, 2019, lifewire.com/how-many-iphones-have-been-sold-1999500.

59 See, for example, Sam Biddle, "Samsung Exposes Blatant iPhone Jealousy," Gizmodo, August 7, 2012, gizmodo.com/474052195.

60 Schlender and Tetzeli.

61 Ibid.

62 The email is reprinted in Schlender and Tetzeli.

63 Ibid.

64 "Apple's Secret Launch Team," youtube.com/watch?v=xxBc1c3uAJw.

65 Fred Vogelstein, Dogfight (New York: Farrar, Strauss and Giroux, 2013), 36.

66 Isaacson.

67 Ibid.

68 Ibid.

69 Ibid.

70 "iPhone 1—Steve Jobs Macworld keynote in 2007," youtube.com/watch?v=VQK-MoT-6XSg.

71 Vogelstein, 36.

72 John William Ward, "The Meaning of Lindbergh's Flight," American Quarterly, Vol. 10, No. 1 (spring, 1958), 8.

73 Vogelstein, 124.

74 Schlender and Tetzeli.

75 Ibid.

76 Caroline Cakebread, "People will take 1.2 trillion digital photos this year—thanks to smart phones," Business Insider, August 31, 2017, https://www.businessinsider.com/12-trillion-photos-to-be-taken-in-2017-thanks-to-smartphones-chart-2017-8.

77 "Ballmer Laughs at iPhone," youtube.com/watch?v=eywi0h_Y5_U.

78 "Bill Gates on making 'one of the greatest mistakes of all time,'" TechCrunch.com. June 22, 2019, techcrunch.com/2019/06/22/bill-gates-on-making-one-of-the-greatest-mistakes-of-all-time/.

79 "Bill Gates says his 'greatest mistake ever' was failing to create Android at Microsoft," www.aol.com/ article/ finance/June 24, 2019.

80 David A. Hounshell and John Kenley Smith, Jr., Science and Corporate Strategy: Du Pont R& D, 1902–1980 (Cambridge England: Cambridge University Press, 1988), 272.

81   "iPhone 1—Steve Jobs Macworld keynote in 2007."

82   Schlender and Tetzeli.

83   Isaacson.

84   Ken Kocienda, Creative Selection: Inside Apple's Design Process during the Golden Age of Steve Jobs (NY: St. Martin's Press, 2018).

85   Ibid.

86   Ibid.

87   Ibid.

88   Ibid.

89   "Steve Jobs Introduces the iPad – 2010," youtube.com/watch?v=zZtWlSDvb_k.

90   "iPad history," Wikipedia; Apple press release, "Apple Launches iPad 2," March 2, 2011.

91   William C. Shiel, Jr., MD, "Medical Definition of Cachectic," medterms medical dictionary, medicinenet, medicinenet.com/cachectic/definition.htm.

92   Cynthia A. Montgomery and David B. Yoffie, "Teaching Note" for "Steve Jobs: Leader Strategist," HBS case number 5-716-413; November 5, 2015.

93   The authors are Emma Bell and Scott Taylor, journals.sagepub.com/doi/10.1177/1350508415605109.

94   Catmull.

95   Kocienda.

Chapter 14

1   Matt Stevens and Matthew Haag, "Jeffrey Skilling, Former Enron Chief, Released after 12 Years in Prison," New York Times, February 22, 2019.

2   Bethany McLean and Peter Elkind, The Smartest Guys in the Room: The Amazing Rise and Scandalous Fall of Enron (New York: Penguin, 2013).

3   Jeffrey Skilling, "Meet the Psychopaths," youtube.com/watch?v=VQe1MOv9Z7E.

4   "The Fall of Enron," Bloomberg, December 26, 2001, bloomberg.com/news/articles/2001-12-16/the-fall-of-enron; McLean and Elkind.

5   McLean and Elkind.

6   Ibid.

7   Ibid.

8   Ibid.

9   Ibid.

10   Kimberly Amadeo, "Mark-to-Market Accounting; How It Works, and Its Pros and Cons," thebalance.com/mark-to-market-accounting-how-it-works-3305942.

11   McLean and Elkind.

12   "The Fall of Enron," Bloomberg, https://www.bloomberg.com/news/articles/2001-12-16/the-fall-of-enron.

13   McLean and Elkind.

14   Ibid.

15   Ibid.

16   "Enron Scandal," Wikipedia.

17   McLean and Elkind.

18   McLean and Elkind.

19   Ibid.

20   Ibid.

21   Ibid.

22   "Enron's Skilling Answers Markey at Hearing; Eyes Roll," youtube.com/watch?v=hPqH3DrWEEU.

23   McLean and Elkind.

24   Susan Donaldson James, "John Taylor Skilling, Ex-Enron Chief's Son, Dies of Possible Overdose," ABC News, February 4, 2011.

25   Fortune, June 12, 2014.

26   Roger Parloff, "This CEO Is Out for Blood," Fortune, June 12, 2014.

27   Ibid.

28   John Carreyrou, Bad Blood: Secrets and Lies in a Silicon Valley Startup (New York: Knopf, 2018).

29   Kimberly Weisul, "How Playing the Long Game Made Elizabeth Holmes a Billionaire," Inc., inc.com/magazine/201510/kimberly-weisul/the-longest-game.html.

30   "The Dropout, Part I, Where ex-Theranos CEO Elizabeth Holmes got her start," ABC News, March 16, 2019.

31   Carreyrou.

32   Mad Money, August 22, 2018.

33   Alexia Fernandez, "Who is Sunny Balwani," People, March 27, 2019.

34   Paige Leskin, "Theranos founder Elizabeth Holmes has reportedly gotten married in a secret wedding," Business Insider, June 17, 2019, businessinsider.com/elizabeth-holmes-theranos-everything-about-fiance-william-billy-evans-2019-3.

35   Peter Blumberg, "Elizabeth Holmes Loses Request to Throw Out Criminal Charges," Bloomberg, October 13, 2020, bloomberg.com/news/articles/2020-10-13/elizabeth-holmes-loses-request-to-throw-out-criminal-charges.

36   "Out for Blood," Fortune.

37   Morgan Baila, "Phyllis Gardner warned everyone about Elizabeth Holmes—but no one listened," Refinery29, March 19, 2019, refinery29.com/en-us/2019/03/226452/phyllis-gardner-elizabeth-holmes-professor-interview-the-inventor.

38   Lydia Ramsey, "The Stanford professor who rejected one of Elizabeth Holmes early ideas explains what it was like to watch the rise and fall of Theranos," Busi-

ness Insider, March 18, 2019, https://www.businessinsider.com/stanford-professor-phyllis-gardner-on-theranos-and-elizabeth-holmes-2019-3.

39 "Theranos CEO Elizabeth Holmes: Firing Back at Doubters," Mad Money, CNBC, October 16, 2015.

40 "Winston Churchill Quotes," brainyquote.com.

41 Matthew Josephson, The Robber Barons: The Great American Capitalists, 1861–1901 (New York: Harcourt, Brace & World, 1934), 194.

42 Ibid., v.

43 "Daniel Drew," Wikipedia.

44 McLean and Elkind.

45 Ronald Reagan, "Inaugural Address," Reaganlibrary.gov, January 20, 1981.

46 McLean and Elkind.

47 Sarbanes-Oxley Act of 2002 Publ. L. 107-204, 116 Stat. 745, enacted July 30, 2002.

48 Carreyrou.

49 Benjamin Franklin, "The Way to Wealth," in Chandler et al., Management, 1–11

Chapter 15

1 "Wall Street (1987 Film)," Wikipedia.

2 Nicholas, VC.

3 Stuart W. Bruchey, Robert Oliver: Merchant of Baltimore (Baltimore: The Johns Hopkins University Press, 1956), 135–141.

4 Tyler Clifford, "Capitalism 'will fundamentally be in jeopardy' if business does not act on climate change, Microsoft CEO Satya Nadella says," CNBC, January 16, 2020; Mad Money with Jim Cramer, https://www.cnbc.com/2020/01/16/microsoft-ceo-capitalism-is-in-jeopardy-if-we-do-not-act-on-climate-change.html; "Microsoft CEO talks sustainability, artificial intelligence, privacy, and satisfying shareholders," CNBC, January 16, 2020, https://www.cnbc.com/video/2020/01/16/microsoft-ceo-cfo-on-getting-a-return-on-investment-in-sustainability.html

5 Steven Levy, Facebook: The Inside Story (NY: Penguin, 2020).

6 "Facebook CEO Mark Zuckerberg testifies before Financial Services Committee –10/23/2019," CNBC, October 23, 2019, https://www.youtube.com/watch?v=B1a5h-5KncNM.

7 Donie O'Sullivan, "Pelosi calls Facebook a 'shameful' company that helped in 'misleading the American people'," CNN, January 16, 2020, https://www.cnn.com/2020/01/16/tech/pelosi-shameful-facebook/index.html.

8 Nick Bilton, "'He's F---king Destroyed This Town': How Mark Zuckerberg Became the Most Reviled Man in Tech," Vanity Fair, November 6, 2019, vanityfair.com/news/2019/11/how-mark-zuckerberg-became-the-most-reviled-man-in-tech.

9 Richard S. Tedlow, Andy Grove: The Life and Times of an American Business Icon (NY: Penguin, 2006), 99.

10 Geoffrey Colvin, "The Ultimate Manager," Fortune, November 22, 1999.

11 James B. Stewart, "Did Jack Welch Model Sow Seeds of G.E. Decline?" New York Times, June 15, 2017.

12 Robert H. Wiebe, Businessman and Reform: A Study of the Progressive Movement (Chicago: Quadrangle, 1962), 17–18.

13 Bell sees charisma as "an integral, inescapable part of modern political life.... We will always have charismatic leaders."

14 Steve Jobs, "Computers are like a bicycle for our minds," youtube.com/watch?v=ob_GX50Za6c.

15 Levy, Perfect.

16 Ralph Waldo Emerson, "Self-Reliance" in Essays: First Series (1841), 10, emersoncentral.com/texts/essays-first-series/self-reliance/. For an instructive discussion of the different views of Carlyle and Mazzini on this issue, see Bell, Horseback.

17 Quoted in Potts, 3.

18 Mad Money, April 27, 2015.

19 Daniel J. Boorstin, The Americans: The National Experience (New York: Knopf, 1965), 127.

20 Hans Christian Andersen, "The Emperor's New Clothes," H.C. Andersen Centre, Andersen.sdu.dk, andersen.sdu.dk/vaerk/hersholt/TheEmperorsNewClothes_e.html.

21 Stephen Manes and Paul Andrews, Gates (NY: Simon & Schuster, 1994), 130.

22 Brian Lamb, interview with Bethany McLean, C-Span, May 19, 2005, youtube.com/watch?v=3C8tC_0dsDI.

23 John Antonakis, Marika Fenley, and Sue Liechti, "Learning Charisma," Harvard Business Review, June 2012.

INDEX